Understanding Governance

Series Editor
R. A. W. Rhodes
Professor of Government
University of Southampton
Southampton, UK

Understanding Governance encompasses all theoretical approaches to the study of government and governance in advanced industrial democracies and the Commonwealth. It has three long-standing objectives:

1. To develop new theoretical approaches to explain changes in the role of the state;
2. To explain how and why that role has changed; and
3. To set the changes and their causes in comparative perspective.

The origins of the series lie in the renowned Whitehall Research Programme funded by the Economic and Social Research Council. Since 1997, it has published 27 books by the best known names in the field including Colin Hay, David Marsh, Edward Page, Guy Peters, R. A. W. Rhodes, David Richards, Martin Smith and Patrick Weller.

Over the past twenty years the 'Understanding Governance' book series has constantly defined the state-of-the-art when it comes to the analysis of the modern state. From accountability to agencies, party politics to parliamentary power and from crisis-management to the core executive this book series continues to set the agenda in terms of world-class scholarship.
—**Matthew Flinders**, Professor of Politics and Director of the Sir Bernard Crick Centre at the University of Sheffield

More information about this series at
http://www.palgrave.com/gp/series/14394

R. A. W. Rhodes
Editor

Narrative Policy Analysis

Cases in Decentred Policy

Editor
R. A. W. Rhodes
University of Southampton
Southampton, UK

Understanding Governance
ISBN 978-3-319-76634-8   ISBN 978-3-319-76635-5 (eBook)
https://doi.org/10.1007/978-3-319-76635-5

Library of Congress Control Number: 2018934643

© The Editor(s) (if applicable) and The Author(s) 2018
This work is subject to copyright. All rights are solely and exclusively licensed by the Publisher, whether the whole or part of the material is concerned, specifically the rights of translation, reprinting, reuse of illustrations, recitation, broadcasting, reproduction on microfilms or in any other physical way, and transmission or information storage and retrieval, electronic adaptation, computer software, or by similar or dissimilar methodology now known or hereafter developed.
The use of general descriptive names, registered names, trademarks, service marks, etc. in this publication does not imply, even in the absence of a specific statement, that such names are exempt from the relevant protective laws and regulations and therefore free for general use.
The publisher, the authors and the editors are safe to assume that the advice and information in this book are believed to be true and accurate at the date of publication. Neither the publisher nor the authors or the editors give a warranty, express or implied, with respect to the material contained herein or for any errors or omissions that may have been made. The publisher remains neutral with regard to jurisdictional claims in published maps and institutional affiliations.

Cover credit: Luciano Lozano/Alamy Stock Photo

Printed on acid-free paper

This Palgrave Macmillan imprint is published by the registered company Springer International Publishing AG part of Springer Nature
The registered company address is: Gewerbestrasse 11, 6330 Cham, Switzerland

Titles in the 'Understanding Governance' Series, 1997–2017

1. Rhodes, R. A. W. (Ed.) *Narrative Policy Analysis: Cases in Decentring Policy* (2018).
2. Theakston, Kevin and Connelly, Philip *William Armstrong and British Policy Making* (2017).
3. Fitzpatrick, Daniel *The Politics of Regulation in the UK: Between Tradition, Contingency and Crisis* (2016).
4. Richards, D., M. Smith, and Hay, C. (Eds.) *Institutional Crisis in 21st Century Britain* (2014).
5. Gauja, A. *The Politics of Party Policy: From Members to Legislators* (2013).
6. Skelcher, C., Sullivan, H. and Jeffares, S. *Hybrid Governance in European Cities: Neighbourhood, Migration and Democracy* (2013).
7. Rush, M. and Giddings, Philip *Parliamentary Socialisation Learning the Ropes or Determining Behaviour?* (2011).
8. 't Hart, Paul and Uhr, John (Eds.) *How Power Changes Hands. Transition and Succession in Government* (2011).
9. Hazell, Robert, Worthy, B. and Glover, M. *The Impact of the Freedom of Information Act on Central Government in the UK* (2010).
10. Theakston, K. *After Number 10. Former Prime Ministers in British Politics* (2010).
11. Scott, Anne *Ernest Gowers: Plain Words and Forgotten Deeds* (2009).

12. Richards, D. *New Labour and the Civil Service: Reconstituting the Westminster Model* (2008).
13. Page, E., and Wright, V. (Eds.) *From the Active to the Enabling State: The Changing Role of Top Officials in European Nations* (2007).
14. Elder, N. and Page E. *Accountability and Control in Next Steps Agencies* (2006).
15. McLean, Iain *The Fiscal Crisis of the United Kingdom* (2005).
16. Pemberton, Hugh *Policy Learning and British Governance in the 1960s* (2004).
17. James, Oliver *The Executive Agency Revolution in Whitehall: Public Interest versus Bureau-Shaping Perspectives* (2003).
18. Marsh, David, Richards, David and Smith, Martin J. *Changing Patterns of Governance in the United Kingdom: Reinventing Whitehall?* (2002).
19. Bulmer, S., Burch, M., Carter, C., Hogwood, P., Scott, A. *British Devolution and European Policy-Making* (2002).
20. Peters, B. Guy, R. A. W. Rhodes and Wright, Vincent *Administering the Summit: Administration of the Core Executive in Developed Countries* (2000).
21. Rhodes, R. A. W. (Ed.) *Transforming British Government, Volume 1: Changing Institutions* (2000).
22. Rhodes, R. A. W. (Ed.) *Transforming British Government. Volume 2: Changing Roles and Relationships* (2000).
23. Theakston, K. (Ed.) *Bureaucrats and Leadership* (2000).
24. Smith, M. J. *The Core Executive in Britain* (1999).
25. Theakston, Kevin *Leadership in Whitehall* (1999).
26. Deakin, N. and Parry, R. *The Treasury and Social Policy: the Contest for Control of Welfare Strategy* (1998).
27. Weller, Patrick, Bakvis, Herman and Rhodes, R.A.W. (Eds.) *The Hollow Crown: Countervailing Trends in Core Executives* (1997).

Preface and Acknowledgements

The main aim of this book is to show how decentred analysis contributes to the study of public policy, both theoretically and practically. We seek to substantiate the claim that it offers novel theory and methods with a clear practical application. However, the book has two subsidiary purposes.

First, it displays research at the University of Southampton in this field. All the contributors are based at Southampton or they are colleagues at other universities who are working with us. The University has established a Centre for Political Ethnography recently that will serve as the home for future work.

Second, the book is part of the 'Understanding Governance' series published by Springer-Macmillan. The first book came out in 1997 so this volume commemorates 20 years of publishing. We have published 25 books with 2 in the pipeline, and counting. We have also developed a subsidiary line in administrative biographies with three to date. There is no danger that any of the books will enter *The Times* bestseller list but we persist, and many an author is in print because we do. Here's to our silver wedding anniversary.

Every editor incurs debts. I would like to thank John Boswell and Jack Corbett for their help over and beyond producing their chapters. I would like to thank all the contributors for responding promptly to my many requests for revisions or information. They helped me also with the summaries of their chapters, although the versions in Chapter 1 are my take on their research for which they cannot be held responsible. I must thank Mark Bevir also because it is our books together that underpins this collection. Finally, I must thank Jenny Fleming for her continued support in a year which saw the death of our cat, Towzer (aged 18), major knee surgery, and illness in the family. We made it.

Southampton, UK
December 2017

R. A. W. Rhodes

Contents

1	**What Is Decentred Analysis?** R. A. W. Rhodes	1
2	**What is Penal Policy? Traditions and Practices in the UK Ministry of Justice** Harry Annison	23
3	**What Makes a Zero Carbon Home Zero Carbon?** Heather Lovell and Jack Corbett	47
4	**What Are the Hidden Dimensions to Parliamentary Scrutiny—The Ghosts in the Machine?** Tony McNulty	71
5	**How Are Children's Rights (Mis)Interpreted in Practice? The European Commission, Children's Rights and Policy Narratives** Ingi Iusmen	97
6	**How Do You Go From Demonising Adversaries to Deliberating with Them?** John Boswell	121

7   How Have Narratives, Beliefs and Practices Shaped
    Pension Reform in Sweden?   141
    Karen Anderson

8   What Are the Consequences of Incessant Reform?
    Losing Trust, Policy Capacity and Institutional
    Memory in the Queensland Core Executive   165
    Anne Tiernan

9   How Do Local Government Chief Executives
    Engage with Policy Dilemmas?   197
    Kevin Orr and Mike Bennett

10 How Do the Police Respond to Evidence-Based
    Policing?   221
    Jenny Fleming

11 What Do UK Citizens Understand About Austerity?   241
    Anna Killick

Index   267

Editor and Contributors

About the Editor

Prof. R. A. W. Rhodes is Professor of Government (Research) and Director of the Centre for Political Ethnography at the University of Southampton. Visiting Professor, Utrecht School of Governance, University of Utrecht, The Netherlands; and Adjunct Professor, Centre for Governance and Public Policy, Griffith University, Queensland, Australia. He is the author or editor of 42 books including, most recently *Networks, Governance and the Differentiated Polity. Selected Essays. Volume I* (Oxford University Press, 2017), *Interpretive Political Science. Selected Essays. Volume II* (Oxford University Press, 2017), and the *Routledge Handbook of Interpretive Political Science* (with Mark Bevir, Routledge, 2015). He is a Fellow of the Academy of the Social Sciences in Australia, and a Fellow of the Academy of Social Sciences (UK). In 2015, the ECPR awarded him their biennial Lifetime Achievement Award for his 'outstanding contribution to all areas of political science, and the exceptional impact of his work'.

Contributors

Assoc. Prof. Karen Anderson Department of Sociology, Social Policy and Criminology, University of Southampton, Southampton UK.

Dr. Harry Annison Lecturer, Southampton Law School, University of Southampton, Southampton, UK.

Mike Bennett School of Management, University of St Andrews, UK.

Assoc. Prof. John Boswell Department of Politics and International Relations, University of Southampton, Southampton, UK.

Assoc. Prof. Jack Corbett School of Social Sciences, University of Southampton, Southampton, UK.

Prof. Jenny Fleming is Professor of Criminology and Head of Department, Department of Sociology, Social Policy and Criminology, University of Southampton; and Director of the Institute of Criminal Justice Research.

Dr. Ingi Iusmen Department of Politics and International Relations, University of Southampton, Southampton, UK.

Anna Killick Ph.D. Candidate, University of Southampton, Southampton, UK.

Assoc. Prof. Heather Lovell School of Social Sciences, University of Tasmania, Hobart, Australia.

Tony McNulty is the former Member of Parliament for Harrow East and Minister of State in both the Blair and Brown governments. Most recently, he was Minister for London (2008–2009).

Prof. Kevin Orr is Professor of Management, and Head of School, School of Management, University of St Andrews, UK.

Prof. Anne Tiernan is Dean (Engagement) and Director of the Policy Innovation Hub, Griffith University, Brisbane, Australia.

List of Figures

Fig. 8.1   The central networks of Queensland's core executive   169
Fig. 8.2   Queensland governments—1989 to present   170

List of Tables

Table 1.1	The interpretive approach	5
Table 1.2	Decentred analysis	6
Table 1.3	Bricolage	9
Table 1.4	Advantages of decentred analysis	15
Table 3.1	Examples of UK policy documents citing BedZed, 2002–2004	53
Table 6.1	Sites of policy advocacy on obesity	125
Table 9.1	Interviews: by number and type of authority	203
Table 11.1	Interview questions relevant to austerity	247

CHAPTER 1

What Is Decentred Analysis?

R. A. W. Rhodes

INTRODUCTION

Policy analysis provides information, evaluation, advice and advocacy for policymakers and is typically a species of naturalist or 'scientific' or positivist social science. It has some distinguished proponents, including Yehezkel Dror (1968), Harold Lasswell (1971), and Aaron Wildavsky (1980). Among the multitude of definitions, Hill (2013: 5) is representative. He distinguishes between analysis *of* the policy process and analysis *for* the policy process. The former is descriptive and analytical seeking to explain the origins of policy and how it was implemented. The latter is prescriptive using the analytical techniques often associated with economics to provide information and evaluations for policymakers.

Naturalism refers to the idea that 'The human sciences should strive to develop predictive and causal explanations akin to those found in the natural sciences' (Bevir and Kedar 2008: 503). For example, evidence-based policymaking is the latest fashion in policy analysis. It favours randomised controlled trials (RCTs). In brief, RCTs involve identifying the new policy intervention, determining the anticipated outcomes and specifying ways of measuring those outcomes.

R. A. W. Rhodes (✉)
University of Southampton, Southampton, UK
e-mail: r.a.w.rhodes@soton.ac.uk

© The Author(s) 2018
R. A. W. Rhodes (ed.), *Narrative Policy Analysis*, Understanding Governance, https://doi.org/10.1007/978-3-319-76635-5_1

Following this, the investigator chooses control groups, whether comprised of individuals or institutions. The policy intervention is randomly assigned to the target groups with a designated control group. Using a randomly assigned control group enables the investigator to compare a new intervention with a group where nothing has changed. Randomisation is considered appropriate to eradicate the influence of external factors and potential biases (Cartwright and Hardie 2012; Haynes et al. 2012). With its roots in clinical trials, the influence of the natural sciences' experimental method and the ambition to be 'scientific' are clear for all to see.

This book rejects such naturalism and argues for decentred policy analysis rooted in an anti-naturalist epistemology. First, it rejects the naturalist thesis that we can explain actions by allegedly objective social facts about people. Meanings are largely irrelevant to mainstream political science and policy studies. Beliefs are, at most, intervening variables. Actions can be correlated with, and explained by, social categories such as class, economic interest or institutional position. These analytical moves suppress or deny human agency. Second, it rejects the naturalist thesis that the relation between antecedent and consequent in political explanation is a necessary causal one—that is it is law like as in the natural science. Political science seeks psychological or social laws, rather than historical narratives or understanding webs of meaning.

Naturalism has been widely criticised for its faith in pure experience. Political scientists recognise that we cannot approach objects from a theory-neutral position. They seem far less aware that the impossibility of pure experience also undermines the two theses just discussed. First, because people do not have pure experiences, they always construct their identities, interests and beliefs in part through their particular theories. Therefore, political scientists cannot explain behaviour by reference to given interests or objective social facts. Second, because social facts do not fix people's identities, interests and beliefs, we have to explain actions by referring to the intentionality of the actors. Therefore, political scientists cannot appeal to causal laws (and for a more detailed discussion see Bevir and Rhodes 2003, 2015b).

In sharp contrast, anti-naturalists argue that 'constitutive features of human life set it apart from the rest of nature to such an extent that the social or human sciences cannot take the natural sciences as a model'. Instead, 'the relevant features of human action are that it is meaningful and historically contingent' (Bevir and Kedar 2008: 505). I develop these points in the next section.

Although naturalist policy analysis has paid some attention to narratives,[1] anti-naturalism underpins most narrative policy analysis, which has existed in the study of public policy since the 1990s.[2] It is one of the few subfields of political science where interpretive approaches have had some traction. Wagenaar (2011) provides an authoritative overview of the field, and there seems little point in covering the ground again. Instead, I focus on the key characteristics of our approach at Southampton: interpretive theory, decentring and fieldwork, especially ethnographic fieldwork. I discuss each in turn.

The rest of this chapter outlines the specific interpretive approach developed by Mark Bevir and R. A. W. Rhodes. It explains what we mean by 'decentring' and unpacks the ethnographic toolkit we employ. It provides brief descriptive summaries of the individual chapters but focuses on how each relates to the overall themes of the book. Finally, it discusses what we can learn from a decentred approach. I suggest that it delivers edification because it offers a novel alliance of interpretive theory with an ethnographic toolkit to explore policy and policymaking from the bottom-up.

INTERPRETIVE THEORY

All political scientists offer us interpretations. Interpretive approaches differ in offering interpretations of interpretations. They concentrate on meanings, beliefs and discourses, as opposed to laws and rules, correlations between social categories or deductive models. An interpretive approach is not alone in paying attention to meanings. It is distinctive because of the extent to which it privileges meanings as ways to grasp actions. Its proponents privilege meanings because they hold, first, beliefs have a constitutive relationship to actions and, second, beliefs are inherently holistic.[3]

First, an interpretive approach holds that beliefs and practices are constitutive of each other. As Clifford Geertz (1973: 5) famously claimed, social science needs to be 'not an experimental science in search of law but an interpretive one in search of meaning'. For example, when other political scientists study voting behaviour using attitude surveys or models of rational action, they separate beliefs from actions to find a correlation or deductive link between the two. In contrast, an interpretive approach suggests such surveys and models cannot tell us why, say, raising one's hand should amount to voting, or why there would be uproar if someone forced someone else to raise their hand against their will. We can explain such behaviour only if we appeal to the intersubjective beliefs that underpin the practice. We need to know voting is associated with free choice and, therefore, with a particular concept of the self. Practices could not exist if people did not have the appropriate beliefs. Beliefs or meanings would not make sense without the practices to which they refer.

Second, an interpretive approach argues that meanings or beliefs are holistic. We can make sense of someone's beliefs only by locating them in the wider web of other beliefs that provide the reasons for their holding them. So, even if political scientists found a correlation between a positive attitude to social justice and voting Labour, they could not properly explain people's voting Labour by reference to this attitude. After all, people who have a positive attitude to social justice might vote Liberal if they believe Labour will not implement policies promoting social justice. To explain why someone with a positive attitude to social justice votes Labour, we have to unpack the other relevant beliefs that link the attitude to the vote. To explain an action, we cannot merely correlate it with an isolated attitude. Rather, we must interpret it as part of a web of beliefs.

Third, human action is historically contingent. It is characterised by change and specificity. We cannot explain social phenomena if we ignore their inherent flux and their concrete links to specific contexts. Such historicist explanations work not by referring to reified correlations, mechanism or models, but by describing and locating contingent patterns of meaningful actions in their specific traditions. Historicists argue that beliefs, actions and events are profoundly contingent because choice is open and indeterminate. They question the possibility of either a universal theory or ahistorical correlations and typologies. In addition, they argue that if we are to understand and explain actions and beliefs, we have to grasp how they fit within wider practices and webs of meaning. Historicism promotes forms of understanding and explanation that are inductive studies of human life in its historical contexts. Its explanations are not only temporal in that they move through time; they are also historical in that they locate the phenomena at a specific time.

Proponents of an interpretive approach incline to bottom-up forms of social inquiry. They usually believe people in the same situation can hold different beliefs because their experiences of that situation can be laden with different prior theories. No abstract concept, such as a class or institution, can explain people's beliefs, interests or actions. Such a concept can represent only an abstract proxy for the multiple, complex beliefs and actions of all the individuals we classify under it. So, for these reasons,

Table 1.1 The interpretive approach (*Source* Geddes and Rhodes 2018)

Concept	Definition
Beliefs	Beliefs are the basic unit of analysis, in that they are the interpretations of individuals of their world and their surroundings
Practices	Sets of actions that often exhibit stable patterns across time. Practices are the ways in which beliefs and traditions manifest themselves in everyday life
Traditions	Traditions are 'webs of belief' and form the background of ideas in which agents find themselves. Agents will adopt beliefs from traditions as a starting point, but may amend them
Situated agents	Individuals are situated in wider webs of beliefs, or traditions, which largely shape their beliefs. Yet they keep a capacity for agency in that they respond to traditions, beliefs and dilemmas in novel ways
Dilemmas	A dilemma is an idea that stands in contradiction to other beliefs, therefore posing a problem. Dilemmas are resolved by accommodating the new belief in the present web of beliefs or replacing old beliefs with new beliefs
Narratives	Narratives are a form of explanation that works by relating actions to individual beliefs and desires that produce them

practices need bottom-up studies of the actions and beliefs out of which they emerge. An interpretive approach explores the ways in which social practices are created, sustained and transformed through the interplay and contest of the beliefs embedded in human activity.

Interpretive theories come in several guises (see Bevir and Rhodes 2015a: Chapters 2–10). This collection of essays draws on the approach developed by Mark Bevir and R. A. W. Rhodes. Their key concepts are summarised in Table 1.1.

Decentring

To decentre is to unpack practices as the contingent beliefs and actions of individuals. Decentred analysis produces detailed studies of people's beliefs and practices. It challenges the idea that inexorable or impersonal forces drive politics, focusing instead on the relevant meanings, the beliefs and preferences of the people involved. A decentred account of public policy is distinctive in seven ways (Table 1.2).

A core technique of decentring is recovering stories. Policy narratives are non-fiction stories with characters and plots. Decentred analysis identifies the beliefs and practices of the characters. The plot is the reasons

Table 1.2 Decentred analysis (*Source* Rhodes 2017)

1. It represents a shift of *topos* from institutions to *meanings* in action
2. Institutions whether a policy network or a prime ministerial office or a policy do not have essentialist features, only *family resemblances* that are *constructed, contested, and contingent*
3. Decentred analysis explains shifting patterns of policy and policymaking by focusing on the actors' own interpretations of their *beliefs and practices*, not external causes such as a global financial crisis
4. The everyday practices arise from agents whose beliefs and actions are informed by *traditions*
5. It explores the diverse ways in which *situated agents* are changing policies by constantly remaking practices as their beliefs change in response to *dilemmas*
6. It reveals the *contingency* and *contestability* of policy narratives. It highlights both the importance of local knowledge and the diversity of policymaking and its exercise
7. It provides instrumental knowledge expressed in *stories*

the characters give for their actions. Storytelling can be seen as an exercise in academic whimsy. However, Van Eeten et al. (1996) distinguish between storytelling by administrators and storytelling by scholars to make the important point that this academic fashion has its feet firmly on the ground. In both public and private organisations, managers use stories not only to gain and pass on information and to inspire involvement but also as the repository of the organisation's institutional memory (Czarniawska 2004; Hummel 1991; Rhodes 2011).

So, recovering stories can be treated as a technique like a survey—a means for acquiring data for policymakers. It is about providing information for policymakers so they can make rational decisions (Van Willigen 2002: 150 and Chapter 10). For example, Torfing et al. (2012: 156–159 and Chapter 7) argue that network governance requires new skills in managing the mix of bureaucracy, markets and networks. Such meta-governing involves devising policy narratives that span organisational boundaries and build collaborative leadership.

Writing a story is about inscribing complex specificity in its context (Wolcott 1995). Inscribing means recovering, recounting and reviewing the stories. We recover the stories told to us by politicians, public servants and citizens. We systematise these accounts, telling our version of their stories and recounting them. Our version is reviewed jointly by storywriter and storyteller to identify errors, divergences and lessons. The aim is a fusion of horizons that covers both agreement and where we agree to disagree. Both are reported. We derive practical lessons from lived experience—an interpretive equivalent of evidence-based policymaking (and see Rhodes and Tiernan 2014). We can choose to be servants of power and help the state win consent, but it is not required. We can choose to contribute to debates that will enhance the capacity of citizens to consider and voice differing perspectives in policy debates. It is an alternative normative choice.

Bricolage

Given the actor-centred character of decentred analysis, it favours fieldwork and methods that focus on the beliefs and practices of actors. An interpretive approach does not necessarily favour particular methods. It does not prescribe a particular toolkit for producing data. Rather, it prescribes a particular way of treating data of any type. It should treat data as evidence of the meanings or beliefs embedded in actions. However, the interpretive approach with its emphasis on recovering meaning does have implications for how we collect data. It leads to a much greater emphasis on qualitative methods than is common among naturalist political scientists. It favours ethnographic fieldwork.

The ethnographer studies people's everyday lives. Such fieldwork is unstructured. The aim is to recover the meaning of their actions by deep immersion, whether looking at a Congressional district or a government department. For Wood (2007: 123), it is 'research based on personal interaction with research subjects in their own setting', not in the laboratory, the library or one's office. It is intensive immersion in the everyday lives of other people in their local environment normally for a substantial period. Such 'deep immersion' or deep hanging out has been challenged. In sociology, ethnographers have long practised 'partial immersion' (Delamont 2007: 206). In the anthropological 'culture wars' of the 1980s, the contributors to Clifford and Marcus (1986) denied deep hanging out's claim to ethnographic authority in representing other cultures. It was said to produce colonial, gendered and racist texts with a specious claim to objectivity. The classic immersive study was challenged by 'hit-and-run ethnography' (Geertz 2001: 141). So, today, we 'study through' by conducting 'yo-yo-research' in multi-local sites. 'Studying through' refers to following events such as making a policy through the 'webs and relations between actors, institutions and discourses across time and space' (Shore and Wright 1997: 14). 'Yo-Yo research' refers to both regular movement in and out of the field and to participant observation in many local sites (Wulff 2002; Marcus 1995: 6–7). Marcus (2007) describes the current practices of ethnography as 'baroque' as even partial immersion becomes dispersed over several sites.

We do not dismiss the value of an immersive approach to ethnography. Rather we stress there is a menu of ethnographic tools. The choice of tools will depend on the access the researcher can negotiate. For example, elite ethnography is difficult because we attempt to enter a closed and secretive world, a hidden world, occupied by people who are more powerful than the researcher. Access can be denied. We have to find other ways of 'being there' (see also Nader 1972: 306–307). For example, focus groups can give access to a group of elite actors. We can observe them in action when observation is not possible at the workplace, especially when the relevant individuals are no longer in office. Focus groups are another way of 'being there' and sidestepping the problems of access and secrecy (see Rhodes and Tiernan 2014).

The several ways of 'being there' are not stand-alone methods. Ideally, we would supplement each method with shadowing. Most important, the data generated by focus groups and other methods require an 'ethnographic sensibility' for interpreting the conversations (Agar and MacDonald 1995; Schatz 2009). The various ethnographic methods suggested in Table 1.3 are still about recovering meaning and locating that meaning in its broader context. So, focus groups are an ethnographic method because ethnography is now a diverse set of practices linked not by a shared method—participant observation—but by a shared focus on the recovery of meaning—the ethnographic sensibility.

Just as are there are many tools in the toolkit, so there are many field roles that the researcher can play. For example, Adler and Adler (1987) distinguish between peripheral, active and complete roles. Thus, peripheral members observe but do not participate in core activities of the group under study. Active members take part in such core activities while complete members become group members; they 'go native'. Each role opens up its own opportunities and imposes its own constraints. For example, complete members are emotionally engaged with the group and find it hard to detach themselves. Within each role, there are also choices to be made. Kedia and Van Willigen (2005: 11) distinguish between 'policy researcher or research analyst; evaluator; impact assessor, or needs assessor; cultural broker; public participation specialist; and administrator or manager'. Applied ethnography can serve many masters, and in identifying the role to be played, a key question is for whom is the research being done.

Table 1.3 Bricolage (*Source* Boswell et al. 2018)

Ethnographic methods	Definition	Potential sources of data	Examples
Hit-and-run fieldwork	Repeated, short bursts of intensive observation as researchers move in-and-out of the field	Legislatures, constituency offices, campaign events	Crewe (2015) and Rhodes (2011)
Ethnographic interviewing	Repeated, semi-structured and unstructured interviews with the same participant	Recently retired politicians and public officials	Corbett (2015) and Reeher (2006)
Memoirs	First-person reflections on governing	Autobiographies and authorised biographies; radio and television interviews	Rhodes (2017) and Richards and Mathers (2010)
Elite focus groups	Group reflections that encourage elites to flesh out and challenge each other's claims	Recently retired politicians and public officials	Rhodes and Tiernan (2014)
Para-ethnography	Ethnographic interviews with a decision-maker to explain a specific decision or event (see Holmes and Markus 2005)	Focused on particular legislative documents, departmental files	Novel in political science but see Holmes and Marcus (2005)
Visual ethnography	Using video recordings as a form of remote observation (see Pink 2013)	C-SPAN (and similar footage elsewhere); press conferences, parliamentlive.tv	Novel in political science but see Pink (2013)

As ever dichotomies mislead. They can become straitjackets. We do not see deep hanging out and hit-and-run fieldwork as mutually exclusive. That is why we talk of 'bricolage'—that is constructing research data from diverse methods and materials (Denzin and Lincoln 2011: 4; and Table 1.3)—and bringing an 'ethnographic sensibility' to bear on the data, however collected (and for a more detailed account see Rhodes 2017: Chapters 3–5).

The Chapters

The remainder of the book examines policies through the eyes of the practitioners. We start with the beliefs and practices of national governing elites before moving through the state governmental to local government before, finally, we turn to citizens. We introduce a different angle of vision on the policy process; we look at it from the standpoint of the individual actor, not institutions. In other words, we look at policies from the other end of the telescope. I provide a short descriptive summary of each chapter but focus on drawing out the relevance of each chapter to the book's themes of interpretation, decentring and bricolage. I explore what the chapters tell us about a decentred approach.

Harry Annison decentres the UK Ministry of Justice (MoJ) in Chapter 2. Using some 80 research interviews conducted with senior policymakers, supported by the analysis of relevant documents, he traces the four traditions that underpin the department and the four dilemmas policy participants encounter. The four Ministries of Justice are: a liberal MoJ centred upon justice and fairness; a MoJ determined to achieve the rehabilitation of offenders; a MoJ obsessed with public protection; and a MoJ that is steeped in new managerialism. They collide around the four dilemmas of: judicial representative vs. government minister; departmental coherence vs. the autonomy of its parts; policy vs. operations; and patient implementation vs. political responsiveness. Decentring reveals that we are faced not with a monolithic institution but *Ministries* of Justice. The label 'Ministry of Justice' is a convenient reification and that decentring reveals the combination of, and competition between, contrasting traditions.

In Chapter 3, Heather Lovell and Jack Corbett uncover the different meanings of a 'zero carbon' housing policy. Drawing on some 60 interviews and site visits, they show that contest over meaning was a strong feature of the ZCH policy. It enabled the deep green environmental advocates to challenge the dominant framing of housing policy as a form of ecological modernisation. The case highlights a housing sector that includes environmentalists, architects, large- and small-house builders and private contractors, among others, each with their own problem definition and their own (often bespoke) solution. When, in mid-2015, the UK government abolished the Zero Carbon policy, it signalled the end of the formal policy but not the end of the policy, which continues to attract support from diverse organisations. The case demonstrates the value of a decentred approach because it addresses perennial public policy concerns about multi-actor policy arenas and implementation delays and failures—the problem and opportunities of too many hands.

Tony McNulty was a former Minister of State under Prime Minister, Gordon Brown. He draws on his insider experience as the lead minister for the Counter-Terrorism Bill (2008) and on interviews with over 50 MPs, ministers, civil servants, special advisers and other public officials. He examines the parliamentary scrutiny of the Bill, which sought to extend the period of pre-charge detention for terrorist suspects from the existing 28 days to 42 days. He argues that to understand parliamentary scrutiny, we need to explore the traditions, beliefs and practices of each set of actors in the process. He argues that there are hidden dimensions to parliamentary scrutiny, and we need to understand such 'ghosts in the machine'. Decentring reveals a novel, multidimensional narrative that unearths these hidden dimensions.

In Chapter 5, Ingi Iusmen explores the implementation of the UN Convention on the Rights of the Child. The EU has endorsed the promotion of children's rights, and she focuses on how EU institutions interpreted and misinterpreted 'child participation' and 'the best interests of the child'. She examines the extent to which institutional narratives, beliefs and practices shaped the meanings attached to these two principles and how these meanings affected policy instruments and implementation. She shows that the Commission drove a protection, needs-based approach, which marginalised children's voices, rather than a prevention and child empowerment approach. The Commission's narrative was not a shared narrative. It was not persuasive among children's rights stakeholders and activists because EU policymakers preferred their interpretation rather than listening to the voices of the children and their spokespersons. As a result, the Commission ended up paying only lip service to the Convention on the Rights of the Child.

In Chapter 6, John Boswell examines those present-day practices of democratic governance that require policy actors to engage across many settings. Some, like the media, are adversarial. They reward simple messages and emotive rhetoric. Others, like expert committees, are more consensus-oriented. They reward sober analysis and technical mastery. Yet in practice, it is often the same actors participating across these diverse settings. Theories of democratic governance typically presume that policy actors advance their best interests at all points of the policy process. However, given this complex patchwork of settings, it is not at all clear how they ought to go about doing this. How do actors negotiate divergent settings to best promote their policy claims? How do they go from publicly demonising adversaries to privately deliberating with them? The chapter explores these questions through a decentred analysis of the obesity debates in Britain and Australia. It is an example of bricolage in that it draws together over 40 interviews with policy actors, 25 hours of video footage of hearings and meetings and thousands of documentary sources. It presents a decentred account of how individuals act in a network, and shows that all actors are not equally capable of advancing their cause across policy debates. The most experienced political operators refer to back-stage practices of 'orchestrated conflict' that enable them to pursue their interests without harming personal relationships. The most inexperienced and peripheral actors—mostly in the public health lobby—can be naïve, and their naivety can be exploited to mask conflict. They either remain adversarial or peripheral in influencing networks. Decentring reveals another way in which the 'dark side' of networked governance can exacerbate asymmetries of access and influence.

In Chapter 7, Karen Anderson explores how narratives, beliefs and practices shaped pension reform. Existing accounts of pension reform processes in Sweden emphasise the impact of political partisanship, institutional constraints and demographic and economic pressures in shaping the direction of policy. It focuses on how the beliefs and practices of policymakers in specific historical contexts shaped the actions associated with pension reform and the reform packages that resulted. To capture the beliefs and practices of key actors, the analysis draws from six semi-structured interviews with relevant policymakers undertaken in May 1994, March 1995 and February 2000 and on documentary sources such as memoirs, published interviews and official documents. The chapter shows how important pension reform struggles in the past shaped policymakers' beliefs and shared narratives about the appropriate design and role of the pension system. Outcomes were much more open and contingent than existing research allows, shaped by the legacy of previous conflicts and hinging on such events as the abstention in the Second Chamber of one Liberal MP.

In Chapter 8, Anne Tiernan presents an 'insider's account' of working with the Queensland state government in Australia to explore the consequences of successive waves of public-sector reform for the Queensland core executive. From 2007 to 2015, the author was an 'active member researcher', participating in the social activities of the group. She took 'part in the core activities of the group'. 'Instead of merely sharing the status of insiders, they interact as colleagues: co-participants in a joint endeavour' (Adler and Adler 1987: 50). Therefore, she worked closely with the members of the political-administrative networks at the centre of Queensland government. Her roles included a member of the Board of the Queensland Public Service Commission; a consultant; a professional educator; a researcher; a confidante; and now a 'critical friend'. The chapter draws on documentary and interview data, as well as informal conversations and observational data, collected in the course of her evolving relationship with Queensland's elite decision-makers. She demonstrates that fieldwork data can be collected in many ways other than those commonly employed by the academic researcher. She explores the implications of frequent, discontinuous change on the beliefs, traditions and practices of central core executive networks and for the quality and efficiency of governance. She shows how it destroyed trust, policy capacity and the 'storage locations' of institutional memory. Reform destabilised the senior ranks of the state's public service, and Tiernan became the one constant. She watched ministers and public servants come and go. She taught, mentored, supported and consulted to officials, ministerial staff and occasionally ministers. She offered a plank of continuity (once the *raison d'être* of a career civil service) from her position at the University.

In Chapter 9, Kevin Orr and Mike Bennett explore how local government chief executives use storytelling to cope with policy dilemmas in the complex arenas of policy networks. It employs a relational perspective that directs attention to communicative practices, such as stories and narratives, through which policy 'realities' are constructed. It employs a decentred approach that collects and learns from the stories of front-line actors. The stories are drawn from 80 interviews conducted with local council chief executives between 2008 and 2016 during which time Bennett was also the director of the chief executive's professional association; he was a complete member researcher. For many years, researchers and practitioners have observed how the policy process has become more decentred—pluralistic or fragmented—involving communities groups, think tanks, media and business groups. In turn, public leaders changed the ways in which they operated. Storytelling emerges as a facilitative resource in policymaking that enables actors to understand the everyday dilemmas of local government actors. The authors suggest that networks are significant for understanding the policymaking practices of local government chief executives. Decentring these networks shows how chief executives frame their accounts of the dilemmas posed by: political values; officer–member relations; relations between members of the council and wider stakeholders, including central government departments and inspectorates. Focusing on the practices of chief executives shows them as actors responding to the flux embedded in policy networks, as they interpret and respond to the competing expectations, actions and experiences of others.

In Chapter 10, Jenny Fleming explores the response of police officers to evidence-based policing. The 'What Works' initiative in the UK aimed to improve the way government and its agencies create, share and use high-quality evidence. *What Works* is based on the principle that good decision-making should be informed by the best available evidence. This evidence should be 'translated' into practical insights that police officers can use. The chapter discusses police officers' response to this evidence-based agenda and the organisational change that would result from its implementation. The chapter draws on data from all ranks, across four police organisations in the UK. The data were obtained through focus groups conducted in 2014, which were attended by 160 police officers from the ranks of constable, sergeant and inspector. The silent voices were not so silent in the focus groups. They were cynical about what they saw as the relentless cycle of change and the senior officers whose careers were based on its implementation. Fleming decentres the inherited beliefs and practices about hierarchy and shows how the divide between the rank and file and management undermines reform. Identifying such bottom-up narratives allows for an understanding of the webs of belief that drive their practices. They unearth the dilemmas and unintended consequences that beset reform and shed light on how existing beliefs are continuously created and sustained even when continuously challenged.

In Chapter 11, Anna Killick asks what UK citizens understand by 'austerity'. At the height of austerity in the UK, many writers argued that the public accepted painful debt reduction policies because they chimed with 'common sense' experience of personal debt. However, while surveys showed public acceptance of austerity, there was little political research asking people what they believed. This interpretivist study is based on interviews with 60 residents of a southern city. It finds that the political economists were right about the 'common sense' of higher income participants, but that lower-income participants did not share such views. They do not believe personal debt and government debt are comparable, that debt is caused by profligacy, or that debt can be reduced quickly. Above all, the chapter demonstrates that social scientists should not assume that they know the beliefs of citizens or that surveys provide an adequate picture of those beliefs. There is not a single dominant version of economic 'common sense'. It is context dependent. People know what they need to know. They learn from their everyday economic experiences. We should always explore particular voices, especially the silent voices of the more marginalised members of society. Moreover, we need an ethnographic sensibility and detailed interviews, not surveys, to draw out such beliefs.

Conclusions

Previous sections of this chapter explain interpretive theory, decentring and bricolage. The summary of the chapters identified the specific contribution of a decentred analysis to several, diverse policy areas. A further summary would try not only the reader's but also the writer's patience. Table 1.4 provides a brief reminder of the advantages of using decentred analysis.

The decentred approach delivers edification—that is 'new, better, more interesting, more fruitful ways of speaking about' policymaking and policy analysis (Rorty 1980: 360). It does so because it is actor centred. It sees policy as enacted by individuals and explains the actions of policymakers by appealing to their beliefs and preferences. In this sense,

Table 1.4 Advantages of decentred analysis (*Source* Modified from Rhodes 2017: 209)

1. It provides data not available elsewhere
2. It identifies key individuals and core processes
3. It identifies 'voices' all too often ignored
4. By disaggregating organisations, it opens 'the black box' of internal processes
5. It recovers the beliefs and practices of actors
6. It gets behind the surface of official accounts by providing texture, depth and nuance, so our stories have richness as well as context
7. It lets interviewees explain the meaning of their actions, providing an authenticity that can only come from the main characters involved in the story
8. It allows us to frame (and reframe) questions in a way that recognises that our understandings about how things work around here evolve during the fieldwork
9. It admits of surprises—of moments of epiphany, serendipity and happenstance—that can open new research agendas
10. It helps us to see and analyse the symbolic, performative aspects of political action

it is a bottom-up approach. In addition, it has a distinctive toolkit. Bricolage is not a standard part of the toolkit of either political scientists or policy analysts. Kapiszewski et al. (2015: 234) concluded that 'political science has yet to embrace ethnography and participant observation wholeheartedly'. Indeed, there is a '*double absence*: of politics in ethnographic literature and of ethnography in the study of politics' (Auyero and Joseph 2007: 2, emphasis in the original). Therefore, decentring offers a novel alliance of interpretive theory with an ethnographic toolkit to explore policymaking and policy analysis from the bottom-up.[4]

Storytelling is also practical. Inscribing complex specificity in its context provides information for policymakers so they can make rational decisions. Recovering, recounting and reviewing the stories are all practical techniques. Although practitioners will not use these labels, they will be familiar with the practices because in many instances they will be part of their everyday life.

This collection shows that decentred analysis can be conducted in a wide range of policy areas across several countries. It travels well. In addition, it shows that it can produce studies both *of* the policy process and *for* policymakers. For example, Anderson (Chapter 7) shows that conventional institutional accounts of welfare policy in Sweden leave out far too much, not allowing for such contingencies as one abstention. Boswell's (Chapter 6) account of policy network in obesity policy arena reveals the dark side of that network. Indeed, by producing new accounts of the policy process, decentred analysis opens new possibilities for the policymakers. It suggests different ways of acting for the practitioner. For example, Tiernan's account (Chapter 8) of continuous reform in Queensland highlights the adverse consequences of losing institutional memory and the importance of the public service for continuity. The policy prescriptions arising out of her account are blindingly obvious. Similarly, Orr and Bennett (Chapter 9) highlight the centrality not only of storytelling but also of the facilitative skills of local authority chief executives in managing networks.

What does this approach add? It identifies the silent voices. At the heart of the storytelling, approach is the collection of the several voices in a policy arena—in effect, increasing the voices heard. It does not exclude evidence-based policymaking. It treats it as another way of telling a story alongside all the other stories. Proponents of evidence-based policymaking in the UK cannot present themselves as neutral scientists with objective evidence. Rather, they must recognise they are protagonists in a political game—*partisan evidence advocates* (cf. Schultze 1968: 101) or policy entrepreneurs, but *not* bearers of truth. Like any other actor in the policy process, they must persuade, negotiate and compromise—be political actors, not scientists. By recording, recovering and reviewing our version of their stories, decentring encourages the forensic interrogation of these different stories. Such an interrogation focuses attention on the criteria for choosing between stories. It seeks to make the tacit criteria for evaluating and comparing stories transparent. It challenges the notion that efficiency or cuts or austerity are the most appropriate criteria for adjudicating between policy options.

In short, decentred analysis offers novel theory and methods with a clear practical application.

Acknowledgements I must thank John Boswell, Jack Corbett and Jenny Fleming for the helpful comments on the first draft. The chapter draws on my previous work with Mark Bevir (see Bevir and Rhodes 2003, 2006, 2010 and 2015b).

Notes

1. See Denning (2005), Dietz and Silverman (2014), Gabriel (2000), Jones and McBeth (2010), Jones et al. (2014), and Roe (1994).
2. Early examples include Bobrow et al. (1987), Dryzek (1993), Fischer and Forester (1993), Healy (1986), Hummel (1991), Jennings (1987), Van Eeten et al. (1996), and Yanow (1999). More recently, see: Bevir (2011), Czarniawska (2004), Fischer (2003), Fischer et al. (2006), Hajer (2009), Hajer and Wagenaar (2003), Stone (2001), and Wagenaar (2011). In the UK, there is also a dedicated journal, *Critical Policy Studies,* and an annual interpretive policy analysis conference.
3. This section paraphrases Bevir and Rhodes (2003, 2006, 2010 and 2015b) and Rhodes (2017).
4. It would require another chapter to discuss the strengths and weakness of both interpretive theory and of ethnographic methods. See, for example, Rhodes (2017: Chapters 2, 3 and 12) and Turnbull (2016).

References

Adler, P. A., & Adler, P. (1987). *Membership Roles in Field Research*. Newbury Park, CA: Sage.

Agar, M., & MacDonald, J. (1995). Focus Groups and Ethnography. *Human Organization, 54,* 78–86.

Auyero, J., & Joseph, L. (2007). Introduction: Politics Under the Ethnographic Microscope. In L. Joseph, M. Mahler, & J. Auyero (Eds.), *New Perspectives on Political Ethnography* (pp. 1–13). New York: Springer.
Bevir, M. (2011). Public Administration as Storytelling. *Public Administration, 89,* 183–195.
Bevir, M., & Kedar, A. (2008). Concept Formation in Political Science: An Antinaturalist Critique of Qualitative Methodology. *Perspectives on Politics, 6,* 503–517.
Bevir, M., & Rhodes, R. A. W. (2003). *Interpreting British Governance.* London: Routledge.
Bevir, M., & Rhodes, R. A. W. (2006). *Governance Stories.* London: Routledge.
Bevir, M., & Rhodes, R. A. W. (2010). *The State as Cultural Practice.* Oxford: Oxford University Press.
Bevir, M., & Rhodes, R. A. W. (Eds.). (2015a). *The Routledge Handbook of Interpretive Political Science.* Abingdon, Oxon: Routledge.
Bevir, M., & Rhodes, R. A. W. (2015b). Interpretive Political Science: Mapping the Field. In M. Bevir & R. A. W. Rhodes (Eds.), *The Routledge Handbook of Interpretive Political Science* (pp. 3–27). Abingdon, Oxon: Routledge.
Bobrow, D. B., & Dryzek, J. S. (1987). *Policy Analysis by Design.* Pittsburgh: Pittsburgh University Press.
Boswell, J., Corbett, J., Flinders, M., Jennings, W., Rhodes, R. A. W., & Wood, M. (2018). What Can Political Ethnography Tell Us About Antipolitics and Democratic Disaffection? *European Journal of Political Research* (forthcoming).
Cartwright, N., & Hardie, J. (2012). *Evidence-Based Policy Making: A Practical Guide.* Oxford: Oxford University Press.
Clifford, J., & Marcus, G. E. (Eds.). (1986). *Writing Culture: The Poetics and Politics of Ethnography.* Berkeley: University of California Press.
Corbett, J. (2015). *Being Political. Leadership and Democracy in the Pacific Islands.* Honolulu: University of Hawaii Press.
Crewe, E. (2015). *The House of Commons: An Anthropology of MPs at Work.* London: Bloomsbury.
Czarniawska, B. (2004). *Narratives in Social Science Research.* London: Sage.
Delamont, S. (2007). Ethnography and Participant Observation. In C. Seale, G. Giampietri, J. F. Gubrium, & D. S. Silverman (Eds.), *Qualitative Research Practice* (pp. 205–227). Thousand Oaks, CA: Sage.
Denning, S. (2005). *The Leader's Guide to Storytelling: Mastering the Art and Discipline of Business Narrative.* San Francisco: Jossey-Bass.
Denzin, N. K., & Lincoln, Y. S. (2011 [1994]). Introduction: The Discipline and Practice of Qualitative Research. In N. K. Denzin & Y. S. Lincoln (Eds.), *Handbook of Qualitative Research* (4th ed., pp. 1–19). London: Sage.
Dietz, K., & Silverman, L. (2014). *Business Storytelling for Dummies.* Hoboken, NJ: Wiley.

Dror, Y. (1968). *Public Policymaking Re-examined*. San Francisco: Chandler Publishing.
Dryzek, J. S. (1993). Policy Analysis and Planning: From Science to Argument. In F. Fischer & J. Forester (Eds.), *The Argumentative Turn in Policy Analysis and Planning*. Durham: Duke University Press.
Fischer, F. (2003). *Reframing Policy Analysis*. Oxford: Oxford University Press.
Fischer, F., & Forester, J. (Eds.). (1993). *The Argumentative Turn in Policy Analysis and Planning*. Durham: Duke University Press.
Fischer, F., Miller, G. J., & Sidney, M. S. (2006). *Handbook of Public Policy Analysis: Theory, Politics, and Methods*. Abingdon, Oxon: Routledge.
Gabriel, Y. (2000). *Storytelling in Organizations: Facts, Fictions, and Fantasies*. London: Oxford University Press.
Geddes, M., & Rhodes, R. A. W. (2018). Towards an Interpretive Parliamentary Studies. In J. Brichzin, D. Krichewsky, L. Ringel, & J. Schank (Eds.), *The Sociology of Parliaments* (pp. 87–107). Wiesbaden: Springer VS.
Geertz, C. (1973). Thick Description: Toward an Interpretive Theory of Culture. In *The Interpretation of Cultures* (pp. 3–30). New York: Basic Books.
Geertz, C. (2001). *Available Light*. Princeton NJ: Princeton University Press.
Hajer, M. A. (2009). *Authoritative Governance*. Oxford: Oxford University Press.
Hajer, M. A., & Wagenaar, H. (Eds.). (2003). *Deliberative Policy Analysis. Understanding Governance in a Networked Society*. Cambridge: Cambridge University Press.
Haynes, L., Service, O., Goldacre, B., & Torgerson, D. (2012). *Test, Learn, Adapt. Developing Public Policy with Randomised Controlled Trials*. London: Cabinet Office.
Healy, P. (1986). Interpretive Policy Inquiry: A Response to the Limitations of the Received View. *Policy Sciences, 19*, 381–396.
Hill, M. (2013). *The Public Policy Process* (6th ed.). Abingdon, Oxon: Routledge.
Holmes, D. R., & Marcus, G. E. (2005). Refunctioning Ethnography: The Challenge of an Anthropology of the Contemporary. In N. K. Denzin & Y. S. Lincoln (Eds.), *Handbook of Qualitative Research* (3rd ed., pp. 1087–1101). London: Sage.
Hummel, R. P. (1991). Stories Managers Tell: Why They Are as Valid as Science. *Public Administration Review, 51*, 31–41.
Jennings, B. (1987). Interpretation and the Practice of Policy Analysis. In F. Fischer & J. Forester (Eds.), *Confronting Values in Policy Analysis* (pp. 128–152). Newbury Park, CA: Sage.
Jones, M. D., & McBeth, M. K. (2010). A Narrative Policy Framework: Clear Enough to Be Wrong? *Policy Studies Journal, 38*, 329–353.
Jones, M. D., Shanahan, E. A., & McBeth, M. K. (Eds.). (2014). *The Science of Stories: Applications of the Narrative Policy Framework in Public Policy Analysis*. Basingstoke: Palgrave Macmillan.

Kapiszewski, D., MacLean, L. M., & Read, B. L. (2015). *Field Research in Political Science*. Cambridge: Cambridge University Press.
Kedia, S., & Van, W. J. (2005). Applied Anthropology: Context for Domains of Application. In S. Kedia & W. J. Van (Eds.), *Applied Anthropology: Domains of Application* (pp. 1–32). Westport, CT: Praeger.
Lasswell, H. D. (1971). *A Preview of Policy Sciences*. Amsterdam: Elsevier.
Marcus, G. E. (1995). Ethnography in/of the World System: The Emergence of Multi-Sited Ethnography. *Annual Review in Anthropology, 24*, 95–117.
Marcus, G. E. (2007). Ethnography Two Decades After Writing Culture: From the Experimental to the Baroque. *Anthropological Quarterly, 80*, 1127–1145.
Nader, L. (1972). Up the Anthropologist—Perspectives Gained from Studying Up. In D. H. Hymes (Ed.), *Reinventing Anthropology* (pp. 284–311). New York: Pantheon Books.
Pink, S. (2013). *Doing Visual Ethnography* (3rd ed.). London: Sage.
Reeher, G. (2006). *First Person Political*. New York: New York University Press.
Rhodes, R. A. W. (2011). *Everyday Life in British Government*. Oxford: Oxford University Press.
Rhodes, R. A. W. (2017). *Interpretive Political Science: Selected Essays* (Vol. II). Oxford: Oxford University Press.
Rhodes, R. A. W., & Tiernan, A. (2014). *Lessons in Governing: A Profile of Prime Ministers. Chiefs of Staff*. Carlton, VIC: Melbourne University Press.
Richards, D., & Mathers, H. (2010). Political Memoirs New Labour: Interpretations of Power the "Club Rules". *British Journal of Politics International Relations, 12*, 498–522.
Roe, E. (1994). *Narrative Policy Analysis: Theory and Practice*. Durham: Duke University Press.
Rorty, R. (1980). *Philosophy and the Mirror of Nature*. Oxford: Blackwell.
Schatz, E. (2009). Introduction. In E. Schatz (Ed.), *Political Ethnography: The Difference Immersion Makes* (pp. 1–22). Toronto: University of Toronto Press.
Schultze, C. L. (1968). *The Politics and Economics of Public Spending*. Washington, DC: The Brookings Institution.
Shore, C., & Wright, S. (Eds.). (1997). *The Anthropology of Policy: Critical Perspectives on Governance and Power*. London: Routledge.
Stone, D. A. (2001). *Policy Paradox: The Art of Political Decision Making* (Rev. ed.). New York: W.W. Norton.
Torfing, J., Peters, B. G., Pierre, J., & Sorensen, E. (2012). *Interactive Governance: Advancing the Paradigm*. Oxford: Oxford University Press.
Turnbull, N. (Ed.). (2016). *Interpreting Governance, High Politics and Public Policy: Essays Commemorating Interpreting British Governance*. New York: Routledge.

Van Eeten, M. J. G., Van Twist, M. J. W., & Kalders, P. R. (1996). Van een narratieve bestuurskunde naar een postmoderne beweerkunde? (M. van Twist, English Trans.). *Bestuurskunde*, 5(4), 168–189.

Van Willigen, J. (2002). *Applied Anthropology: An Introduction* (3rd ed.). Westport, CT: Bergin & Garvey.

Wagenaar, H. (2011). *Meaning in Action: Interpretation and Dialogue in Policy Analysis*. Armonk, NY: M.E. Sharpe.

Wildavsky, A. (1980). *The Art and Craft of Policy Analysis*. London: Palgrave Macmillan.

Wolcott, H. F. (1995). *The Art of Fieldwork*. Walnut Creek, CA: Altamira Press.

Wood, E. J. (2007). Field Research. In C. Boix & S. C. Stokes (Eds.), *The Oxford Handbook of Comparative Politics* (pp. 123–146). Oxford: Oxford University Press.

Wulff, H. (2002). Yo-Yo Fieldwork: Mobility and Time in Multi-local Study of Dance in Ireland. *Anthropological Journal of European Cultures, 11,* 117–136.

Yanow, D. (1999). *Conducting Interpretive Policy Analysis*. Thousand Oaks, CA: Sage.

CHAPTER 2

What is Penal Policy? Traditions and Practices in the UK Ministry of Justice

Harry Annison

INTRODUCTION

In this chapter, I depict the Ministry of Justice (MoJ). I draw on research interviews conducted with senior policymakers, supported by the analysis of relevant documents and existing accounts, to trace a number of traditions that underpin the department and a number of dilemmas that policy participants encounter by dint of their involvement with the department.[1] I decentre it, providing my account of policy participants' accounts of what the MoJ *is* and what it is *for*.

Before saying a little more about the approach taken and the methodology utilized, we can provide briefly a more 'standard' account of the department, in order to provide some orientation points for the discussion that follows. It was created on 9 May 2007, assembled from components of the Home Office and the Department for Constitutional Affairs (DCA)—itself a recent reformulation of the historic Lord Chancellor's Department (LCD). Its political head was to hold jointly the positions

---

H. Annison (✉)
Southampton Law School, University of Southampton, Southampton, UK
e-mail: h.annison@soton.ac.uk

© The Author(s) 2018
R. A. W. Rhodes (ed.), *Narrative Policy Analysis*, Understanding Governance, https://doi.org/10.1007/978-3-319-76635-5_2

of Secretary of State for Justice and Lord Chancellor. These developments were highly controversial. The decision to create the department was taken swiftly and with little consultation (House of Lords Select Committee on the Constitution 2014).

Concern was expressed, not least, due to the unusual and historically prominent role played by the Lord Chancellor. The Lord Chancellor was a member of the Cabinet, was responsible for criminal legal aid and oversaw constitutional affairs. The Lord Chancellor was Speaker of the House of Lords, as well as speaking and voting in the House as a member of the government. They could also sit as a judge in the judicial House of Lords (although tended to do so rarely). 'As a figure spanning Parliament, the executive and the judiciary, the Lord Chancellor had a vital role in upholding the rule of law and the independence of the judiciary' (House of Lords Select Committee on the Constitution 2014: 6).

The department comprises a number of executive agencies including the National Offender Management Service (NOMS). On 1 April 2017, NOMS was replaced by a new organization, Her Majesty's Prisons and Probation Service (HMPPS). The department is self-defined as:

> One of the largest government departments, employing around 70,040 people (including those in the Probation Service), with a budget of approximately £9 billion. Each year, millions of people use our services across the UK - including at 500 courts and tribunals, and 133 prisons in England and Wales.[2]

These origins make the MoJ a particularly valuable object of decentred analysis.

A Note on Methods[3]

This chapter draws on four sets of research interviews conducted with senior penal policymakers over seven years, in relation to three distinct projects. The first and second sets comprised interviews conducted between September 2010 and October 2011, and March–June 2014, respectively. Together these totalled 63 interviews. They were centred upon the policymaking relating to the Imprisonment for Public Protection (IPP) sentence targeted at 'dangerous offenders', which had—and continues to have—great significance for both its practical effects and implications for penal theory (Annison 2015). The third set comprised 26 interviews conducted between March 2014 and August 2016. These addressed primarily policymakers' experience of penal policy under conditions of coalition government (Annison 2018). The fourth set comprised five interviews conducted between February 2017 and June 2017, centring specifically on the question of the cultures and practices of the MoJ during its ten-year history. Quotes from interviews are accompanied by an indication of the broad category into which the respondent fits (e.g. civil servant or special adviser) and the year in which the interview was conducted.

There was a degree of overlap between each set of interviews, in terms of individuals interviewed. Due to this fact, taken as a whole these sets of interviews constitute a form of what Rhodes has termed 'ethnographic interviewing' (Rhodes 2015). These repeat interviews, if trust and rapport are successfully developed, can serve as a valuable means of circumventing the barriers to engaging in sustained ethnographic study of a department, as one might ideally wish. In this case, elite policymakers became more relaxed and open with each encounter meaning that the fourth set of interviews, though small in number, provided a wealth of information that expanded on dynamics glimpsed, but not always clearly elucidated, in earlier interviews.

This is an 'elite' account of the MoJ. A 'bottom-up' view, of which there are many accounts spanning prisons, policing, probation and so on provided in the criminological literature, may differ substantially from that presented here. I present here a much less common 'view from the top', based upon research interviews with senior criminal justice policymakers (and informed by interviews with a broader range of participants). An interpretive stance should not be mistaken for one of endorsement. I seek here to understand the perspectives in play, not to favour one position over another.

Traditions

This section identifies a number of competing traditions that underpin practice within the MoJ. In so doing, it also touches on key historical developments in relation to the decade-old UK MoJ. For clarity and emphasis, each tradition is presented in its strongest form.

The Ministry of Justice Is Legal Liberalism

The MoJ is the 'liberal department' (Special adviser 2017). Human rights, due process, fairness and justice are central concerns. The rule of law is sacrosanct.

> You've got the prison reformers and you've got the liberal judges, sentencing, reform people…that is the pigeonhole that a lot of people in the Ministry of Justice find themselves in… The Ministry of Justice was always seen as being a hotbed of liberalism, and compared to the Home Office which was the bulwark of a much tougher law and order approach. That was true not only under David Cameron but also under Gordon Brown and Tony Blair as well. (Special adviser 2017)

While the department was far from being a coherent whole (as discussed below), what these parts had in common was 'by and large, a more liberal ethos, a small 'l' liberal ethos, than say the Home Office':

> So what had happened I think with the separation is that we began to look pretty much like the continental divide between the Interior and Justice Ministries. You talk to any Europeans, and it is always the Interior Ministry are a bunch of semi fascists and the Justice Ministry tend to be peopled by more liberal types. (Civil servant 2017)

There was a 'cultural commonality' between sentencing officials, the senior judiciary and the concerns underpinning sentencing law and penal policy (Civil servant 2016). The officials moving from the Home Office 'were the ones who did…check and balances and all that' (Civil servant 2017)[4]:

> All of the concerns you've just talked about, you know, proportionality and over-population in prisons have generally, with a few exceptions, been concerns shared by the majority of the senior judiciary. (Civil servant 2016)

The 'overt justice tag' was key in facilitating the blocking of 'draconian measures' that may be proposed by the Home Office or Number 10:

> We're responsible for human rights and for maintaining due process in the law as well so I think that there is more of a balance these days than there used to be, though there are inevitably tensions. (Civil servant 2011)

Indeed, as then Lord Chancellor and first Justice Secretary Lord Falconer asserted, 'Justice needs a Ministry of Justice' (quoted in Gibson 2007: x).

Given the Ministry of Justice's role as the 'balancing department' (Civil servant 2017), and its historical emergence from the LCD, it seemed to some senior officials during its formative years that:

> You would have great difficulty putting a full-blooded, Home Secretary-type politician in as a Justice Secretary. Because it's got to be someone who has the confidence of the judiciary, who understands how the law works. (Policy official 2011 interview)

The Ministry of Justice Is Public Protection

The prioritization of public protection, and the concomitant focus upon risk, has been a general trend across Western liberal democracies from the 1990s (Hope and Sparks 2000). For present purposes, this trend involves two distinct, though intrinsically related, concerns. On the one hand, it involves an increasing focus on offender management (and oversight and control). On the other hand, it involves a (continued) determination to avoid prison riots and escapes in particular, and to avoid horrific crimes that may be viewed in hindsight as having been avoidable given appropriate action by the authorities.

The shift towards an offender management paradigm, in which public protection sits as a central goal, is perhaps most starkly seen in the changes imposed on probation over the past two decades. A series of policy papers, legislative bills and ensuing practitioner guidance saw 'clients' become 'offenders' and 'probation officers' become 'offender managers'. Probation's former guiding principles, captured in the motto 'advise, assist, befriend', were radically altered (Raynor 2007).

As one 'elite' policymaker recalled approvingly,

> There was much more emphasis on preventing reoffending which there hadn't been for years because preventing crime was always seen about target-hardening and policing. It wasn't really until the early 2000s that the sort of policy interest started to move towards stopping people reoffending... probation was being changed to become a public protection agency. (Civil servant 2017)

For the prison service, the prioritization of public protection and avoidance of catastrophic events were fully in keeping with its longstanding cultures (Bastow 2013).

> What NOMS is very, very good at and has made an art form of is protection and security of the estate, so you aren't going to breach the walls. And that's NOMS's primary concern. (Special adviser 2016)

The prison service is 'best at…gold command and crisis management, sending in the heavies when there is a riot' (Civil servant 2017). And this may have been to the detriment of efforts to address reoffending:

> They had all the programmes and so on, and it is not as if the top of the NOMS didn't care about those programmes, they did. But it wasn't what their skillset was really about. (Civil servant 2017)

While NOMS (now HMPPS) is only one component of the MoJ, its head—and by extension the organization itself—is regarded by some as:

> An incredibly powerful individual. Within the MoJ he is the most powerful [Director General], with nine tenths of all the resources. (Senior official, quoted by Bastow 2013: 167)[5]

They are 'incredibly underrated'; they 'control the system' (Special adviser 2016).

For many informed observers, the two traditions set out so far are inherently incompatible as departmental bedfellows. It is for this reason that the roles of Lord Chancellor and Justice Secretary have been viewed by many policy participants to be in unavoidable and unacceptable conflict (House of Lords and House of Commons Joint Committee on Human Rights 2014: 22–23).

The Ministry of Justice Is Rehabilitation

This rehabilitative tradition, perhaps most of all of the traditions set out here, operates at the level of aspiration and rhetoric. Rehabilitation can further, of course, be understood and enacted in dramatically different forms. Robinson and Crow are undoubtedly right to note first that rehabilitation has tussled with a 'new punitiveness' as a central driver of policymaking (Robinson and Crow 2009: Chapter 10). Second, they correctly note that where rehabilitation may cast offenders (or 'clients', as previously conceived) as the primary beneficiaries of advice and support (and indeed arguably did so during the highpoint of the 'rehabilitative ideal' up to the 1970s (Robinson and Crow 2009: Chapter 2)), the justification is now generally 'unreservedly utilitarian'. It 'emphasises its crime reduction benefits' with 'communities and potential victims' as the main beneficiaries (Robinson and Crow 2009: 162).

The MoJ from its inception aspired to reduce reoffending (Ministry of Justice 2007): rehabilitation of offenders has served as a thread weaving through the department from (in modern times) the New Labour years before its creation, through to the present day. For example, for the Labour government in 2001, it was imperative that:

> We have a correctional system which punishes but also reduces reoffending through the rehabilitation of the offender and his or her successful reintegration into the community. (Home Office 2001: 87)

This carried through to the department's 2007 Carter Review, which set out proposed reforms that sought to 'allow for greater attention to be given to the rehabilitation of offenders whilst they are in prison' (Lord Carter of Coles 2007: 16). Further, the Coalition government in 2010 proposed a 'rehabilitation revolution' (HM Government 2010), flowing from the Conservative Party's stated goals to 'reduce the prison population...break the cycle of re-offending and reduce crime' (Conservative Party 2008).

Some policymakers shared this view of rehabilitation as a thread running through the MoJ's self-identity:

> The focus on reducing re-offending even predates the Ministry of Justice, I mean it was there in the Home Office and the PSA targets, they were set. So people thought it was a good, noble aim. What I think we then did was make something of that with the Transforming Justice programme, because we wanted to reduce demand pressures on the system. (Civil servant 2017)

For others, it was often seen to be the case that in practice 'those that work on the rehabilitation side of things have been shoved to a "nice to have"' (Special adviser 2016). From 2012, the prison service has been pushed increasingly towards crisis by severe staffing and resource cuts (Garside and Ford 2015; HM Chief Inspector of Prisons 2017). Even in the relatively well-resourced years of the late 2000s, one senior Prisons Inspectorate official described the position as being a 'worst place' scenario:

> You are resourced to do a lot more than containment [of prisoners], but you are not resourced well enough to do the real rehabilitation work… That would require more space, fewer prisoners, more headroom. (Senior Prisons Inspectorate official, quoted by Bastow 2013: 95)

Even the avowedly hard-line Justice Secretary, Chris Grayling (2012–2015), cast his reforms in terms of it being 'not enough just to be tough':

> [Prisons] also need to be places that begin to change the lives of those inside in a more positive way. It's where we need to be as a Party… We have to address our stubbornly high reoffending rate. It costs us £13 billion a year. To say nothing of the emotional and mental toll on victims. (Grayling 2014)

Post-coalition government 2016–2017 Justice Secretary Michael Gove wanted prisons to be guided by a 'moral purpose…[a] mission to change lives for good', 'to make prisons much more effective at rehabilitation' (Gove 2016).[6]

However, even prior to its recent privatization, probation—for many the spiritual home of the rehabilitative ideal—had been 'swallowed up into prisons' (Civil servant 2017). The failure of the practice to match the rhetoric therefore left many to 'feel very aggrieved' (Civil servant 2017).

The Ministry of Justice Is New Managerialism

New Public Management (NPM) has spread over the public sector during the last three decades or so, bringing with it 'a certain kind of legitimacy'. It is based on 'concepts of performance management, strong centralized policy coordination, the devolution of operational tasks, and the use of target regimes, which essentially set the parameters of success and failure of the system' (Bastow 2013: 47).

This shift is demonstrated for example in the benchmarking exercise undertaken in the early 2010s in relation to prison costs:

> It was a very hard edge thing of actually what's the staff ratio- in prisons, and can we look at private sector prisons which have lower staff ratios and essentially emulate those and make the whole system cheaper. (Civil servant 2016)[7]

In government itself, these priorities were reflected in the type of Permanent Secretary sought for the department in its early years:

> Someone who was not necessarily steeped in the justice system, but someone who is known as a leader manager. And because [the Department for International Development] had been somewhat transformed in the period [he] was there, and had come top of the capability reviews in Whitehall, [Sir Suma Chakrabarti] was brought in essentially to lead and manage the change in the MOJ and make it a department that worked well. (Civil servant 2017)

There was a sustained effort to bring in 'people who thought much more deeply about management':

> Whether it is financial or how we provide these services in a more efficient and effective way. [The MoJ] didn't have enough of those, procurement types, people who knew about contracting, and have built those parts of the department up… [It was a] genuine attempt to build up a sort of more professional cadre of managers who may or may not have cared a jot about re-offending before that. (Civil servant 2017)

This tradition further lay behind the first Justice Secretary's desire for:

> A single department [being] responsible for delivering an end-to-end criminal justice system from first appearance in court right through to rehabilitation or release. (Constitutional Affairs Committee 2007: Ev32)

A governmental Capability Review in 2008 revealed, in the language of NPM, a number of capability gaps in the department. It received the lowest ratings for 'Strategy' and 'Delivery' of all the UK government departments assessed (Gash and McCrae 2010: 12). This, in part, reflected its development from the old DCA:

> Which was largely left alone, because of the judge's independence… It had to become much more grown up, professionalised, a well-run organisation. It is a completely different set of skills required. (Civil servant 2017)

A major departmental change programme, 'Transforming Justice', was developed, 'aimed at achieving a better justice system at less cost to the public' (Gash and McCrae 2010: 6). One indicator of the increasing influence of the NPM tradition to departmental working was the manner in which policymaking was reformed,

> With policy teams having been brought together to form a single group with much greater focus on how resource is deployed to meet business critical requirements… This has been captured in the new Policy Plan process, which is the department's systematic attempt to prioritise its policy workload against the operational needs of the rest of the department. (Gash and McCrae 2010: 20)

The department has increasingly looked to the private sector as the solution to emerging policy problems, based on largely unquestioned assumptions of the inherent superiority of private sector solutions. Developing markets—and finding ways to sustain existing ones—was central to policy in England and Wales during the coalition period (Garside and Ford 2015). This was vividly demonstrated by the centrality of marketization to the Transforming Rehabilitation of probation reform (Burke and Collett 2016).

DILEMMAS

> You have got to bring this leviathan together somehow. (Civil servant 2017)

We have seen, so far, that the MoJ contains liberal, public protection, rehabilitation and new managerial traditions. They coexist and clash; complement and compete. I now survey a number of key dilemmas that have been in play since the creation of the department. Indeed, most of these dilemmas predate the MoJ, with some informing its creation. Ultimately, what I survey in this section are issues which are buffeted by competing ideas about what the MoJ *is* and what it is *for*.

Judicial Representative or Government Minister?

> [The Secretary of State] affects the whole tenor of the place. Because everything flows from those Secretaries of State. They are the boss. The permanent secretary knows they are the boss. (Civil servant 2017)

The office of Lord Chancellor has existed for over 900 years and has evolved substantially during this time (Woodhouse 2001). The position is firmly entrenched in the unwritten constitution, holding responsibility for a range of both crucial and obscure duties (House of Lords Select Committee on the Constitution 2014). Crucially, the Lord Chancellor historically acted (paradoxically) as a point where the separation of powers between the legislature, executive and judiciary was protected by being fused.

The combining of the Lord Chancellor role with that of a newly established Secretary of State for Justice has woven this dilemma into the very fabric of the MoJ. For some within the department, in particular those whose roots are in the LCD, the MoJ *is* the LCD with additional responsibilities.

> [The Lord Chancellor's Department] was an organisation which was brought up never to say boo to a judge, and those of us from the Home Office tended to regard judges as mortals... I think the difference has eroded gradually over the years but it has been very gradual. (Civil servant 2017)

In contrast to the historical power of the Lord Chancellor as head of the judiciary—and the department itself operating as something of a 'sleepy place' largely protected from political interference (Civil servant 2017)—came a radically different dynamic:

> ...Whereas before, so far as the Lord Chancellor was concerned, the running of the courts was really probably his primary concern, now he has taken on board an enormous portfolio, and it seems to us, looking at it realistically, that his primary concern is bound to be prisons and offender management. (Lord Phillips evidence to Constitutional Affairs Committee 2007: 21)

The Lord Chancellor (as Justice Secretary) was emphatically a government minister, with governmental concerns. No longer primarily a judicial representative, he was instead responsible for one of the UK's 'most complex departments' (Gash and McCrae 2010: 10). At a quotidian level, there was substantial concern by the DCA that it would 'be swamped by this new beast that was joining them':

> Because it was a totally different machine, so for example all the administrative systems they tried to shoehorn into the DCA's administrative system, it just didn't work. (Civil servant 2017)

By 2010, the Lord Chancellor role had become 'more and more ceremonial', 'a faintly comic and outdated bit of pomp' (Special adviser 2017).

> And then [on the other hand there were] the managerial and technocratic parts of the department, of running this vast empire, with the complexities of sentencing policy and financing the prisons and the courts, and managing individual cases that were, in and of themselves, intractable and complex. It didn't really fit. (Special adviser 2017)

This dilemma was initially held in balance primarily by reference to the personal qualities of the Justice Secretary. A politician of some standing, with a legal pedigree:

> That was seen as an essential component of the job ... we had always assumed, particularly because you're there to uphold the independence of the judiciary, that we needed someone who understood why, legally, that was really, really important. (Civil servant 2017)

More recently, this has been seen to be breaking down. This was starkly illustrated by the failure of then Justice Secretary Elizabeth Truss in November 2016 swiftly to defend the judiciary against the *Daily Mail's* demonization of them as 'Enemies of the People'.

> It's just an understanding of the performance, the significance, the importance of it. And the judges have this saying, they say, "You get us. You understand." But I think from their point of view, there's a series of people who don't get it and that's worrying. (Civil servant 2017)[8]

Departmental Coherence or Autonomy of Parts?

Is the MoJ a centralized department, or an assortment of largely discrete parts? While for some what had been created in 2007 was, in effect, a 'multi-agency partnership' (Gibson 2007: 126), for others 'the Ministry of Justice is much more unified than many [government] departments' (Civil servant 2017). This dilemma, longstanding across all government departments, was exacerbated in the early days of the MoJ by pragmatic decisions regarding utilization of space within available Whitehall buildings:

> We were shipped out of the nice, new Home Office – well, much of NOMS, into Selborne House and gradually we brought people with us. But again, it wasn't ideal because [the Director-General] was running the operational [prison] service [from a different building] and NOMS was the frontend with ministers, you know? So, to be detached away from all the people who are dealing with the [prison capacity] crisis was not ideal. (Civil servant 2017)

An absence of 'joined-up' coherence played out in terms of the lack of alignment between 'new' MoJ elements of the department (largely coming from the Home Office) and 'old' parts enduring from the predecessor DCA:

> A whole load [of policy officials] came over from the Home Office…and for a while the two sort of almost operated in parallel within the same department. (Civil servant 2017)

It was a 'department which wasn't a department!'

> Like a conglomerate, in a holding company atop called the Ministry, and lots of different bits [underneath]. (Civil servant 2017)

For the majority of its history, the former narrative—the autonomy of component parts—has prevailed:

> You certainly had these different cultures getting used to each other, but operating quite independently because lots of these policies were, you know, you could operate the prisons service almost independently of operating the sentencing policy development, for example, although the two

obviously interact, but the day-to-day running of the prisons or the courts is something which has a completely separate rhythm of its own. (Special adviser 2017)

For a long time, there were many people in particular parts of the department 'who could speak intellectually about the need for whole system benefits', but when faced with a need to make trade-offs, 'would choose their [part of the] system' (Civil servant 2017).

In the mid-2010s, in some areas the pendulum then swung in the other direction. The physical concentration of staff increased, with the department moved into 102 Petty France, the former Home Office headquarters (formerly known as 50 Queen Anne's Gate). NOMS was moved 'in house', having been 'over the road' in Clive House for some time (Civil servant 2017). The 'brilliant' 102 Petty France, a 'prestige building' (Civil servant 2017), seemed to reflect a growing sense of departmental confidence and coherence.

At the same time, fragmentation and dispersal of responsibilities have continued to occur in some areas of departmental competence. For example, probation services have been splintered, with public, private and third sector actors all involved in an unwieldy array of processes and responsibilities (Burke and Collett 2016). Further, the departmental direction of travel has, at least at the level of aspirational rhetoric, been towards greater autonomy for individual prison governors (Ministry of Justice and Prime Ministers Office 2016).

Policy and Operations: Fusion or Separation?

A related dilemma is that of the approach to be taken to managing policy and operations. This is 'one of these great pendulums' (see Bastow 2013: 158):

> That goes from, "Policy and operations must be located together so that their policy is informed by operations and vice versa" to "We must make sure that policy is completely separate from the people who do it"... and that pendulum just swings all the time. (Civil servant 2017)

One view has policy officials, when separated from operational matters, as too 'abstract', 'They sit there in Whitehall and [develop policy] and they hardly ever get out' (Senior civil servant 2011).

[The way the civil service works] tends to get people at the top who match what ministers need in terms of handling and the feeling of support that they want; it doesn't necessarily encourage people who've got the ability to do things. Ministers also want things doing, so if you get people who are handlers, in charge of what's a very chunky "doing" project, it's potentially quite vulnerable. (Civil servant 2017)

For others, the problem is that the operationally focused NOMS (as it then was) had far too limited horizons, being 'not remotely interested in policy' (Policy participant 2016). One tangible example given was the result seen when responsibility for a grant supporting the criminal justice voluntary sector moved from the MoJ to NOMS.

A policy participant involved in this development reflected that the specification for the grant was subsequently significantly amended. It was considered to reflect that:

Not having had that experience of working with the voluntary sector, they wouldn't have had that understanding that the voluntary sector has quite an awful lot of expertise, a lot of thinking about how your policies could help to reduce the need to rely on support services in the first place. (Policy participant 2016)

Recent efforts have been made to effect a more clear distinction between policy (central MoJ) and operational practice (NOMS, now HMPPS). This, however, has been met with fierce criticism from concerned groups including the Prison Governors Association (PGA), who have argued that this has led to unacceptable ambiguity over responsibilities and decision-making (Khomani 2017). It has further, perhaps ironically, led to some leading prison governors (i.e. operations) being redeployed into the centre in response to the impossibility of developing policy without operational knowledge.

Another element of this dilemma relates to the visibility and perceived relevance (or otherwise) to ministers of specific policy participants. In this regard, policy officials have consistently been regarded as 'first among equals' (McCrae et al. 2011: 19).

I think that one of the downsides, if you like, of the creation of the department is that the operational parts of the business, and prisons and courts, did feel a little bit less important, maybe…I think there was always a sense from the operational departments that they didn't necessarily feel like they had quite the power and the influence that they might want. (Special adviser 2017)

The prison service (and NOMS) was highly influential in a certain sense, but for some policymakers:

> What the influence seemed to me to stretch to the application of the rulebook, and the implementation of the cuts, and they didn't tend to provide much room for change. There just wasn't the capacity in terms of time resource, money, people, for the prison service to adapt to change. So there was a little bit of a disconnect, if you like, between prisons and sentencing policy and Transforming Justice, and all of the, kind of, blue sky thinking. (Special adviser 2017)

Under conditions of austerity and heavily reduced budgets, this 'power dynamic' was 'accentuated' (Special adviser 2017).

> If you're in policy and the request is to cut 33% from the budget, then you can be very influential in policy terms because you've got to come up with all these imaginative solutions. If you're in the implementation side of the business… your room for manoeuvre is very limited, and actually you've just got to, sort of, suck it up. (Special adviser 2017)

As noted above, the department was increasingly organized so as to have a relatively small policymaking 'core', surrounded by the various agencies and other elements of the department. While a number of considerations lay behind this decision, a distrust of senior operational chiefs—or, to put it more moderately, a wearily cynical view of organizations' tendency to resist change and to request ever more money—was one driving factor.

> Every prisons minister used to say, "When so and so says this can't be done, do you think that's really true?" They always felt they were having the wool pulled over their eyes. (Civil servant 2017)

For some, this arrangement was highly beneficial to the minister:

> You might have these people out there in the agencies telling you [that] you couldn't possibly [pursue a certain course of action, or achieve a certain efficiency] but close around you, you had your policy makers who you relied on to be able to say actually, "you should be able to do it because it will do

this or we've looked at the evidence and we think this." And that in a way was more comfortable for ministers to work that way. (Civil servant 2017)

Patient Implementation or Political Responsiveness?[9]

Success is the announcement; and a successful announcement, with lots of glossy brochures and some decent publicity, and pictures of the minister, and good headlines in the right papers: that is success. (Civil servant 2017)

In theory, government departments are about policy delivery, and they are about tangible solutions. However, this view confronts in practice a number of challenges. Efforts at delivering tangible change 'from the centre' often leave even determined policy participants reeling;[10] success is far from guaranteed. Political crises have a way of upsetting efforts at long-term policy development and implementation (see, for example, Sparks 2003). Accentuated by the short tenure of most Secretaries of State, ministers face the temptation to prioritize media perception over on-the-ground reality and to 'deliver' a promised policy, Act of Parliament, or structural change with little concern for the long-term consequences.[11]

One civil servant reflected on a tale of an acquaintance's consternation at meeting with a criminal justice minister about a particular policy area. While the acquaintance, the head of a criminal justice agency, sought to discuss details around the implementation of practice guidelines, the minister was clearly distracted by their pleasure at the good press reception that day to a speech given by a fellow Justice Minister:

If you look at the time-scale of an impact of a big policy change; to make something happen that is real, it probably needs at least two years of work to change computer systems, get rid of staff, recruit staff, train staff, so you can say, "We're now through the phase of implementation – we've got it!" And then, actually, for the next couple of years, you'll be doing it, and getting better at doing it, and you'll find some glitches in the system. So getting the change in, and so it's really bedded down, it's probably a four-year process; and then the results may not show up for two or three years afterwards. No wonder ministers concentrate on the announcement; that's the only bit they'll be there for! (Civil servant 2017)

As regards tabloid pressures, crime is an emotive area that unsurprisingly sees the department constantly buffeted by tabloid outrage and calls for common-sense, 'obvious' solutions. This dynamic has a long history. For example, in 1974–1976, Roy Jenkins reflected in his diaries on the 'barrage of daily bombardment' of public and press hysteria about escapes (quoted in Bastow 2013: 126).

> In the end we had what we called the book. We put together answers on every crackpot scheme you could think of because we just kept being asked and we got tired of telling the same story. (Civil servant 2017)

The tabloid press does not always generate the sense of panic. The pressures of the austerity agenda (from 2010 onwards) at times had a similar effect:

> It was just extraordinary to see, you know, week after week there were charts and things being demonstrated, showing that there was just, particularly for the later years of the spending round, there was no plan at all. They literally didn't know what to do. So when you've got that sense within a department of, "Shit, how are we going to save all this money?" there's very little space to [look beyond this]. (Special adviser 2016)

The chronic capacity stress suffered by prisons is a classic example of the failure to address the long-term practical implications of short-term (often politically compelled) policy decisions (Bastow 2013). One senior policymaker reflected that the ongoing crisis of insufficient prison capacity throughout the mid-2000s was 'a direct consequence of policy':

> A policy that says we want to lock more people up for a variety of offences, and that is a policy that is then pushed particularly hard by the Home Office. ... And at the same time we don't adapt the expenditure, so we can actually build enough places to do that ... either Number 10 Downing Street, or the Home Office, would make draconian statements about the need to lock more people up. Meanwhile, they would never have to face the consequences of that. They would be faced [by the Ministry of Justice]. (Civil servant 2017)

Where the riots of the late 1990s continued to hold great resonance within the prison service (and affected their view of capacity issues accordingly), for many political actors the memories had more swiftly faded (Civil servant 2011).

Impatience, a desire to see near-immediate results from political decisions, was often seen in relation to policy development:

> The trouble is that people see a proposal that looks quite simple, and you can express it in five words or whatever in a manifesto and everyone says, "Oh yes, why don't we just do it," but the reality is that somebody then has to look at it and go, "Okay, how would we express it in a statute?" I mean you know all of this, "how would we express it in a statute, if we express it in a statute like this, is it actually in conflict with human rights and would the Secretary of State need to be judicially reviewed, what would happen if we were successfully judicially reviewed?" Yeah, yeah. "How much would it cost? Where would we get the money from? Is it actually possible to do this thing whatever it is with prisons or probation services or courts structured the way they are? Is it, would we actually want to change the structure to accomplish this objective? If we did that, you know, what are the cost implications of that, what are the long-term impacts of the other objectives that we need to achieve?" and, you know, that's even before you get onto things like the IT … [You have to] say, "You don't understand. It will take five people two months of spending 10 hour days on writing [the policy], and so on and so forth." (Civil servant 2016)

More experienced Justice Ministers 'valued policy advice'. They 'need to know that somebody is working through the detail and they're getting it right' (Civil servant 2017). But more recent Justice Secretaries consider that 'They don't need any advice, they just want people to do their bidding' (Civil servant 2017).

> Why do we want somebody who over-promises and under-delivers? But in the short run, a minister would much rather have a civil servant who over-promises. (Civil servant 2017)

Looking beyond the prioritization (or otherwise) of long-term considerations in relation to specific policy areas, we can note here that the creation of the MoJ was itself in part driven by the desire to respond to media and political pressures of the day. In 2007, the Home Office was beset by multiple scandals and crises: the department was failing to deport foreign prisoners at the end of their prison sentences; the immigration service was in crisis; the Parole Board was failing to protect the public; the prison population was reaching unmanageable levels.

> In the middle of [all of] that, I think [Home Secretary] John Reid decided he'd had enough. He had enough on his plate and so he exported us, the most problematic and from his point of view least interesting bit of his portfolio. He thought maybe the time has come for a Ministry of Justice. And I'm sure somewhere in the back of his brain [he thought], "And I can get rid of these people who are going to get me sacked." So, the idea was hatched very, very quickly. (Civil servant 2017)

Conclusion: The Ministry/s of Justice

In explaining policy developments relating to the MoJ, one former special adviser (2017) considered that an important underlying factor was its lack of 'strategic purpose…it's never known what it is'. Similarly, Conservative politician Damian Green, a joint Home Office-MoJ Minister (2013–2015), has suggested that the MoJ has 'much less of a self-image, partly because it's a new department' (Institute for Government 2015: 6).

These statements recall Laws' aphorism that outsiders studying an organization 'are no more able to offer a single and coherent account of the way in which it orders itself' than its managers (Laws 1994: 263). We must make two important clarifications. First, Laws is making a sociological observation, not offering a critique. Second, in the case of the MoJ here (and likely any organization not on the brink of disintegration), I do not seek to argue that the department does not know what it is, or that I have demonstrated its uniquely incoherent nature. Rather, there are multiple explanations, multiple narratives in play, relating to what the department *is* and what it is *for*.

We have moved, in other words, from a monolithic Ministry of Justice, a department that has intrinsic properties and objective boundaries. Rather, the department, as with any institution, is rightly viewed as a notion whose particular meaning and content are only fully comprehensible within the web of beliefs in which relevant actors are situated (Bevir 2011: 188): a coalescence of 'meaningful activities…a set of cultural practices' (Bevir and Rhodes 2010: 198).

We encounter, in other words, the Ministry/s of Justice. There is a liberal MoJ centred upon justice and fairness; there is an MoJ determined to achieve the rehabilitation of offenders; there is an MoJ that is obsessed with public protection; there is an MoJ that is steeped in new managerialism. They collide and combine; they compete.[12]

We have seen also a department buffeted by a number of dilemmas. Some of these, with which policymakers have to grapple, are unique to the department, most notably the challenges posed by the incorporation of the Lord Chancellor role. Other dilemmas are more general and faced by many departments and indeed many organizations, albeit given particular form in the light of the responsibilities of the MoJ.

Looking to the department's future, we can conclude with an observation that was echoed by many of those interviewed (and in informal discussions with others). Perhaps, the dilemmas buffeting the department, and the austerity agenda's 'dull compulsion to cut and trim' (Garside and Ford 2015: 5), are beginning to take too great a toll. Perhaps, the MoJ is enveloped in an emerging narrative of decline:

> [At the beginning] there was all that sense of mission and you know, "We are the first Ministry of Justice ever and we're going to make this ship fly." For a while, it did… (Civil servant 2017)

Notes

1. Thanks to Rod Rhodes, attendees at the Political Studies Association and European Society of Criminology 2017 annual conferences for helpful comments and two (anonymous) policymakers who provided comments on earlier drafts.
2. https://www.gov.uk/government/organisations/ministry-of-justice/about#priorities. Accessed 8 August 2017.
3. For discussion of the theoretical and methodological framework underpinning this chapter, see Annison (2017, Appendix I; Forthcoming).
4. One could argue that the Home Office–MoJ contrast can be overdone; a liberal thread can plausibly be traced through (parts of) the Home Office's history. Consider, for example, the decriminalization of homosexuality, the abolition of the death penalty and the implementation of the Human Rights Act. I am grateful to Tim Wilson for this observation.
5. This is an overestimate, although prisons and probation (i.e. the areas covered by NOMS/HMPPS) do hold responsibility for a great deal of departmental resources.
6. And see more recently similar statements by current Justice Secretary David Lidington (2017).
7. For a wide-ranging analysis of the role of neoliberalism in criminal justice, see Bell (2011).

8. Such concerns underpinned Westminster gossip in April 2017 that had the department cast as not a 'well-functioning department', with anonymous ministers arguing for the Justice Secretary and Lord Chancellor roles to be split: http://www.telegraph.co.uk/news/2017/04/05/cabinet-ministers-call-prime-minister-strip-liz-truss-lord-chancellor/. The outcome following the June 2017 general election was in fact the installation of David Lidington as Justice Secretary—the fifth in seven years—who was considered to have a better understanding of the judiciary. The Justice Secretary mantle has since changed hands again, to former solicitor David Gauke.
9. For a more detailed consideration of the pressures on penal policymakers and the implications for penal policy, see Annison (2017).
10. For examples, one could consult any number of recent political autobiographies, including those published by David Blunkett, Tony Blair, Jack Straw, Ken Clarke, Alan Johnson and many more.
11. A striking recent example is the successful 'delivery' of the Transforming Rehabilitation changes to probation structures before the 2015 general election and the subsequent serious concerns raised as regards the damaging implications of these changes for probation practice.
12. It is notable that punishment did not feature as a dominant theme in research interviews, notwithstanding its centrality to the work of the department (I am grateful to Phillipa Thomas for this observation). We can suggest that this is because it is seen as a (reluctant?) duty, legitimated through the lens of the traditions discussed in this chapter.

References

Annison, H. (2015). *Dangerous Politics*. Oxford: Oxford University Press.
Annison, H. (2017). Interpreting Influence: Towards Reflexivity in Criminal Justice? In S. Armstrong, J. Blaustein, & A. Henry (Eds.), *Reflexivity and Criminal Justice*. Basingstoke: Palgrave.
Annison, H. (2018). The Policymakers' Dilemma: Change, Continuity and Enduring Rationalities of English Penal Policy. *British Journal of Criminology*. Online First.
Annison, H. (Forthcoming). Towards an Interpretive Political Analysis of Penal Policy. *Howard Journal of Crime and Justice*.
Bastow, S. (2013). *Governance, Capacity and Capacity Stress: The Chronic Case of Prison Crowding*. Abingdon, Oxon: Palgrave Macmillan.
Bell, E. (2011). *Criminal Justice and Neoliberalism*. Basingstoke: Palgrave Macmillan.
Bevir, M. (2011). Public Administration as Storytelling. *Public Administration, 89*, 183–195.
Bevir, M., & Rhodes, R. A. W. (2010). *The State as Cultural Practice*. Oxford: Oxford University Press.

Burke, L., & Collett, S. (2016). Transforming Rehabilitation. *Probation Journal, 63,* 120–135.
Conservative Party. (2008). *Prisons with a Purpose.* London: Conservative Party.
Constitutional Affairs Committee. (2007). *The Creation of the Ministry of Justice.* London: TSO.
Garside, R., & Ford, M. (2015). *The Coalition Years.* London: CCJS.
Gash, T., & McCrae, J. (2010). *Transformation in the Ministry of Justice: 2010 Interim Evaluation Report.* London: Institute for Government.
Gibson, B. (2007). *The New Ministry of Justice: An Introduction.* Winchester: Waterside Press.
Gove, M. (2016). *Making Prisons Work.* London: Ministry of Justice.
Grayling, C. (2014). *Conservative Party Speech.* London: Conservative Party.
HM Chief Inspector of Prisons. (2017). *Annual Report 2016–7.* London: TSO.
HM Government. (2010). *The Coalition: Our Programme for Government.* London: Cabinet Office.
Home Office. (2001). *Justice for All.* London: TSO.
Hope, T., & Sparks, R. (2000). *Crime, Risk and Insecurity.* Abingdon, Oxon: Routledge.
House of Lords and House of Commons Joint Committee on Human Rights. (2014). *The Implications for Access to Justice of the Government's Proposals to Reform Judicial Review.* London: TSO.
House of Lords Select Committee on the Constitution. (2014). *The Office of Lord Chancellor.* London: TSO.
Institute for Government. (2015). *Ministers Reflect: Damian Green.* London: Institute for Government.
Khomani, N. (2017). Prisons in Crisis Due to 'Perverse' Government Overhaul. *The Guardian.* Manchester and London: GMG.
Laws, J. (1994). Organization, Narrative and Strategy. In J. Hassard & M. Parker (Eds.), *Towards a New Theory of Organizations* (pp. 248–268). London: Routledge.
Lidington, D. (2017). Prison Reform Must also Factor in a New Focus on Rehabilitation. *Evening Standard.* London: ES Media.
Lord Carter of Coles. (2007). *Securing the Future.* London: Ministry of Justice.
McCrae, J., Page, J., & McClory, J. (2011). *Transformation in the Ministry of Justice: 2011 Interim Evaluation Report.* London: Institute for Government.
Ministry of Justice. (2007). *Justice: A New Approach.* London: Ministry of Justice.
Ministry of Justice and Prime Ministers Office. (2016). *Biggest Shake-up of Prison System Announced as Part of Queen's Speech.*
Raynor, P. (2007). Community Penalties: Probation, 'What Works', and Offender Management. In M. Maguire, R. Morgan, & R. Reiner (Eds.), *Oxford Handbook of Criminology.* Oxford: Oxford University Press.

Rhodes, R. A. W. (2015). Ethnography. In M. Bevir & R. A. W. Rhodes (Eds.), *The Routledge Handbook of Interpretive Political Science*. Abingdon, Oxon: Routledge.

Robinson, G., & Crow, I. (2009). *Offender Rehabilitation*. London: Sage.

Sparks, R. (2003). States of Insecurity: Punishment, Populism and Contemporary Penal Culture. In S. McConville (Ed.), *The Use of Punishment*. Cullompton: Willan.

Woodhouse, D. (2001). *The Office of Lord Chancellor*. Oxford: Hart.

CHAPTER 3

What Makes a Zero Carbon Home Zero Carbon?

Heather Lovell and Jack Corbett

INTRODUCTION

This chapter analyses policy complexity, uncertainty and meaning ambiguity, drawing on the case of the zero carbon homes (ZCH) policy in the UK. We use scholarship on narrative policy analysis to understand this case. The ZCH policy illustrates well the value of a decentred approach to policy analysis (Bevir and Rhodes 2001, 2003), with its long history and active role of organisations outside of government. We draw here on two strands of empirical research: one conducted prior to the announcement of the ZCH policy in 2002–2003, and a second conducted in its aftermath in 2016–2017. In this way, we seek to explore and better understand the role of influential policy actors (state and

H. Lovell (✉)
School of Social Sciences, University of Tasmania,
Hobart, Australia
e-mail: heather.lovell@utas.edu.au

J. Corbett
School of Social Sciences, University of Southampton,
Southampton, UK
e-mail: j.corbett@soton.ac.uk

© The Author(s) 2018
R. A. W. Rhodes (ed.), *Narrative Policy Analysis*, Understanding Governance, https://doi.org/10.1007/978-3-319-76635-5_3

non-state) over the life course of a policy. More specifically, we show how zero carbon housing was happening before the UK government policy was introduced in 2006, and that it has also continued since the policy was abolished in 2015. A focus purely on government institutions and the policy process would miss this activity. We demonstrate how from some key individuals' perspective the work of the UK government through its ZCH policy has been important, but not as critical as it might first appear. The work of several non-state practitioners was pivotal to the development of ZCH implementation in the UK and has continued to be so during and beyond the formal lifetime of the policy (2006–2015).

In our analysis, we foreground the 'decentred' beliefs that human actors hold about the ZCH homes policy, why it came into being, what it aimed to achieve, and the challenges and opportunities of enacting it. We are interested in not only the narratives—the stories themselves—but also how they have translated into material forms: ZCH (see Hajer and Versteeg 2005; Hajer 2001: for similar discourse and materiality approaches). We take individual stories and experiences from key people directly involved. We consider the differences and similarities between them, across a fifteen-year period. Many of our interviewees had first-hand experience of designing and building ZCH. We search for common narrative patterns as understood by key practitioners, examining the multiple 'storylines' in operation in the ZCH policy area, who is using them and for what purpose, and how they have changed or remained stable over time. We define storylines as 'the essential discursive cement that creates communicative networks among actors with different or at best overlapping perceptions and understandings' (Hajer 1995: 63; see also Bevir and Rhodes 2003, 2006, 2010; Hajer and Wagenaar 2003). In assessing the translation of narratives into material form, we are attentive here to actual cement as well as its discursive variant. The dominant storyline is ecological modernisation, which has been the case over the life course of ZCH policy initiation, implementation and closure, i.e. evident in 2002–2003, as well as 2016–2017.

Our decentred approach follows Bevir and Rhodes (2003, 2006, 2010). Their version of interpretive theory seeks to avoid the types of reification and determinism common to much political science by focusing analysis on the common meanings of 'situated' agents. That is, they claim to explain why people act by reference to their meanings and beliefs, but they are also sceptical of equating agency with autonomy.

Meanings and beliefs are intersubjective and are thus inherently social in nature. The important point, for our purposes, is that while we use interviews (and quotes from them) to parse out the storylines relevant to this policy, our historical focus allows us to place each individual story within a wider canvas of similar narrative accounts. We thus present an 'interpretation of interpretations' that not only aims to shed light on the case study at hand but also contributes to broader arguments about the nature and place of meaning ambiguity in processes of policy change. Further, in our focus on the materiality of policy change, we draw on Hajer's observations about '… the role of meetings and excursions in the process of persuasion …. these practices…can be identified as an essential moment in … policy change. … face-to-face contacts, visits, excursions, and symposia fulfil a key role in the generation of credibility and trust' (Hajer 1995: 271). In our case of the ZCH policy, we identify particular zero carbon housing developments that have been crucial in the development of persuasive policy narratives.

The chapter has the following structure. First, we provide a brief description of our methodology. Second, we give an overview and background analysis of the UK ZCH policy and policy-related activity and events in the period leading up to 2006. Third, we outline changes in the ZCH policy over time. Fourth, we assess the dominant narratives used by practitioners in the pre-ZCH policy period (2002–2003), paying particular attention to the non-state actors who were developing and implementing ZCH in this early period, i.e. in the absence of any formal government policy. Fifth, we turn to consider how the narratives have changed over time, drawing on empirical material comprising ten interviews with key stakeholders (state and non-state) undertaken in 2016–2017. We ask whether the pre-policy storylines are still circulating and evolving. In conclusion, we reflect on the value of a decentred narrative policy analysis and the benefits of a longitudinal research method.

Methodology

Phase One

The empirical research undertaken in the period 2002–2003 comprises a combination of interview and documentary research: approximately fifty in-depth semi-structured interviews were conducted with key people involved in sustainable housing and climate change policy and practice in the UK. Organisations interviewed include local and national government, sustainable housing groups, consultancies, Registered Social Landlords (RSLs), non-governmental organisations, regional government agencies and private-sector house builders. In addition, documentary evidence was compiled and analysed from a range of sources including government policy documents, trade magazines for the housing and energy industries, and the national press. Site visits were conducted of prominent ZCH.

Phase Two

The second phase of interview and documentary empirical research was conducted in 2016–2017. We spoke to 10 key actors—ministers, senior civil servants and key policy makers from across the housing sector—about the implementation of the policy and its final abolition. The documentary research focused on the web archive of the Zero Carbon Hub, as well as policy documents, speeches and select committee inquires.

Background: The Early Development of ZCH

The 1990s and early 2000s were active years for building sustainable homes in the UK. An internet-based survey reveals that over 150 sustainable and low-energy housing developments were built or planned in the UK in the period 1990–2004, comprising more than 24,000 dwellings (Lovell 2005). Most of these sustainable homes were built without government support. They can be characterised as bottom-up or grassroots developments, in the main initiated by individuals and organisations with strong sustainability values and desires (Lovell 2004, 2009; Seyfang and Smith 2007). Two zero-carbon housing developments that gained a significant amount of media attention, and became more widely known outside of green home-building circles, were the Beddington Zero Energy Development (or BedZED) and the Hockerton Housing Development. BedZED, a low-energy development in South London, was completed in 2002. BedZED was the outcome of a joint initiative between the architect Bill Dunster, the

Peabody Trust (a RSL) and the environmental consultancy Bioregional Development Group (Lowenstein 2001; BRECSU 2002). It comprises eighty-two homes, nearly half of which were sold on the private market. The remainder were social housing (i.e. low-income) rentals. BedZED incorporated a number of environmental innovations: an on-site combined heat and power plant (to provide hot water, the homes are so well insulated there is no need for central heating); a car pool for electric vehicles; rainwater tanks; and sedum grass roofs (BRECSU 2002). Hockerton, in contrast, is a much smaller, earth-sheltered housing development near Newark in the East Midlands, completed in 1996. The five terraced homes similarly have no need for central heating: large conservatories collect heat from the sun, and the walls are well insulated. Photovoltaic panels and a wind turbine provide electricity, and all wastewater is treated on-site in a reed bed (BRECSU 2000). Hockerton was built by Nick Martin, the builder who also constructed the Vales' Autonomous House (the UK's first non-grid-connected modern home), in 1993, in the nearby village of Southwell (Vale and Vale 2000). A number of our most recent interviewees claim that BedZED was influential in the formation of the ZCH policy, a point we return to below.

Research has shown that the main motivation for the individuals and organisations initiating and building these sustainable homes was to enable a material demonstration that they worked (Lovell 2007). In other words, they sought to show that it was possible—economically and technically—to build homes sustainably in the UK. The material existence of the homes was hence key to giving confidence and credibility to those advocating housing as a way of mitigating climate change (along with other sustainability problems). The housing they constructed was mostly conceived of, and certainly acted as, tools or devices designed to shape ideas and practices. This point is illustrated, for example, by comments from Robert Vale about why he and his wife—both architects—built the Autonomous House:

> I think having examples is good because it shows that it can be done and that it does work. ... We just wanted to do it to show that it could be done, that it was a reasonable thing to do ... to convince the sceptics as it were. (Interview, Robert Vale, May 2004)

For, with the rise of climate change as an issue on the UK policy agenda during the 1990s (Lovell 2004; Toke 2000), it became increasingly important to have material evidence of low-carbon practice to promote new ideas and gain support. Brenda Vale similarly noted that building homes such as the Autonomous House was 'a way of helping policy change because you can actually see the buildings and you can see that you can do it, and therefore you can legislate to have more insulation because it is based on facts and not on ideas. I think that is important' (Interview, Brenda Vale, May 2004).

The deliberate use of already existing ZCH to enhance the credibility and salience of policy narratives was an effective strategy: these activities caught the attention of the UK government. BedZED was identified by the UK government as an attractive solution to a host of policy problems (Lovell 2004), acting as a focal point for policymakers interested in developing credible solutions to resolve difficult policy problems, in particular climate change, where the UK government had made a number of policy commitments (DTI 2003). In other words, the material existence of this zero-carbon housing is a critical reason why policy makers wished to be associated with it, because it was judged proof that the ideas and technologies embedded in the dwellings worked, thereby giving instant credibility to what otherwise might have been dismissed as rhetoric. Thus, for instance, the authors of a government-commissioned report about BedZED, published a few years before the introduction of the 2006 policy, noted that the BedZED development represents 'a *powerful argument* for the feasibility of a zero-carbon target for all new build' (BRECSU 2002: 11; emphasis added). More generally, in another government-sponsored case study of energy policies and programmes within the Newark and Sherwood District Council in the UK, one of the lessons learnt was that 'exemplar projects bring to life the reality far greater than shelves of strategies' (Energy Saving Trust 2004: 10). The government attempted to associate itself with BedZED by frequent visits, including the launch of new policies. For example, Patricia Hewitt, the then Secretary for Trade and Industry, used it as a location to announce a new government solar power initiative (DTI 2002). Similarly, the Liberal Democrat party leader visited because he 'was making an environment announcement later that day and wanted a photo to go with any publicity' (Bioregional Development Group Communications Officer, 2004, email correspondence with author).

Table 3.1 Examples of UK policy documents citing BedZed, 2002–2004

Policy document	Reference to BedZED
Speech by Energy Minister Brian Wilson, February 2002 (DTI 2003)	'Demonstrations such as the developments… at BedZed… prove that the technologies are available to deliver practical systems'
Royal Commission on Environmental Pollution 22nd Report: 'Energy – Our Changing Climate'	Has a case study box devoted to BedZED and describes it as: 'the most ambitious low energy housing development in the UK to date' (RCEP 2000)
Government Energy Efficiency Best Practice Programme—General Information Report No. 89	'BedZed represent[s] state-of-the-art for sustainable housing in the UK' (BRECSU 2002)
UK 2003: the Official Yearbook of the United Kingdom of Great Britain and Northern Ireland (The Stationery Office 2003)	Double page picture spread (pp. 298–299)
Environment Agency Report—'Our Urban Future' September 2002 (www.environment-agency.gov.uk)	BedZED is cited as an example of a solution to climate change
The Housing Corporation (2004)	It is used as a model case study for RSLs 'to show how sustainable development can be achieved'

Table 3.1 provides further examples of UK policy documents citing BedZED in the period preceding the announcement of the ZCH policy in 2006, indicating the desirability of BedZED to policy makers.

THE 2006 ZCH POLICY AND ITS CHANGES OVER TIME

In 2006, the (then) Housing Minister, Ruth Kelly, announced that 'Our key goal is to achieve zero-carbon new homes within a decade' (DCLG 2006: 1). In a speech at a green building event hosted by the environment group WWF, Kelly explained how:

> It is vital that homes and other buildings are as sustainable and as eco-friendly as possible. … Within a decade I want every new home to be zero-carbon. … This country is the first to set this ambition and we look forward to our international partners matching it.

The 2006 policy document *Building for a Greener Future* set out three main ways in which the zero-carbon target would be achieved: through the planning system; through the building regulations (via Part L, which relates to energy); and through a voluntary, sustainable building standard—the Code for Sustainable Homes. Interim steps for Part L of the Building Standards were proposed: a 25% improvement on energy use on current building regulations by 2010 and a 44% improvement by 2013. Care was taken to specify what was meant by a zero-carbon home:

> For a new home to be genuinely zero carbon it will need to deliver zero carbon (net over the year) for all energy use in the home – cooking, washing and electronic entertainment appliances as well as space heating, cooling, ventilation, lighting and hot water. … It could be at the development or building level. (DCLG 2006: 15)

This definition sought also to provide some flexibility over how 'zero carbon' was interpreted and implemented, i.e. at the 'development or building level'. The ZCH policy had multiple, ambitious policy aims: the zero carbon home would not only mitigate climate change, but also 'driv[e] innovation in the market and reduc[e] costs of technologies' (DCLG 2006: 1), facilitate the building of new homes, and reduce fuel poverty.

In the period 2006–2015, there were many changes to the policy, summarised in Box 3.1 below.

Box 3.1—The UK Zero Carbon Homes Policy Timeline

In 2006, Ruth Kelly MP, Minister for Communities and Local Government, announces the government's intention that all new-build homes will be zero carbon from 2016 (simultaneously launching the holistic Code for Sustainable Homes, the highest level of which enshrines the zero carbon standard).

Subsequently, the 2016 Zero Carbon Task Force is convened and co-chaired by the Housing Minister and Chief Executive of the Home Builders Federation.

The Task Force assigns a group of experts, under the auspices of the UK Green Building Council, to undertake a detailed assessment of the definition of ZCH and provide recommendations.

In May 2008, the Zero Carbon Task Group reports back recommending a hierarchical approach starting with energy efficiency first, followed by carbon compliance (largely on-site) and allowable solutions (largely off-site).

In June 2008, the public–private Zero Carbon Hub is launched with a mandate from government to take day-to-day operational responsibility for coordinating delivery of low and zero carbon new homes reporting directly into the Zero Carbon Task Force.

July 2009—Housing Minister announces that the carbon compliance level will be set at 70% and tasks a specialist group to investigate the minimum energy efficiency standard for new-build homes.

March 2011—Budget announcement by government that ZCH will no longer take into account 'unregulated' energy use within the home.

August 2013—the government launched a consultation specifically about the allowable solutions part of its ZCH policy 'Next steps to zero carbon homes – allowable solutions'. June 2014 in the Queen's Speech allowable solutions were confirmed as a component of the ZCH policy, within the Infrastructure Bill.

July 2014—summary of the governments' consultation on 'Next steps to zero carbon homes – allowable solutions' released.

July 2015—ZCH policy scrapped by the government.

A number of scholars have analysed aspects of the nine-year period (2006–2015) of ZCH policy debate, policy change and refinement. With one exception (see the Addendum by Walker et al. 2016), these analyses were conducted prior to the policy being abolished. However, they are nonetheless valuable because they shed light on the complexity of the policy process, the role of the state (Greenwood 2012) and the tensions and difficulties in implementing the ZCH policy, which were manifested mostly in debates around the definition of zero carbon (Goodchild and Walshaw 2011; Greenwood 2012). For example, McLeod et al. (2012) analyse the changes in definition of 'zero carbon' compared with the European PassivHaus standard (McLeod et al. 2012). In what is mostly a technical analysis, they are critical of the introduction of off-site renewable energy generation to the ZCH policy ('allowable solutions') and the likely negative effects on carbon emissions and meeting UK climate change targets. Goodchild and Walshaw (2011) focus on policy implementation and policy discourse around ZCH, using an ecological modernisation framework alongside science and technology studies theories (actor-network, quasi-object). They view ecological modernisation as including the state, as an 'enabler' (2011: 935). Like McLeod et al. (2012), they are pessimistic about the ability of the ZCH policy to meet its objectives, citing a range of factors including the 2008–2009 recession, and the high cost of applying the ZCH standard to small urban developments. Heffernan et al. (2015) present a detailed account of the ZCH policy—its constitution, the EU policy context and so on. Their analysis is based on interviews with private-sector house builders and assesses why compliance with ZCH was slow in the lead up to the 2016 policy implementation date. Findings from these interviews—which go beyond the large house builders to include small companies—indicate significant unease about the feasibility of the ZCH target, identifying several challenges with implementation such as increased cost, lack of public awareness and the culture of the house-building industry (Heffernan et al. 2015). Greenwood (2012) provides a thoughtful analysis of policy coordination and the role of markets, using the ZCH policy as a case study. He draws on Hayek's ideas about the effectiveness of markets in achieving coordination to investigate whether implementation issues arising with the ZCH policy are a result of poor coordination. Drawing on findings from 38 interviews with a range of stakeholders, Greenwood concludes that coordination problems are evident with the ZCH policy and have created policy distortion, which the state has failed to resolve (Greenwood 2012). Walker et al. (2015) engage with the occupants of ZCH as well as the house-building industry to explore the materiality of zero carbon and how homes are used and occupied in ways not necessarily intended by their designers. They discuss the implications of this for policy outcomes and for our conceptualisation of processes of innovation, drawing on social practice and sociotechnical theories (Walker et al. 2015).

Storylines in the Pre-ZCH Policy Period

We now turn to examine the dominant narratives or 'storylines' used by practitioners in the lead up to the 2006 ZCH policy implementation. In the early 2000s, there was the emergence of an ecologically modern discourse to frame already existing sustainable housing as a ready-made policy solution to climate change, i.e. as low or zero carbon. This discursive work was an important precursor to the development of the ZCH policy, as it reframed existing sustainable housing as a potential mainstream, credible policy solution. As an interviewee described:

> And over that period basically we kind of managed to persuade, not just WWF but stakeholders in the field, persuaded the industry that zero carbon was not crazy and the government [were persuaded] that actually almost the industry didn't care where the standards were set, they just wanted to know where they had to be. So, the government had the confidence to go for it. (Interview, November 2016)

The ecological modernist policy discourse in use here constituted a weak version of ecological modernisation, in that eco-efficiency and technology solutions dominated (Christoff 2000). It thus stood in strong contrast to the deep green values and beliefs (Dobson 2000) of long-standing sustainable housing advocates in the UK—a values-based policy network of non-state organisations and individuals active for decades in building and living in sustainable homes (Lovell 2004).

Those framing sustainable housing as low or zero carbon used two ecologically modern discursive storylines to unite the diverse group—namely housing 'life cycles' and 'smart housing'. These storylines were contested though—not all were happy with government-led reframing of sustainable housing as ecologically modern ZCH. The response from the sustainable housing advocates was to try to widen the discourse from the narrow low-carbon and ecologically modern framing, and tensions were evident between these two coexisting policy networks.

THE LIFE CYCLE STORYLINE

The Ecologically Modern Approach

In the housing sector, a 'life cycle' approach refers to the practice of examining economic (and environmental) costs and benefits over the lifetime of a house or housing development. In other words, taking a long-term view as to when initial investment capital may be recouped. Life cycle storylines are used in response to the (often-posed) question: 'Does sustainable housing cost more?' There remains much confusion about the answer. This is because the answer depends on:

- the timeframe of consideration;
- the type of housing (i.e. private or social sector, or self-build); and
- whether it is new-build housing or refurbishment of old housing (and if so, how old the housing is).

The storyline is a way of making sense of this complex situation through use of familiar metaphor—the life cycle—including terms such as 'pay back periods' and the financial accounting discourse of costs and benefits. The storyline proceeds as follows: it is sensible to invest extra money at the design and construction stages of a house, as it can be recouped when the house is sold, because there is significant consumer demand for low-carbon better-quality housing, and it can therefore be sold at a premium price. Further, better-quality housing leads to lower (or even non-existent) utility bills; thus, over the lifetime of the house, these costs are recouped by the householder.

A local authority manager responsible for planning a large low-carbon housing development near Leicester uses this type of life cycle storyline to justify the council selling the land to a developer at a lower price and their intention to retain a financial stake in the development:

> So the houses are more expensive because they are more popular, because it is a super place to live, well designed very attractive, low energy. ... There will be a premium on the house prices so the [local] authority will get some of that back through each house that is sold off. *So ultimately it will be self-financing*, but there is a cost up front through the land sale. (Interview, December 2002, emphasis added)

The economic life cycle storyline is used in part as a way to remove environmental values from the debate and thus distance policy-focused ZCH housing actors from long-standing sustainable housing activists with strong environmental and social values. In other words, low-carbon housing is portrayed primarily as a sensible financial investment.

Ecological Modernisation Contested

The response of those within the UK sustainable housing movement to the life cycle storyline is to counter the idea that a financial profit must be made for an investment decision to be deemed rational. In particular, the payback on any investment is widened to include environmental and social criteria. For example, a local authority manager involved in planning a sustainable housing development describes a situation of environmental payback through higher capital investment:

> So the [local] authority is ultimately having to pay for the energy efficiency approach. But we accept that the pay back to the environment is worth it, and ultimately it will make Ashton Green….a more attractive place to live, because energy costs will be so much less. (Interview, December 2002)

Another example is the decision-making by the owners and builders of the UK's first autonomous house (i.e. not connected to the utility grid): Robert and Brenda Vale (Vale and Vale 2000). The Vales decided to purchase expensive photovoltaic panels for their house, essentially a non-economically rational decision, as the financial savings in annual energy bills are small, with a payback period at the time of approximately fifty years. A local authority energy manager relates the story told about this decision by members of the sustainable housing advocacy Coalition here:

> … 'The Vales' response to how you can justify spending £15,000 [on photovoltaics (PVs)]… for a £150 [per annum] saving was beautiful… It is normal to have a £20,000 kitchen in a high status house isn't it? Where is the pay back in a £20,000 kitchen or a £2,000 kitchen? 'So I look out the window at my PVs and it gives me great pleasure. £20,000 kitchen annoys me, well what a waste of money.' *It's down to values isn't it*? (Interview, August 2002, emphasis added)

This narrative about the Vales contests the idea that financial payback is the only consideration of a rational purchase decision. The payback for the Vales comprises less tangible, non-monetary returns, such as reducing their consumption of non-renewable resources: a lifestyle decision in keeping with their deep green values.

THE SMART HOUSING STORYLINE

Ecological Modernist Approach

A second storyline that was commonly used by the low-carbon housing discourse Coalition in the early 2000s centres on the notion of 'smart' housing. Smart housing can be narrowly defined:

electronic networking technology to integrate the various devices and appliances found in almost all homes...so that the entire home can be controlled centrally – or remotely – as a single machine. (Pragnell et al. 2000: v)

However, in this context, smart housing is viewed more broadly as housing in which householders are not required to modify their behaviour to become less resource intensive. In other words, one can live in a smart house and continue to behave as normal. Examples of low-carbon smart technology include movement sensitive light switches and low-energy electrical appliances. The smart housing storyline is ecologically modernist in that it is technology focused, and does not involve social or institutional change: one does not have to adopt deep green values and practices in order to live more sustainably.

A sustainable housing manager at an environmental charity involved in building sustainable housing developments describes their approach in smart housing terms:

> So what we're trying to do on our [housing] developments is, *its all in there, you buy the house and its there, you don't have to think about it,* you're not even aware of it. But actually when your water bill comes through its only £50 because you've got a 2 litre flush toilet, and you've got low pressure aerated taps...*And they are all put in in a way that you would be nuts to want to replace them with something else.* (Interview, June 2002, emphasis added)

As does a sustainability manager in the social housing sector:

> We try to promote passive [technologies], so that householders don't even need to know that they're making an environmental saving. (Interview, June 2002)

The chief architect at the well-publicised BedZed sustainable housing development in south London also discusses the approach of the BedZed team using smart housing ideas:

> [we're] trying to come up with a lifestyle that makes it easier and more convenient to live a lower impact existence, than by using conventional alternatives. So what we're saying is that *if you're prepared to work with*

the infrastructure we've provided, you can achieve really quite astonishing things. It's possible to live [at BedZed] and be pretty close to carbon neutrality. [Bill Dunster, quoted in Lowenstein 2001: 16]

Ecological Modernisation Contested

The response of the sustainable housing movement to the smart housing storyline is that such approaches may go some way to reducing resource consumption, but that ultimately some modification of householder behaviour, and greater householder awareness and education is required. Smart housing poses a challenge for sustainable housing advocates, as it is a direct attempt to prove that environmental values are not a necessary component of successful sustainable, or low-carbon, housing. Sustainable housing advocates view adding smart technologies to a house as an 'end of pipe' solution: a short-term technological fix to a problem that requires institutional and social change (Christoff 2000).

Another response is that without an ideological commitment by the householder (i.e. deep green values), and an associated level of knowledge and motivation, the smart technology in the houses will simply not function properly. The sustainable housing manager at a UK charity describes the difficulty of making the technologies work in their holiday cottages:

> we started making [the holiday cottages] green, because we thought it would be an attraction....And we found that actually the systems that we were putting in were just that little bit too different, so that somebody coming to stay never learnt how to use it properly. (Interview, June 2002)

Further, this attitude often finds expression in a 'simplicity is best' argument. Removing the need for energy consumption in the first place is advocated as the best low-carbon approach. Thus, energy conservation, rather than energy efficiency, should be the first area of attention, followed lastly by increasing energy supply. A local authority energy manager complains about the dominant perception of energy efficiency as boring, with renewable energy technologies given priority:

[the renewable sector] are focusing on that which is exciting … the technology and everything else, and in fact it's all the boring basic stuff that should be done first. (Interview, August 2002)

The perception that these simple energy conservation and energy efficient approaches are boring is perhaps in part a recognition of the fact that calls for householder behaviour change are politically unpopular—i.e. in opposition to the ecological modernist ZCH framing.

Narratives in the Post-ZCH Policy Period

Ecological modernisation remains the dominant narrative for the ZCH policy. However, the storyline has become nuanced—a reflection of ten hard years at the policy coalface. The claim is that the housing sector has made progress, despite the recent setback, and that there has been a lot of learning, particularly among industry, along the way. The key concession here is that the implementation of the ZCH policy was far from straightforward. The ecological modernisation narrative has had to adapt to incorporate this.

For the most part, actors highlighted the technical challenges associated with achieving zero carbon. For many, the 'zero' language, while useful as a rhetorical device, became a hindrance to the successful implementation of the policy:

> So when we started to look at what it involved, the idea of zero was a bit of challenge … to achieve zero is probably a bit too much like utopia. So very early on, my influence was to say we can only actually deliver low carbon emissions. Low emissions, I should be calling it. And in a pragmatic way which must be technically achievable on a mass scale, cost effectively by an average tradesman. (Interview, February 2017)

In recognition of this shift, in August 2013, the Coalition government launched a consultation specifically about the possibility of 'allowable solutions'. For advocates, 'allowable solutions' meant that the policy was practically achievable:

> It was just the beginning that it was never zero carbon, always low carbon. So to achieve zero, you had to come up with some sort of concocted

methodology, which in this particular case was these allowable solutions. Now, the problem with allowable solutions was that it became incredibly complex to work out what allowable solutions meant, and then how you might input it into a policy. (Interview, February 2017)

For critics, it involved watering down the 2006 commitment. Echoing this, the Queen's Speech in June 2014 confirmed allowable solutions as a component of the ZCH policy, within the Infrastructure Bill, and a summary of the government's consultation on 'Next steps to ZCH – allowable solutions' was released the following month. For many, the ability of the housing sector to reach any sort of consensus on this issue was an ecological modernist, technical triumph that demonstrated the viability of the policy—delivering environmental benefits at no (or few) extra costs:

> I think what was interesting was this kind of tide of innovation, wave of innovation, because the industry felt like it had the direction of travel set out for it. And even though they might have known about it and complained about it they were kind of surfing it. At least the forward thinking ones were … Quite a lot of house builders and developers put quite a lot of money into R and D to work out how to do it … There is no evidence that the zero carbon requirements … were holding up development. No evidence. And actually the costs were falling quite rapidly as people did it. (Interview, November 2016)

Indeed, the view that, technically, the policy could be made to work in an environmentally and economically successful way was widespread among our interviewees.

> [ZCH] got caught up in the classic assumption that all regulation, really, is a burden on business … that [it] would get in the way of bigger priorities around housing delivery and the irony was that, really, we had fought those battles and most of those battles had been won because, whereas early estimates of the cost of zero carbon homes had estimated a figure in the 30 odd per cent sort of premium, by the time we packed up, it was, to quote one house builder who probably wouldn't want to be named, but sort of said, 'Look, this is in the roundings'. In the roundings, you know … we have worked through this and like all things, costs are hugely contingent on economies of scale … the incremental cost was almost negligible. (Interview, February 2017)

While the emphasis on the primacy of a cost-effective technical solution fits within the general ecological modernisation narrative, it also extends it because it sees strong policy direction from government, combined with the steering function of the public–private organisation the Zero Carbon Hub, as essential to policy success. Indeed, many within the sector see themselves as now biding their time until a more favourable political environment emerges in which they can relaunch the policy:

> So Osborne, as Chancellor, was more interested in reducing the influence of the state and reduc[ing] deficit than he was looking at an actually circular economy - if you employ people to reduce energy use, you are tending to employ people local to where your buildings are, for example. And it reduces your energy you need to import into the country, therefore - those subtleties were too subtle for the blunt instrument he was using. Whereas, the government now, early feelings are they are looking at a world post-Brexit and, therefore, ideas for how we have to change, how we have to move forward and we are beginning to see re-engagement of a lot of these issues. It was greatly helped by, for example, the Mayor of London saying we will implement the zero-carbon to the original program … And therefore, the indications are there that this ain't going away, there's just been a temporary blip in central government. (Interview, January 2017)

The key point is that while ecological modernisation has tended to be a market-based narrative, this experience of ZCH has somewhat altered that view among some actors. Indeed, while the 'zero' carbon rhetoric is seen by many as unhelpful, sector insiders seemed much more comfortable with government setting out a stringent policy platform (with a long lead in time) in order to provide market certainty, something that house builders in particular welcomed.

> It was … key … that there was going to be a 10-year timetable for implementation … that there would be three main step changes in building regulations and requirements so that we weren't trying to do it all in one go and we could learn as we went along. (Interview, April 2017)

One consequence of this shift is that the main alternative to this narrative remains straight economic modernisation, i.e. without the state setting the long-term policy framework. When the Coalition government announced in July 2015 that it was formally abandoning the policy, its main rationale was that the ZCH policy was stymying the housing industry, thus contributing to critical housing shortages across the UK. Insiders highlight two additional explanations: the end of Coalition government at the 2015 election; and the fragmentation of the housing industry.

The first explanation is a political one and is relatively straightforward: the Liberal Democrats were perceived to be more invested in the policy than their Conservative partners. Don Foster, former Minister for Housing, recalls some of his battles with the Chancellor, George Osborne, in the following terms:

> It became increasingly apparent the Conservatives - and particularly the Chancellor - wanted to really put a stop to Zero Carbon Homes ... Behind the scenes [I] went to some of the major house builders ... and managed to coordinate them writing a letter of complaint about me. So they wrote a letter basically dictated by me saying how disappointed they were with me for not getting on with Zero Carbon Homes, given it's what they wanted. And they wanted the certainty. They'd started to gear up for it, and it was getting - it was pissing them off, no end. And that letter actually played quite a key role because I then circulated it within government, again behind the scenes. (Interview, March 2017)

Efforts like this kept the policy going under the Coalition, but with the Liberal Democrats out of the way, this view was marginalised.

The second explanation speaks directly to the broader issue of the role of government in pushing this type of policy. The point, insiders argue, is that while the technical solutions worked for the large house builders (who wrote the above letter), who were able to absorb any increased costs, smaller house builders and sub-contractors—'men in white vans'—were less able to adapt to the changing technology. Here is a former Minister of Housing on this point:

> Well, the building industry is fragmented and dysfunctional. ... Big firms, particularly, even the non-housing firms, tended to think it was a good thing because it's marketable if you've got high environmental quality buildings. ... And clearly, the extent to which the cheap and cheerful end of the market has to provide high standards is a benefit to the top end of the market. ... But, the big volume housing providers, of whom there are too few in this country ... means that there are only a few voices. (Interview, March 2017)

This latter point further reiterates the explanatory purchase of the decentred explanation offered in this chapter. It highlights a housing sector that includes environmentalists, architects, large and small house builders, and private contractors, among others, each with their own problem definition and their own (often bespoke) solution. Ecological modernisation is a narrative that provides them with common ground, but this consensus is always much more contingent and indeed relational than theorisations of the policy process that emphasise fixed interests presume.

What is more, many actors do not consider the policy to be finished, despite government having ostensibly abandoned it. The people who staffed the Zero Carbon Hub are still working on these issues, for example, as the below quote illustrates:

> When the Hub finished, I formed another company called The Buildings Hub, and that still runs today. It's still doing much of the work that the Zero Carbon Hub did. With the same operational directors, the same technical director, the same project director, myself as managing director. And we still carry on that work. (Interview, February 2017)

Indeed, there has been discussion within the industry about whether to continue funding ZCH despite government having walked away from the policy. And other parts of government, like the Great London Area, are still pursuing zero carbon targets. In which case, the narratives persist within the sector despite the absence of national government interest or direction.

Discussion and Conclusions

In this chapter, we have used a decentred narrative policy analysis approach to examine the UK's ZCH policy (2006–2015). A core objective has been to trace the policy over the whole of its lifetime, including from the period before it was formally announced, and since its demise, through the eyes of practitioners and with a focus on the narratives or 'storylines' they use to explain ZCH. By doing so, our analysis encompasses both long-standing community action on sustainable housing, which catalysed policy initiation pre-2006, as well as the ZCH policy and practices, which have continued in a variety of forms since the national policy was abolished in 2015. We have explored how the ZCH policy narratives have translated into material form and the resulting effects.

The benefit of a longitudinal methodological approach is an ability to see what policy implementation activity takes place in the absence of the state, pre- and post-policy. What we have uncovered is a considerable amount of work from non-state actors (private-sector house builders, advocacy organisations, etc.) to achieve zero carbon housing. This action in the absence of policy continues a long-standing tradition at the fringes of the UK housing sector of self-build and using already existing homes to effect change, as evidenced by the sustainable housing movement that predated the ZCH policy, and had significant influence on it, as well as the continuation of ZCH activities post-2015. The ZCH policy is thus a good example of a decentred approach to policy, wherein the state sets the framework—inspired and informed in this case by work already done by non-state organisations and practitioners—and then allows state and non-state organisations/practitioners to work out how to implement it.

The main discursive 'story line' running through the lifetime of the ZCH policy has been ecological modernisation—a belief that it is possible to achieve both environmental (climate change) and economic goals (profit). However, this ecological modernist storyline has been heavily contested. In particular, in the early preconception stages of the ZCH policy, the ecological modernist storyline competed with, and emerged out of, an alternative storyline used by deep green environmental advocates, who had strong environmental and social values, and opposed the idea that economic value is more important than other values, such as environmental protection and community-based action. Nevertheless, analysis of the ZCH policy over its lifetime demonstrates how the ecological modernist objective of profit and environmental protection has (more or less) been achieved. This conclusion is supported by, for example, the continuation of ZCH building practices and local policies post-2015, i.e. even in the absence of the national ZCH policy target.

Contest over meaning has been a strong feature of the ZCH policy from the outset: despite the clarity of the ZCH policy ten-year goal and framework, there was still a huge amount of uncertainty about the detail of implementation, e.g. defining 'zero carbon', the cost of doing it, and how it affected smaller house builders. These difficulties in implementation—felt and experienced by practitioners rather than government—were ultimately listened to closely by the Conservative government and led to the termination of the policy. However, there continues to be a feeling of unrest in the industry, and, more positively, practitioners continue with aspects of the ZCH implementation, even in the absence of the formal policy.

References

Bevir, M., & Rhodes, R. A. W. (2001). Decentering Tradition: Interpreting British Government. *Administration & Society, 33,* 107–132.
Bevir, M., & Rhodes, R. A. W. (2003). *Interpreting British Governance.* Abingdon, Oxon: Routledge.
Bevir, M., & Rhodes, R. A. W. (2006). *Governance Stories.* Abingdon, Oxon: Routledge.
Bevir, M., & Rhodes, R. A. W. (2010). *The State as Cultural Practice.* Oxford: Oxford University Press.
BRECSU. (2000). New Practice Profile 119: The Hockerton Housing Project—Design Lessons for Developers and Clients (Watford, BRE).
BRECSU. (2002). General Information Report 89: BedZED—Beddington Zero Energy Development, Sutton (Watford, BRE).
Christoff, P. (2000). Ecological Modernisation, Ecological Modernities. *Environmental Politics, 5,* 476–500.
DCLG. (2006). *Building a Greener Future: Towards Zero Carbon Development.* Consultation Paper, Department of Communities and Local Government (DCLG), London, UK.
Dobson, A. (2000). *Green Political Thought.* London and New York: Routledge.
DTI. (2002). First Stage of Major PV Demonstration Programme Launched. *New Review, 52,* 1.
DTI. (2003). *Energy White Paper 'Our Energy Future—Creating a Low Carbon Economy'.* Department for Trade and Industry (London, HMSO).
Energy Saving Trust. (2004). *Newark and Sherwood District Council Case Study: A Guide for Local Authorities* (London, Energy Saving Trust for the Energy Efficiency Best Practice in Housing Programme).
Goodchild, B., & Walshaw, A. (2011). Towards Zero Carbon Homes in England? From Inception to Partial Implementation. *Housing Studies, 26,* 933–949.
Greenwood, D. (2012). The Challenge of Policy Coordination for Sustainable Sociotechnical Transitions: The Case of the Zero-Carbon Homes Agenda in England. *Environment and Planning C: Government and Policy, 30,* 162–179.

Hajer, M. A. (1995). *The Politics of Environmental Discourse: Ecological Modernisation and the Policy Process.* Oxford: Clarendon Press.

Hajer, M. A. (2001). *A Frame in the Fields: Policy Making and the Reinvention of Politics.* European Consortium for Political Research Conference (Workshop 9—Policy Discourse and Institutional Reform). Grenoble, France. http://www.essex.ac.uk/ecpr/jointsessions/grenoble/papers/ws9.htm.

Hajer, M., & Versteeg, W. (2005). A Decade of Discourse Analysis of Environmental Politics: Achievements, Challenges, Perspectives. *Journal of Environmental Policy & Planning, 7,* 175–184.

Hajer, M. A., & Wagenaar, H. (2003). *Deliberative Policy Analysis: Understanding Governance in the Network Society.* Cambridge: Cambridge University Press.

Heffernan, E., Pan, W., Liang, X., et al. (2015). Zero Carbon Homes: Perceptions from the UK Construction Industry. *Energy Policy, 79,* 23–36.

Lovell, H. (2004). Framing Sustainable Housing as a Solution to Climate Change. *Journal of Environmental Policy & Planning, 6,* 35–56.

Lovell H. (2005). *The Governance of Emerging Socio-technical Systems: The Case of Low Energy Housing in the UK* (Unpublished Ph.D. thesis). Department of Geography, Cambridge University, Cambridge.

Lovell, H. (2007). The Governance of Innovation in Socio-technical Systems: The Difficulties of Strategic Niche Management in Practice. *Science and Public Policy, 34,* 35–44.

Lovell, H. (2009). The Role of Individuals in Policy Change: The Case of UK Low Energy Housing. *Environment and Planning C, 27,* 491–511.

Lowenstein, O. (2001). From BedZed to Eternity. *Building for a Future, 11*(3), 16–21.

McLeod, R. S., Hopfe, C. J., & Rezgui, Y. (2012). An Investigation into Recent Proposals for a Revised Definition of Zero Carbon Homes in the UK. *Energy Policy, 46,* 25–35.

Pragnell, M., Spence, L., & Moore, R. (2000). *The Market Potential for Smart Homes.* York: Joseph Rowntree Foundation.

RCEP. (2000). *Energy: The Changing Climate.* 22nd Report of the Royal Commission on Environmental Pollution (RCEP), London, UK.

Seyfang, G., & Smith, A. (2007). Grassroots Innovation for Sustainable Development: Towards a New Research and Policy Agenda. *Environmental Politics, 16,* 584–603.

The Housing Corporation. (2004). *BedZed case study for housing associations.* Retrieved October 22, 2004, from http://www.housingcorp.gov.uk/resources/sustain.htm#tools.

Toke, D. (2000). Policy Network Creation: The Case of Energy Efficiency. *Public Administration, 78,* 835–854.

Vale, B., & Vale, R. (2000). *The New Autonomous House*. London: Thames & Hudson.

Walker, G., Karvonen, A., & Guy, S. (2015). Zero Carbon Homes and Zero Carbon Living: Sociomaterial Interdependencies in Carbon Governance. *Transactions of the Institute of British Geographers, 40*, 494–506.

Walker, G., Karvonen, A., & Guy, S. (2016). Addendum: Reflections on a Policy Denouement: The Politics of Mainstreaming Zero-Carbon Housing. *Transactions of the Institute of British Geographers, 41*, 104–106.

CHAPTER 4

What Are the Hidden Dimensions to Parliamentary Scrutiny—The Ghosts in the Machine?

Tony McNulty

Introduction—Ghost in the Machine

When asked about the parliamentary scrutiny of the Counter-Terrorism Bill 2008 and the provision for 42-day pre-charge detention, a senior official in the Home Office said, in a rather exasperated tone, that resorting to legislation so readily was:

> a complete mystery…because a high amount of effort was put into this legislation… when actually the really important work was being done in parallel.

The official continues by saying that:

> it's a very interesting example of what happens in government, you have these great iconic battles…about things and it takes attention away from the things that are being done to strengthen security services, to improve coordination across government. (Interview)

T. McNulty (✉)
Queen Mary University, London, UK

© The Author(s) 2018
R. A. W. Rhodes (ed.), *Narrative Policy Analysis*, Understanding Governance, https://doi.org/10.1007/978-3-319-76635-5_4

For this official, the government was implementing a whole range of policies on counter-terrorism that were improving and enhancing the government, police and security services and their respective capabilities in this area—but legislation wasn't one of them. Central to the theme of this chapter is the simple question—if this was so clear to this senior official, why did the government pursue legislation in this area at all?

This chapter uses my experience as a key participant in counter-terrorism policy as a government minister at the time and over fifty interviews that have been carried out with the key actors and players in the Home Office and across government. Geddes and Rhodes (2017) have argued that academic research on parliament has overlooked actors' individual beliefs, everyday practices, and wider traditions because they are often perceived to be inconsequential to the institutional dynamics at play'.

This chapter argues that such beliefs, practices and traditions are far from inconsequential, and they are central to a comprehensive understanding of parliament and the processes in parliament. Interpretivism and ethnography—particularly auto-ethnography—can help us to unpack, understand and analyse the beliefs, practices and traditions of the actors involved. Using this approach, we can discern a new narrative for the Counter-Terrorism Bill and the 42-day provision specifically, and the parliamentary scrutiny process in general.

In order to fully understand what went on during this scrutiny process, a decentred analysis is used. This interpretive approach helps explain how the beliefs, practices and traditions of all the actors within the parliamentary scrutiny processes of the UK Parliament play such a crucial role in our ability to understand such processes. It argues that we need to go beyond a normative, quantitative study of parliamentary scrutiny if we are to understand how the impact of these varying beliefs, practices and traditions—the 'ghosts in the machine'—helps to shape the responses of parliamentary actors to the events, choices, decisions—the dilemmas—that they face (see Chapter 1 above).

Bevir and Rhodes use ethnographic studies designed to examine how 'actors develop their beliefs', and the ethnography makes available the 'formation of individual beliefs out of confrontation between 'situated actor' and changing external world' (Finlayson 2007: 549–550). Finlayson also argues that in politics one cannot simply choose the 'best idea or the one that is most coherent or congruent with our own traditions.' He argues that we have to deal not only with the sorts of 'dilemmas' identified by Bevir and Rhodes, but also with contingency and uncertainty on at least two further levels—'the uncertainty of the world, the need to act despite a lack of full and final information; and that caused by the presence of others who think in different ways, rooted in different traditions' (Finlayson 2007: 549–550).

Bevir and Rhodes argue that central to such an approach is the ability to 'tell stories about other people's stories' and to do this 'we have to recover their stories and explain them' (Bevir and Rhodes 2003: 5–6).

Geddes and Rhodes (2017: 14–16) draw on three sources of information in their research—documents, interviews and observation. Parliamentary documents are 'meat and drink' to the interpretive analyst and provide a treasure trove for those seeking to recreate the stories and narratives under review. This is complicated further when the analyst is also a participant and has had a role, sometimes 'minor', sometimes 'starring' in the documents under review. The participant also has the advantage of access to some papers and documents that are beyond the reach of the outside academic researcher. As a former minister, I have access to any papers that I utilised as a minister when making decisions or developing policies.

Interviews allow the researcher to, as Geddes and Rhodes (2017: 17) contend, give the parliamentary 'actor' the opportunity to 'narrate their experiences, tell us about their beliefs, and explain how they negotiated dilemmas in Parliament.' This again is further complicated when the researcher is also one of the 'actors'. Difficulties arise when the actor as academic interviews other 'actors' about events in which they both took part. I have interviewed over fifty key participants for this chapter and the wider study of which it forms a part.

The third element of their research—observation—enables them to 'observe behaviour directly; to see everyday practices as they happen; to open what is ordinarily hidden in official documents and accounts; and provide a deep immersion that no other method can.' (Geddes and Rhodes: 17) For a researcher who had also been a participant, observation is again quite complex. It has great value and adds an insight that the non-participant could not possibly have or ever obtain, but the researcher/participant has his/her own set of beliefs, traditions and values—and their own version of the stories and narratives under review.

The three central concepts of Bevir and Rhodes' interpretivism—narrative, tradition and dilemma—are useful here in helping us understand what is really going on in the world of parliamentary activity, rather than what seems to be going on (Bevir and Rhodes 2003: 26 and Chapter 6. Also see Chapter 1 above).

These constructs can help understand and recognise that the emerging data from these scrutiny activities need to be fully analysed and assessed before it can be seriously treated as data at all—and that there are 'ghosts in the machine' that may be the key to such an understanding and recognition. As Geddes and Rhodes argue, 'academic research on parliaments and legislatures has often overlooked actors' individual beliefs, everyday practices and wider traditions because they are often perceived to be inconsequential to the institutional dynamics at play' (Bevir and Rhodes 2003: 17). By adding the participant's viewpoint to this study of parliamentary scrutiny, this research adds an important dimension to the study of parliaments and, notwithstanding the ontological difficulties, can help us explain further the efficacy of scrutiny as a parliamentary function.

Context Is Everything

Throughout this period, separate beliefs, narratives and dilemmas were routinely generated and adhered to that would colour and shape how Parliament would interpret the language and issues of the Counter-Terrorism Bill 2008—and ultimately determine how people would vote. While it is impossible to 'operationalise' these dimensions of parliamentary life, their impact on subsequent debates, choices and ultimately votes in Parliament is clear—and needs to be understood further in the contact of the emerging data and its value. Each bill, each vote and each choice of action need to be understood within a range of differing 'worlds, contexts and needs.'

Nothing about the passage of the Counter-Terrorism Bill 2008 can be understood without a complete comprehension of the broader context. In terms of the broadest context, three key elements prevail. Firstly, the relationship and rivalry between Blair (Prime Minister 1997–2007) and Brown (Chancellor of the Exchequer 1997–2007, Prime Minister 2007–2010) (see Richards 2010; Rawnsley 2010; Boulton 2008). Secondly, the government's relationship with the USA and its consequent reaction to events after the attack on the World Trade Centre in September 2001, including the Iraq War and the attacks on Afghanistan (see Blair 2010; Seldon 2008; Rawnsley 2010). Thirdly, the emerging and all too real counter-terrorism threat at home in the UK (see Omand 2010).

Everything about the Labour Government from 1997 to 2010 should be seen through the prism of the relationship between Blair and Brown. Richards (2010: 2) maintains that '…suddenly in the mid-1990s there were Blairites and Brownites springing up from nowhere in large numbers'. Many of those interviewed for this chapter and the wider study that it forms a part of are clear that this is the case. Interviewees stated repeatedly that all decisions, all developments of policy and ultimately decisions were looked at through the prism of the Blair–Brown relationship.

As an active participant on the political side, I was aware of this in the political context, but did not fully understand that it mattered so much to the civil service and other public servants. It was only after carrying out the interviews for this study that I began to understand how redolent and all-important the relationship was for them. Indeed, it was clear that this all-encompassing rivalry between Blair and Brown and the way in which it had the potential to impact across the domestic policy agenda had a real influence on the 'beliefs and practices' of the civil service, as well as on the key actors within the government.

If much of the foreign policy of the first parliamentary session of the Labour Government from 1997 to 2001 was influenced by the close and strong relationship between Blair and Clinton, then the subsequent period of government—all the way up to 2010 and the ultimate defeat of that government—was coloured by the 9/11 attack and the government's subsequent decision to join in the war in Iraq. Up to, and in the immediate aftermath of 9/11, there had been some rather limited legislative interventions around counter-terrorism to deal with the perceived terrorist threat. The *Terrorism Act 2000* confirmed 7 days as the maximum period of detention but required judicial approval for extension rather than ministerial authorisation.

Following the 9/11 attack on the twin towers of the World Centre on New York, the UK passed the *Anti-Terrorism, Crime, and Security Act 2001*—which included provision for the indefinite detention of terrorist subjects who were non-UK citizens. The *Criminal Justice Act 2003* amongst other things doubled the period for pre-charge detention for terrorist suspects from 7 days to 14 days.

In December 2004, Charles Clarke replaced David Blunkett as Home Secretary. The next day, the Law Lords ruled that detaining foreigners without trial was unlawful. The appeal was made on behalf of nine men who were detained under the Part 4 provisions of the 2001 Act. These provisions were due to expire in March 2005—hence the speed with which the *Prevention of Terrorism Act 2005* was introduced. The Act was secured three days before the provisions expired.

So, prior to the attack in London on 7/7, there had been a history of legislative interventions that were increasingly more serious in import and direction. One senior government minister at the time stated that 'I … understood the instinctive reaction of many parliamentarians …that actually the state has too much power and it should not be increased… we were always trying to reconcile those two irreconcilable principles: the security of the country and individual liberty' (Interview). This reconciliation was to be sorely tested on a number of occasions during the government's lifetime.

7/7—The Road to 90 Days

Much of the work to prevent such terrorist acts went on unnoticed by the public. The attack on 7/7 in London did succeed—and the death of 52 people with hundreds injured, many severely—brought home clearly the nature of the threat. The reaction to it was more pronounced because it soon emerged that the perpetrators were young men born and bred in the UK (Herrington 2015; Malik 2007).

The immediate reaction to these attacks was from an operational policing perspective. The 7/7 attack had brought a new phenomenon to the UK—suicide bombers. Police and lawyers would agree that one of the most vulnerable elements of any crime—including planting bombs—is the proposed escape route, that is, how the perpetrators intend to get away from the scene. If escape is no longer a factor, there are profound ramifications for the respective roles of the intelligence services, the police and the law. Two weeks later, on 21/7, there was a further attack involving bombs on London's trains, but it failed and a more traditional 'flee and pursue' scenario developed—ending in the capture of the terrorists.

The first substantial political response was a press conference by Tony Blair on 5 August 2005 (*The Guardian* 2005a). The framework outlined built on the government's approach to counter-terrorist the policy direction for the rest of the governments' time in office. He announced a twelve-point plan. The plan framed the government response in terms of politics, legislation and policy. It was a mixture of measures already in train, measures already discussed but in abeyance and new measures—both practical and aspirational. The last two points of the plan were a promise that 'new anti-terrorism legislation would be introduced in the autumn (of 2005)' and 'the government would seek to meet the "police and security services request that detention, pre-charge of terrorist suspects" be significantly extended'.

If the plan set the context, then four elements coloured the progress of the government on the way to legislation. Firstly, as we have seen, the whole issue of the relationship between Blair and Brown is central to the analysis. However, there was little disagreement between them on either how to tackle counter-terrorism in these early years or, indeed, foreign policy. Although, at this stage, the two significant leaders of the government were in full agreement, the roots of subsequent discord started here. The ghosts were stirring.

Secondly, Blair was clear that there needed to be legislative change. This option was not up for debate and it was clear that it was going to be fast-tracked too. Within the context of the 7/7 attack, the government was clear that legislation was an option that 'goes without saying' because it comes 'without saying', as Bourdieu (1977: 167) would have it. An official close to the development of the government counter-terrorism strategy (Contest Strategy 2006) at the time has since said that 'Ninety days was clearly in breach of the spirit of the counter-terrorism strategy' (Interview). The interviewee argued further that actually in 'Contest terms that is completely counter-productive because what you are emphasising is abnormality. Terrorists have forced us to do this' (Interview).

Thirdly, central to the legislative dimensions of the twelve-point plan was the full support of the police establishment with the implied support of the security services. Indeed, many challenged what they saw as an 'over-politicisation' of the police (BBC News 2005; *The Guardian* 2005b). This contrasts with the absence of support from the 'uniformed establishment' in 2008. There was a lingering negative view of the role of intelligence because of the war in Iraq in 2003. It proved to be a central feature of the 42-day debate in 2008. Three years prior to the 42-day vote, the support of the police reinforced the foundations of a set of beliefs and practices that would be further articulated in the context of another scrutiny clash between government and legislature.

Fourthly, the developing government narrative around 90 days was broadly accepted by public opinion and the media. The government was clear that, in the wake of the 7/7 atrocity, it had public opinion on its side, even if it faced a rather strange parliamentary coalition of protagonists—dissident Labour MPs, the Liberal Democrats and the Tories led by the Shadow Home Secretary, David Davis. It was, perhaps, this legacy that led to an absence of narrative in 2008 for 42 days. The assumption was that the same level of support would prevail.

The Terrorism Bill was published (Terrorism Act 2006) specifically seeking to extend pre-charge detention from 14 days to 90 days. The Act also contained other provisions about the encouragement of terrorism, proscription of terrorist organisations, preparations of terrorist acts and definitions of searches and terrorism. The police made clear throughout the process that they had requested the extension and argued that there was a 'compelling case' for it. Critics accused the government of 'politicising' the police (*The Guardian* 2005c). Blair suffered his first defeat in the House of Commons on the issue of the extension of pre-charge detention to 90 days. He lost by a majority of 31, by 322 votes to 291 because there was a substantial rebellion by 60 Labour backbenchers. A backbench compromise of 28-day detention, reviewed on an annual basis, was passed by 323 votes to 290 votes—a majority of 33. The Bill secured Royal Assent—with the 28-day provision in place. The government did not pursue the 90-day provision in the House of Lords and appeared to accept the will of parliament with the 28-day limit.

A member of the government at the time was clear that an extension was the right thing to do, but was not clear about 28 days. They said:

> I don't think I ever thought 28 days was the final position. There were just so many legal, administrative, and judicial complexities involved that it was absolutely necessary to hold people for longer. I just do not believe that we have gotten the right answer in this respect. (Interview)

It is worth saying too that the nature of the compromise during the debate on ninety days also matters. Having arrived at such a compromise, the House would defend it vociferously. The compromise at twenty-eight days was regarded as a 'job well done' by a House of Commons that felt it had recognised the need for some movement but recognised too that the government had gone too far. As one of the key participants related, the origin of the compromise was quite prosaic. It was felt that the provision for pre-charge detention 'had been doubled from seven to fourteen … it should be doubled again' (Interview). The House would jealously guard this position—and the absence of a detailed government narrative as to why things should change would, ultimately, cost the government.

Post 7/7—The Ghosts Gather on the Path from 90 to 42 Days

Despite many thwarted attacks and continued plot activity, there was only limited legislative intervention after the failure of the 2005 Bill. The Crevice and Rhyme plots (BBC News 2007a, b; RUSI 2007) were finally coming to the courts, with much previously unheard detail being placed into the public domain for the first time. The plot to bring down airliners over the Atlantic—Project Overt—was foiled in the summer of 2006, partly as the result of precipitative action by the Pakistani and US authorities (*The Independent* 2008; *The Guardian* 2009). The first half of 2007 saw the foiling of a plot to behead a soldier in the West Midlands—Operation Gamble (Home Office 2006) and the first week of the Premiership of Gordon Brown saw the failed bomb plot of Operation Seagram—that started in the Haymarket in London and ended in flames at Glasgow Airport (Home Office 2011).

For some, the details that emerged in the trails of those involved in either the Crevice or Rhyme plots illustrated how the police and security services could be successful within the existing legal framework. The details that many in the government thought would assist in the justification and rationale behind further legal intervention were being used by the government's protagonists to explain how 'normal' legislation was the best response—and was being successful.

In 2008, although much had changed, there was no agreed government line on the narrative, strategy or beliefs that underpinned the introduction of the Counter-Terrorism Bill or indeed the need for legislation at all. The government assumed that there would be a consensus on which to go forward—but there was none. Worse than this, as a senior government member now described it 'The absence of a narrative … allows a counter-narrative to prevail' (Interview).

The counter-narrative of the government's opponents wrote itself. Richards reports that Brown's close allies Ed Miliband and Ed Balls were both opposed to the extension of pre-charge detention to 42 days and had 'assumed that Brown had come under pressure from Blair to show how tough he was on terrorism' (Richards 2010: 334–335). Others went further. One senior backbencher said that it 'just came out of nowhere' (Interview). A senior former member of the government said 'I thought the reason… for returning to it was utterly pathetic… he (Gordon Brown) was trying to demonstrate that he was tough and could get things through that Tony (Blair) couldn't get through' (Interview). For others, the view was that 'Parliament had already decided … Why would anybody vote differently in the new situation…well the answer to that was forty-two is different to ninety…and I never really believed forty-two was different to ninety' (Interview). Another senior former member of the government thought that even after the horror of the airline plot—Project Overt—many in the police and security forces didn't call for a change in the law perhaps because they were 'once bitten, twice shy' after their role in the 90-day debate (Interview). The former minister felt that the services should be 'put on the spot because of what happened last time' (90 days—author) and that the proposal should not proceed unless there was a 'clear operational demand from the police' (Interview). Throughout this period, the 'ghost' of the 90-day debate lay heavy over all the government's deliberations on counter-terrorism, not just the potential legislation. There was a feeling from some inside government not only that the issue of legislation was 'unfinished business' that needed redressing but also that it was a matter that needed to be resolved before the government could develop a serious narrative around its efforts (Personal recollection).

Frustratingly at the time, I felt that all the elements of such a coherent narrative existed and were rooted in four significant elements of a narrower counter-terrorism context (Personal recollection). Firstly, alongside the seemingly endless plot attempts, parliamentary committees maintained a steady interest in all matters to do with counter-terrorism. There was a steady drumbeat of criticism of much of the work of government by both the Home Affairs Select Committee and the Joint Committee on Human Rights (JCHR). Both committees were particularly concerned with any new legislative initiatives in the area by the government and produced a range of reports throughout this period (e.g. JCHR 2007; Home Affairs Select Committee 2007). The government might well be determined to revisit some aspects of the legislative agenda—but it would not be allowed to do so in a vacuum. Both committees constantly referred to the 'settled will' of Parliament as 28-day detention—and ensured on the run-up to the introduction of the new bill that there would be, at the very least, a competing narrative to the government's narrative. Both committees, and the opposition parties, were clear in their own belief that there was no need to revisit the legislation. Often the government is able to craft and frame the narrative for a new piece of legislation, but there is a strong view that on this occasion it was simply a rerun of the 90-day debate that the government had lost some years before.

Secondly, as the new Home Secretary in 2006, John Reid made it clear that he wanted to instigate a comprehensive review of the government's counter-terrorism effort and he did so. He also wanted to establish a national security council and made it clear to that he favoured a 'European-style' split of responsibility between a security-focussed

Home Office and a Ministry of Justice that would be responsible for offender management and prisons. This marked new territory in a UK context. He began his review of all aspects of the government's counter-terrorism policies, resources and structures, and all government departments remotely involved in counter-terrorism were invited to attend a high-level series of meetings over the course of late 2006 and into 2007.

The fact that the Home Office should be the centre of the government's counter-terrorism effort is entirely uncontroversial today, but the prospect of this outcome was both deeply controversial and fiercely contested across government at the time. One participant suggested that the 'Cabinet Office didn't want it to be based in the Home Office because they thought their job was coordinating things, but they weren't up to the task…the Foreign Office thought it was a great idea, but of course they were the lead department for MI6 …. And didn't want anything to threaten their position' (Interview). Once, however, it became clear that the review had the full support of Prime Minister and the Chancellor of the Exchequer, all participants worked with the review to get the best they could from the outcome. I was a member of the review and attended all the meetings. For the first few meetings, some departments sent some junior civil servants or ministers and this practice ceased only when it became clear that Number 10 fully supported Reid's initiative (Personal recollection).

The review reported in May 2007, and as expected, the Home Office took full responsibility for the government's counter-terrorism strategy for the first time and a new Ministry of Justice was created by a merger between the Department for Constitutional Affairs and the offender management, probation and prison elements of the Home Office. Also, a new Office of Security and Counter-Terrorism was formed (OSCT) reflecting the new Home Office responsibilities. The Foreign Office remained in control of GCHQ and MI6, the Cabinet Office still serviced COBRA when it met, and some elements of the community functions of the Home Office were moved to the Department for Communities and Local Government. Some of these moves proved successful and largely remain in place today. Most interestingly of all though is the absence of any declared and concrete proposals for legislative change. So, the government's senior minister in the policy area, after a lengthy detailed and comprehensive review of the government's counter-terrorism capacity, did not choose to highlight further legislation around the issue of pre-charge detention as a necessary way forward to enhance the country's capacity to resist terrorism. The conclusions and outcome of the review were another 'ghost' that would return to haunt the scrutiny process.

Thirdly, soon after all these changes of the government machinery at the Home Office and elsewhere, Blair resigned as Prime Minister and was replaced by Gordon Brown: a month after Reid's review and the implicit rejection of legislation, the new Prime Minister designate made clear that he was going to look at the legislative route again. Brown made a statement on security to Parliament some weeks after the plot to bomb a nightclub in the Haymarket was foiled. He announced that he was going to 'explore whether a consensus could be built on the most measured way to deal with (the) …remaining risk' (Hansard 2007). He made clear that he would consult on four options—a state of emergency option rooted in the Civil Contingencies Act; an extension of the pre-charge detention limit; an extension but with a vote in Parliament before implementation; and the development of a European-style investigative magistrate system (Home Office 2007). The options were considerably influenced by the output of the JCHR and the influence of Liberty. The relative success of both Liberty and the JCHR in framing the limitations of the legislative discourse was, in my opinion at the time, rooted in the absence of a comprehensive government discourse (Interview and personal recollection).

The case for new legislation had not, however, been made in the view of many within Parliament including those who fully understood the importance of beliefs, traditions and narratives. With the case not made, not only would the policy appear to be flawed, but the nature of the scrutiny process would also be challenged. This view was shared by a senior government member at the time who reported that, 'We had not done the groundwork, we'd not prepared the ground sufficiently. We just assumed after Glasgow … it becomes a rerun of ninety days with no real substantial basis' (Interview). There was a growing view that the push for new legislation was coming from Number 10—the Prime Minister—rather than from the Home Office—and that it might have its origins in the 'ghost' of the TB/GBs rather than a coherent policy direction. (TB/GBs was a phrase first coined by the deputy Prime Minister, John Prescott, to describe the ongoing fraught relationship between Blair and Brown.)

It would prove difficult to sustain the government narrative on the need for legislative change when the cumulative impact of these three events—the 'drumbeat' of negative committee reports, the reality of Reid's counter-terrorism review findings and Brown's 'instant' decision to go forward—was so apparently contradictory.

Fourthly, and just for good measure, the retired Director-General of MI5 took her seat in the House of Lords in the summer of 2008 just before the Bill, having completed its passage in the House of Commons, was about to go into the Lords for a far more contentious debate. She declared in her maiden speech that 'Since 9/11, we have had a great deal of terrorism legislation. One point that has not been made so far is that successful counter-terrorism work depends on many things, but in particular on good intelligence and good police work, not necessarily on changes in the law. That said, all the legislation has had some important and enabling provisions'. The government would have been happy with this intervention, but the speech had a sting in its tail. She continued by saying 'In deciding what I believe on these matters, I have weighed up the balance between the right to life—the most important civil liberty—the fact that there is no such thing as complete security and the importance of our hard-won civil liberties. Therefore, on a matter of principle, I cannot support the proposal in the Bill for pre-charge detention of 42 days' (Hansard 2008e: col. 648).

All of these factors—but especially the 'ghost' of the previous proceedings on the provisions for ninety days—haunted the development and eventual scrutiny of the Bill and its proposals. Most deliberative legislative bodies take its activities seriously, and the House of Commons is no exception. The beliefs and traditions of the Commons start from the belief that governments are always seeking to undermine their functions and roles—particularly its key role of holding the government to account and imposing scrutiny on it. If the pervading view, on such an important matter as security, is that the government is seeking to 'politicise' the process of legislation and offers no significant narrative or reasons why new legislation should be introduced, then the traditions of the Commons dictate that the government will get a rough ride during the passage of such legislation. It appears that the government decided on this occasion that it could ignore the beliefs and traditions of the Commons—notwithstanding that many in its own ranks knew and understood their importance. Certainly, the 'ghost' of the 90-day process haunted the committee and Commons proceedings of bill completely. Context, again, is everything.

42 Days—It's Déjà vu All Over Again

A government minister lives in a world at once removed yet intensely part of daily parliamentary life. When a bill is under scrutiny, the entire committee, but especially the government minister, 'live and breathe' a process in what must be surely one of the narrowest confines of that life—the committee room—carrying out one of the narrowest of parliamentary processes—the line-by-line scrutiny of a bill. The committee would meet every Tuesday and Thursday, in the morning and in the afternoon, for the number of sessions allotted to it. The lead minister will spend much of Mondays and Wednesdays preparing for these sessions and the weekend preparing for the sessions the following week. Thus, for anything up to ten to twelve weeks, the busy life of a government minister will be taken over by the scrutiny process of the bill. Then, usually, the role of lead minister will be handed to the department's cabinet minister at report and third reading stage. I was the lead minister for this bill.

The government minister and the business managers (the Whips Office and the Leader of the House Office) have an overriding goal to deliver the government's full business—including all legislation—on time and intact. Each of the decisions will impact on their ability to deliver this goal. The Counter-Terrorism Bill, like all remotely contentious bills, began its passage in the Commons. The government feels that it can control the destiny and timing of a bill far more readily if it starts in the Commons. The bill was not in any manifesto, had no pre-legislative scrutiny (for although there was a consultation process of sorts, it was felt that the government was clear which option it would choose in the end) and was substantive rather than tinkering. Although it was not strictly a retread bill, the House has already discussed the important issue of pre-charge detention in real detail only a short while ago—and arrived at a 'settled will' on such a contentious matter. Further, it achieved this 'settled will' by taking on and defeating the government on 90 days. Many felt it was incumbent on the government to offer substantive reasons, a detailed narrative, about why there should be changes to the legislation at all given the 'settled will' of the House on twenty-eight days.

It was felt by many, particularly by those Labour backbenchers who felt no loyalty to the new Prime Minister, that the government was not taking the Commons seriously if it thought it could reintroduce these matters, without detailed reasons as to why it was doing so (Interviews).

A senior backbencher argued that 'it's mad, completely mad. There is no and, to my knowledge never has been, a strong demand from the police for this. They don't want to be dragged back into this. Why is he (Brown) doing this?' (Interview). These issues were swirling around the parliamentary estate prior to the introduction of the bill.

There were three key decisions made by the government that coloured the entire process of the bill. As we have seen, despite indicating that he wanted to proceed on consensual basis, the Prime Minister and the new Home Secretary, Jacqui Smith announced a consultation on four options for legislation (Hansard 2007; Home Office 2007). One backbencher commented on the potential for new legislation by saying that 'I think a number of us were really quite surprised … we could not see what could happen to change the settled will' (Interview).

There was a strong view from those who did not support the legislation that it was wrong to consult, if you were going to do what you wanted anyway. Yes, there was a consultation process, but 'the trouble is a lot of the responses to the consultation came out saying, "Don't do it!"' (Interview). Notwithstanding the consultation, a senior official thought at the time that the government was 'on heightened alert and therefore our mind-set is still, and probably Gordon Brown's as well, we need to all the powers we can get. In truth, there wasn't that much evidence for going beyond twenty-eight days was there?' (Interview).

Secondly, by opting in the end for an elaborate extension to 28 days based on a stated 'emergency' without resorting to emergency legislation, the government opened itself up to criticism based on the confusion between making law and implementing law. Quite reasonably, many of the detractors of the bill argued that, as drafted, it confused the role of the Commons as a legislative body with the role of the courts to discharge the law. If the police could not proceed with an extension to the period of pre-charge detention until Parliament has determined that there was a situation urgent enough to warrant such an extension, then how could the defendants have any guarantee of due process in the courts? Only by basing the legislative change on 'emergency-style' provisions could the government end up in such a difficult position with some of the concessions that it made to get the bill through.

Thirdly, by the time of the report and third reading stages of the bill, the political imperative had become simply winning the vote in the Commons. As has been said, the government needs to get its business through the House—and on this bill, the focus became securing the position of the government, not the passage of the bill. Sometimes the ability of governments to make concessions to secure its business is seen as a virtue—the result of a confident but listening government. Sometimes concessions are the result of panic and an inability to understand that securing the bill in the Commons is not the whole process. There was never any significant discussion across government about how it would deal with the Lords stages of the bill (Personal recollection).

In normal circumstances, any proposal for legislation goes through a detailed internal government scrutiny process that includes both extensive consultation across government departments and an exhaustive process under the aegis of the Legislative Programme (LP) cabinet sub-committee. As part of this process, one essential document concerns how the government will handle the bill in the House of Lords. I remember clearly taking the bill through this part of the process and there was little debate over how to deal with the issues that would be raised in the Lords. Usually this is an essential document for any remotely controversial bill. I remember that, unusually, there was an intense debate at the committee about the legal coherence of the 42-day provisions and whether it was really the right way to go for the government—but no significant debate on the Lords handling at all (Personal recollection).

This was, I think, a debate by proxy about the poor quality of the bill and the absence of a government narrative. Key senior politicians on the committee knew that the Prime Minister wanted the bill so challenged the details, not the proposals themselves. Practice and belief dictated that a Prime Minister's wishes should prevail, especially a relatively new Prime Minister. But this conflicted with their beliefs and practices as parliamentarians, which dictated that they should still resist in some form or other, if only rather passively. I remember being furious that they challenged the bill at all and thought—wrongly as it turned out—they should have simply rubber-stamped the bill and the handling strategy for the Lords—however feeble (Personal recollection).

Ghosts in the Machine

The ghost of the 90-day debate was not on the parliamentary order paper of the 42-day debate. It was in the committee room and the Commons chamber nonetheless. Time after time, a range of participants—government and opposition, frontbenchers and backbenchers, old hands, and new recruits—said that if the government had understood the political capital exhausted in achieving the 28-day compromise, then it would have never come back with further changes (Interviews). It may have been the result of not only the change in Prime Minister halfway through this crucial three-year phase from 2005 to 2008, but also the fact that the government had a total of three different chief whips over the period. These individuals were experienced and heavyweight politicians. Every aspect of what they sought to do in the role of Chief Whip would have been shaped by their:

> Individual interpretation of what the Prime Minister of the day wanted;
> Personal views about the importance of the beliefs and practices of the Commons;
> Personal views on how the government should react to the Commons to secure the legislation;
> Assessment of the government's capacity for both agency and its ability to secure change; and
> Assessment of the government's power to deal with dilemmas that arose when new ideas stood in opposition to existing beliefs and practices. (Bevir and Rhodes 2010: 73)

To fully understand the importance of the 28-day settlement in 2005, one needs to understand what it costs parliament to reach that compromise. The government maintained that it sought to legislate on 90 days in a spirit of agreement. Some of those involved in government were clearly willing to go further than others in forging a compromise—and were not 'fixated on the number 90' (Interviews). It became clear, however, that the Prime Minister, Blair, wanted to stick with 90 days and 'thought it was more important to stand with the position that we had' (Interview). It was reported that 'Tony wants this to be a binary issue' meaning 'a polarised issue on which there can be no possible compromise' (Seldon 2008: 398; Blair 2010: 583–584). Defeating the government but responding to public concerns over terrorism by alighting on the 28-day compromise mattered to the tradition of Parliament. Parliamentary beliefs and practices accepted that there was indeed a threat that needed responding to in 2005–2006 and that it would have been irresponsible and counter to these beliefs and practices to defeat the government. The compromise of 28 days was a reaction to the heavy handedness of the government's 90-day proposal—but also a recognition that something had to be done to allay the fears of the public and to address the threat.

One of the provisions of the compromise on 28 days was that the order had to be agreed by Parliament on an annual basis. I was the minister who had to put the renewal order before parliament for renewal in the three years after it had passed. While always anticipating trouble and a rerun of the old debate on the manner of pre-charge detention, it was never forthcoming, and renewal was secured with relative ease. I reflected that this was because of the way in which the compromise had been secured. In other words, Parliament did not defeat the government lightly and felt that it collectively 'owned' the 28-day compromise as its 'settled position' (Personal recollection). Revisiting the issue on what appeared to be a flimsy basis devoid of even a substantive government narrative would have irked Parliament.

Theatrical Endeavours: Ghostbusting Tradition and Dilemma

Ironically, scrutiny becomes less important when there are set positions and little room for flexibility or compromise, and this needs to be understood when simply counting the number of votes or number of committee sessions. A simple count of each aspect of the scrutiny process is useful, but limited if taken out of context. If we take a reductionist approach to the scrutiny of the Counter-Terrorism Bill, there were 20 speeches at Second Reading. However, they belonged more to the realms of either theatrical endeavour or 'shadow boxing' than to any notion of coherent parliamentary debate (Hansard 2008a, b, c, d, e). Minds were clearly made up, and no one was listening to anybody else. Often in these situations, members know that the big set piece debate of the bill—in this case the provision on 42-day pre-charge detention—will happen in the Commons at report stage and not in committee, so the scrutiny function of the committee was undermined as well.

Fifteen witnesses were called and gave evidence to the bill committee—all of whom had already declared for one side or other of the debate. None of the witnesses moved minds or informed those willing to be informed further, and all were rehearsing arguments and debate that had been in the public domain for months. Thompson (2014) quotes the then Labour MP Martin Salter, who had been a member of the Home Affairs Select Committee as well as a member of the bill committee, as describing the evidence sessions for the Counter-Terrorism Bill 2007–2008 as being like 'Groundhog Day' as the bill 'heard from the same people who gave evidence to the Home Affairs

Committee' (Thompson 2014: 387–389). The arguments, and relative positions, of many people concerned with counter-terrorism and the provisions of the bill have, apparently, been well rehearsed and fully articulated—another recipe for rather limited debate and discourse within the committee.

There were twelve votes in committee—none of them on any of substance. This was largely because everybody knew that the 'ghosts in the machine' had determined that real debate, the real contest, would be on the floor of the House of Commons and, ultimately, up in the Lords. There were 182 amendments to the bill presented at the committee stage—50 from the government and 132 from the opposition. Two of the opposition amendments were accepted—they changed the word 'may' to 'must'. These were not trivial amendments, but they were not decisive either and it costs the government little to concede them.

On some 17 occasions, clarity was asked for and given, or the minister said he would look at the issue and might bring the matter back at report stage. The minister made provision for opposition spokespeople to discuss some of the bill's provisions with government civil servants—especially on the issue of coroners and inquests without juries. So, 130 opposition amendments were either withdrawn or defeated, and the government secured all its amendments; there was a set debate on the key issue of 42 days but clearly within the context of government concessions to come and a more substantive debate on report stage. So, while these numbers—votes, sessions, concessions, etc.—are relevant, their usefulness is limited if considered out of context.

Through a Glass Darkly—Chasing Concessions

The scrutiny in committee was indeed 'shadow boxing' and would always have been so given the nature of the bill and all the surrounding processes. As most of those on the committee, including myself, as minister, respected the practices, beliefs and traditions of the House, the nature of the committee proceedings was conducted in a civil fashion, as was noted in the prelude to the report stage debate. One opposition member noted that 'to be fair, the Minister engaged at all times with the Committee, and we had good debates', and another reported that 'the Committee Stage was undertaken in good spirit' (Hansard 2008e: cols. 165–178). They were, it should be said, contrasting the time taken at committee stage, with the time being offered for the report stage.

As the minister taking the bill through the committee stage, I was clear that I had to be as amenable, polite, indulgent and inclusive as I could possibly be. I had to ensure that there was still scope for proper debate and, where possible, agreement. I was keenly aware too that, in anticipation of the more focussed debate to come on the issue of 42 days at report stage on the floor of the House of Commons, every word that I said in committee was being carefully interpreted and analysed by an audience far beyond the handful of observers in the committee room itself. For the minister in charge of a bill, a misplaced word or phrase, a temper tantrum or a verbal attack on an opponent, could cost the government an agreement, compromise or deal farther down the line of the scrutiny process. Opposition members expected respect and courtesy—longstanding beliefs of the Commons. It is axiomatic that every member has a valuable contribution to make. This is part of the basic anthropology of politics (Crewe 2015). When I was a Councillor on a local London Borough Council, the leader of the Conservatives once said to me that the louder I spoke in proceedings, the more he learnt not to listen as 'volume meant partisanship'. He would only worry, he said, when I both spoke softly and sounded reasonable (Personal recollection).

As mentioned previously, it had become clear that there would be a set piece of parliamentary theatre—an all-day debate on just the pre-charge detention provisions. Such a debate, it was clear, was also going to be about provisions for 42-day pre-charge detention that bore little relation to those in the bill or those discussed in committee.

By indicating that almost all the provisions of the bill around the issue of 42 days were up for grabs and could be looked at again, the government gave the impression of a degree of cynicism motivated by getting the bill through the Commons no matter what it took. Many of the apparent concessions only complicated matters further. There was to be a reserve power, in the original bill, only to be used in times of emergency. The 'exceptional circumstances' of the emergency would have to be invoked by the police and the Crown Prosecution Service and approved by the Home Secretary. It was to be available for up to 60 days with no renewal and would have to be approved by both Houses of Parliament within 30 days. As with the existing provision for up to 28 days, a senior judge would have to extend the period of detention in blocks of 7 days.

The government insisted throughout the period of scrutiny that this package of measures was essential for the safety and security of the nation.

Now, at report stage, the government changed the entire package. There was to be a 'trigger' to the period being extended arising out of 'grave and exceptional terrorist threat', it was to be available for only 30 days and parliament had to approve the decision within seven days. This opened the entire process—nominally an operational matter for the police—to instant political scrutiny. The Director of Public Prosecutions had to approve any extension beyond 28 days—which some contended might threaten his position as the independent prosecuting authority. A statement had to be laid before the Commons within two days—again potentially confusing the operational and the political. The government had to seek independent legal advice before the order to extend the pre-charge detention period—and publish this advice with the statement. This too might jeopardise the balance between the operational and the political. Further, the government had to notify the chairs of the Home Affairs, Intelligence and Security and JCHR before taking the order forward.

Superficially, this looked like a government ready and willing to work with its opponents and detractors to secure the legislation. Others thought it was more readily the actions of a government determined to secure victory in the Commons. During a discussion on this package of concessions, I asked one of the Home Office lawyers in the meeting if a provision 'makes sense legally?' and in a rather unguarded moment she said something like 'well half of the rest of the bloody bill doesn't so you may as well throw that in as well' (Personal recollection).

The government won the crucial vote by 9 votes on 11 June 2008—by 315 to 306. Thirty-six government MPs voted against the proposal, but importantly 9 MPs from the Democratic Unionist Party voted with the government leading to instant accusations about some sort of deal being done between the government and the DUP. The bill was passed at third reading and went up to the House of Lords where the 42-day provision, as amended, was unceremoniously dumped out of the bill. The Lords passed an amendment that read 'No extension of pre-charge detention: For the avoidance of doubt, nothing in this Act allows the Secretary of State to extend the maximum period of pre-charge detention beyond 28 days'. This amendment was passed by 309 votes to 118, a majority of 191 (Hansard 2008e). The government subsequently withdrew the provisions on 42-day pre-charge detention and the rest of the bill proceeded through both Houses.

The new Prime Minister secured the victory in the Commons by 9—that had eluded his predecessor—but at what cost? One senior backbencher when asked if 'Gordon would have been better off not dealing with (42-days) at all', answered 'Oh yes, absolutely' (Interview). Another thought that 'nothing of value came out of the process', and agreed it was 'a complete waste of time, effort and an indulgence' (Interview).

Ghosts in the Machine—Revisited

As has been seen, there is clear evidence of the presence of what has been described here as 'ghost in the machine'—a host of factors such as prior decisions, previous issues, foreseen and unforeseen events. These factors have all been the result of the way in which parliamentary beliefs, traditions and practices have endured, changed, shifted or transformed in the context of responding to previous dilemmas that parliament has had to face.

Dilemmas such as the relationship between Blair and Brown, the various terrorists plots culminating in 7/7, Blair's twelve-point counter-terrorism plan, the assumption that legislative change was essential and had been requested by the police who fully supported the measure, the absence of a counter-terror narrative by the government, all had an impact on the decision-making process that culminated in the production of the Counter-Terrorism Bill 2008. Brown took from Blair's earlier response that legislation should be central to the government's response. Others subsequently disagreed. One has said since that they were 'proud of both the policy structure and the results of (our)…counter-terrorism work—and that's one of the reasons why I think 42-days was a distraction' (Interview).

The contexts that were relevant reflected the changing times in the government and the counter-terrorism world. Some things remained the same—such as the constant drumbeat of the reports from various committees that were resolutely against further legislation on pre-charge detention. Some things were completely new—a new Home Secretary, a new Prime Minister and another new Home Secretary. Finally, as the former Director-General of MI5, took her seat in the Lords, she made clear that she was not favourably disposed to any extension in the period of pre-charge detention. These levels of complexity and layers of context and nuance, beliefs and practices are essential to understand and analyse this Bill.

Brown opted for the legislative route, at least in part, because Blair had done so and failed. Brown was determined to succeed where

Blair had failed. The government put great store on the process of consultation, but it was already clear which option it was going to take. The government decided that it would listen to critics to the extent that what it proposed at report stage had little or nothing to do with the provisions in the bill. Every decision on the bill was influenced by the decisions already made. Numeric data on the votes, the divisions in committee and in the Commons can only be seriously used with a full understanding of these contexts.

CONCLUSIONS

This account of the *Counter-Terrorism Bill 2008* suggests several conclusions. The most important debates on the bill were predetermined long before any scrutiny by parliament. The concessions made were either meaningless because there was no plan to deal with the Lords' objections to the principles of the bill or made to secure a victory in the Commons. The building block of a 'quasi-emergency' approach was fundamentally flawed, although it was a device much praised by groups such as Liberty and the JCHR. The government resisted plans for either a European-style investigative magistracy or the notion of a 'state of emergency' as alternatives (JCHR 2007).

Many of the conversations that mattered took place everywhere except in parliament and certainly not in the scrutiny process. The key to future work in this area is to understand how to regularise the study of the procedural, cultural and unacknowledged ghosts in the machine. The scrutiny process on this bill was shaped and informed by several contexts and nuances described above. Further, I suggest that the beliefs and practices embedded in the government department and the House of Commons also shaped and influenced these processes. Indeed, every actor interpreted events from the confines of their own set of beliefs and practices, and their corresponding reaction to such events and the dilemmas they face influenced every stage of the scrutiny process. These beliefs, practices and traditions—the ghosts in the machine—colour and influence every choice made, every decision taken and every response to the dilemmas faced in the scrutiny process. Only by understanding these ghosts—and the beliefs, traditions and practices behind them—can we better understand the nature of the human activity that goes on in our legislative chamber in our name.

REFERENCES

Anti-Terrorism, Crime, and Security Act 2001. Available at: http://www.legislation.gov.uk/ukpga/2001/24/contents (Accessed 6 May 2015).
BBC News. (2005). *MPs Probe Police 'Politicisation'*, 11/11/05. Available at: http://newsvote.bbc.co.uk/mpapps/pagetools/print/news.bbc.co.uk/1/hi/uk_politics/4426024.stm (Accessed 12 May 2016).
BBC News. (2007a). *Timeline—Operation Crevice*, 30/4/07. Available at: http://news.bbc.co.uk/1/hi/uk_politics/6207348.stm (Accessed 12 May 2016).
BBC News. (2007b). *Fertiliser Bomb Plot—The Story*, 30/4/07. Available at: http://news.bbc.co.uk/1/hi/6153884.stm (Accessed 12 May 2016).
Bevir, M., & Rhodes, R. A. W. (2003). *Interpreting British Governance*. London: Routledge.
Bevir, M., & Rhodes, R. A. W. (2010). *The State as Cultural Practice*. Oxford: Oxford University Press.
Blair, T. (2010). *A Journey*. London: Hutchinson.
Boulton, A. (2008). *Tony's Ten Years: Memories of the Blair Administration*. London: Simon & Schuster.
Bourdieu, P. (1977). *Outline of a Theory of Practice*. Cambridge: Cambridge University Press.
Contest Strategy. (2006). *Contest Strategy Summary*. Available at: https://www.gov.uk/government/uploads/system/uploads/attachment_data/file/97994/contest-summary.pdf (Accessed 15 June 2015).
Counter-Terrorism Act 2008, 22/4/08. Available at: http://www.publications.parliament.uk/pa/cm200708/cmpublic/counter/080422/am/80422s01.htm (Accessed 6 May 2015).
Crewe, E. (2015). *The House of Commons: An Anthropology of MPs at Work*. London: Bloomsbury Academic.
Criminal Justice Act 2003. Available at: http://www.legislation.gov.uk/ukpga/2003/44/contents (Accessed 6 May 2015).
Finlayson, A. (2007). From Beliefs to Arguments: Interpretive Methodology and Rhetorical Political Analysis. *British Journal of Politics and International Relations, 9*, 545–563.
Geddes, M., & Rhodes, R. A. W. (2017). Towards an Interpretive Parliamentary Studies. In J. Brichzin, D. Krichewsky, L. Ringel, & J. Schank (Eds.), *The Sociology of Parliaments*. Wiesbaden: Springer VS. (forthcoming).
Hansard. (2007). PM Statement on Security, 25/7/07. HC col. 842–848.
Hansard. (2008a). Eliza Manningham-Buller Maiden Speech, col. 648. House of Lords, 8/7/08.
Hansard. (2008b). Second Reading, Counter-Terrorism Act 2008, 1/4/08. HC col. 647–736.

Hansard. (2008c). Report Stage, Counter-Terrorism Act 2008, 10/11-6/08. HC col. 1650178, 180–280, col. 313–401.
Hansard. (2008d). 42 Day Vote, Counter-Terrorism Act 2008, 6/11/08. HC col. 313–401.
Hansard. (2008e). Counter-Terrorism Act 2008, 13/10/08. HL cols. 491–545.
Herrington, L. (2015). British Islamic Extremist Terrorism: The Declining Significance of Al-Qaeda and Pakistan. *International Affairs, 91*, 17–35.
Home Affairs Select Committee. (2007). *The Government's Counter-Terrorism Proposals.* First Report 2007–08 Session.
Home Office. (2006). *Home Office Media Briefing Relating to West Midlands Anti-terror Operation.* Available at: https://www.gov.uk/government/uploads/system/uploads/attachment_data/file/100280/6292-op-gamble-reply_pdf.pdf (Accessed 12 May 2015).
Home Office. (2007). Options for Pre-charge Detention in Terrorist Cases, 25 July.
Home Office. (2011). *Report on the Operation in 2010 of the Terrorism Act 2000 and of Part 1 of the Terrorism Act 2006 by David Anderson Q.C.* Available at: https://www.gov.uk/government/uploads/system/uploads/attachment_data/file/243552/9780108510885.pdf (Accessed 12 May 2015).
JCHR. (2007). Joint Committee on Human Rights. Twenty-Fourth Report Counter-Terrorism Policy and Human Rights.
Malik, S. (2007, June). My Brother the Bomber. *Prospect,* pp. 30–41.
Omand, D. (2010). *Securing the State.* London: Hurst & Company.
Prevention of Terrorism Act 2005. Available at: http://www.legislation.gov.uk/ukpga/2005/2/contents (Accessed 6 May 2015).
Rawnsley, A. (2010). *The End of the Party: The Rise and Fall of New Labour.* Harmondsworth: Penguin.
Richards, S. (2010). *Whatever It Takes.* London: Fourth Estate.
RUSI. (2007). *Operation Crevice Trial Ends.* Royal United Services Institute. https://rusi.org/commentary/operation-crevice-trial-ends.
Seldon, A. (2008). *Blair Unbound.* London: Simon & Schuster.
Terrorism Act 2000. Available at: http://www.legislation.gov.uk/ukpga/2000/11/contents (Accessed 6 May 2015).
The Guardian. (2005a). The Prime Minister's 12-Point Plan. Available at: https://www.theguardian.com/politics/2005/aug/05/uksecurity.terrorism2 (Accessed 12 May 2015).
The Guardian. (2005b). Police Support Blair on Terror Detentions, 7/11/07. Available at: http://www.theguardian.com/politics/2005/nov/07/terrorism.uksecurity (Accessed 12 May 2015).
The Guardian. (2005c). A Failure of Political Judgment, 11/11/05. Available at: http://www.theguardian.com/politics/2005/nov/11/terrorism.lab (Accessed 12 May 2015).

The Guardian. (2009). Rashid Rauf: Missing 'Mastermind' of the Airline Bomb Plot. Available at: https://www.theguardian.com/uk/2009/sep/08/rashid-rauf-airline-bomb-plot (Accessed 12 May 2015).

The Independent. (2008). The Life and Death of Rashid Rauf. Available at: http://www.independent.co.uk/news/world/asia/the-life-and-death-of-rashid-rauf-1031217.html (Accessed 12 May 2015).

Thompson, L. (2014). Evidence Taking Under the Microscope: How Has Oral Evidence Affected the Scrutiny of Legislation in House of Commons Committees. *British Politics, 9,* 385–400.

CHAPTER 5

How Are Children's Rights (Mis)Interpreted in Practice? The European Commission, Children's Rights and Policy Narratives

Ingi Iusmen

INTRODUCTION

Over the last decade, the EU has developed and promoted measures aimed at upholding the protection of children's rights at the domestic level. By endorsing the UN Convention of the Rights of the Child (CRC) as the main source of inspiration for its child-related policy measures, the EU—led by the European Commission—endeavoured to uphold the CRC's principles and norms in all its relevant actions. However, the EU's commitment to advancing fundamental child rights principles, such as child participation or the best interests of the child, materialised only on paper: in practice, the EU institutions were less successful in implementing the CRC principles in a genuine and meaningful manner. On the contrary, EU institutions, like the Commission, paid

I. Iusmen (✉)
Department of Politics and International Relations,
University of Southampton, Southampton, UK
e-mail: i.iusmen@soton.ac.uk

only lip service to the CRC principles by creating a policy narrative about the EU's endorsement of these principles in the official EU documents but, in practice, this commitment did not translate into concrete actions. Examples of the EU's, particularly the Commission's, interpretations and misinterpretations of children's rights principles are examined in this chapter. I argue that the European Commission, led by Directorate General (DG) Justice, adopted a narrow and tokenistic approach to the interpretation of child rights principles in practice. While in the official legal and policy documents, the Commission endorsed a convincing and far-reaching narrative of the EU's commitment to the CRC principles, the same narrative failed to be transposed effectively in concrete terms. In other words, a disjuncture emerged between the Commission's children's rights narrative on paper—according to the official policy documents—and the pursuit of this narrative in practice. While this may constitute the outcome of a lack of expertise and experience of engaging with complex child rights matters, it could also be described as a pragmatic choice that enabled the Commission to defend its involvement in children's rights if challenged by the Member States for overstepping its legal mandate.

The EU and the UN Convention on the Rights of the Child

This section outlines the significance of the UN Convention on the Rights of the Child for the global endorsement of children's rights as a matter of international law and public policy, as well as the broader acceptance and promotion of children's rights norms and principles. It provides the backdrop for the more recent emergence of the EU as a children's rights actor (Iusmen and Stalford 2016) and for the policies and measures upholding this EU human rights role.

The CRC

The UN Convention on the Rights of the Child (1989) is the most ratified of all the treaties on human rights, and it constitutes the first international instrument to focus on children as autonomous, rights-bearing subjects, possessing individual and inalienable human rights. The CRC provides a new understanding of how children should be addressed in legal, policy and normative terms at the national level. The CRC is based on four key principles, which constitute the cornerstone of the Convention, namely non-discrimination, the best interests of the child, the right to life, survival and development; and respect for the views of the child. Furthermore, the CRC includes a wide range of children's human rights, such as children's right to voice or freedom of expression and thought. Therefore, the CRC provides the main template for the development and implementation of international and domestic laws and policy measures affecting children. The CRC has wide coverage and far-reaching aims 'in recognising the rights of children and young people, and setting out how they are to be promoted and protected is unrivalled in terms of their comprehensive nature, national and international standing and relevance' (Kilkelly and Lundy 2006: 6).

The groundbreaking view endorsed by the CRC is that children should be treated as subjects with rights, rather than objects. They should be regarded as independent, autonomous rights bearers. The CRC focuses on children's human rights and further enshrines a set of fundamental principles specific to children's rights only. For instance, the CRC includes fundamental principles that should underpin all children's rights, such as the 'best interests of the child' (Article 3) and the right to have a say or child participation (Article 12) in all matters affecting them within the family, schools, local communities, public services or judicial procedures, to name just a few. The translation of CRC provisions into concrete rules and policies has to pay heed to an intrinsic tension between children's protectionism and their self-determinism (Lansdown 2005; Stalford 2012). Indeed, children's rights norms have been framed in terms of balancing, namely protecting children by supporting parents and carers, but also advancing children's right to autonomy and their right to self-determination (Melton 2008). It has been shown that the promotion of children's rights has to provide a balanced approach between these two opposing interpretations of children's rights: children's dependency on adults in order to exercise his/her rights, hence 'children's needs-based rights', and children's 'dignity/capacity rights' (or a 'rights-based' approach) which acknowledge that children are individual persons with the same claims to dignity as autonomous adults (Woodhouse 2000). This balance of rights has to be addressed by national and international actors when adopting and implementing CRC-inspired measures.

What the CRC has provided is a global commitment shared by national and international actors to advance the principles and rights enshrined in the Convention, notwithstanding the diversity of contexts within which children may lead their lives across the world. The Convention, therefore, provides a child rights-based narrative that has to be reflected by the relevant national policies and laws of the state parties to the CRC. However, despite its ambitious objectives, the CRC suffers from some significant shortcomings, such as the often vague, ill-defined nature of its key principles such as the 'best interests of the child' (Cordero Arce 2012; Van Bueren 1998; Freeman 2000). Furthermore, the absence of any overarching enforcement mechanism, as well as the prevalent shortcomings in the way in which the Convention has been transposed into domestic law across the signatory states, generates inconsistencies and gaps to its full and effective application (Tomás 2002; Freeman 2000; Gareth 2005). By endorsing the promotion of children's rights in line with the CRC provisions, the EU has set itself a challenging task: namely it committed itself to advancing the child rights narrative—as transpiring from the CRC provisions—by child-proofing all EU legislation and policy measures, and furthermore, to applying the CRC principles, such as the 'best interests of the child' or 'child participation' in all its child-relevant actions and measures. As shown below, the Commission took the lead in both embracing the children's rights narrative in EU policy documents and also in attempting to translate this narrative into practice.

EU Children's Rights Policy

The Commission championed the EU's role in children's rights since the mid-2000s. The Commission is a newcomer in addressing international children's rights. The Commission's intervention in tackling the child rights provision of Easter candidates, as part of EU enlargement, has been widely covered (Iusmen 2012, 2013, 2014; Jacoby et al. 2009) and indeed, the EU's engagement with children's rights matters as part of its external policy is well-established. This situation changed in 2006, when the Commission, at the initiative of DG Justice, adopted the Communication 'Towards an EU Strategy on the Rights of the Child', which constitutes the first coherent statement of intent with regard to future action in the area of children's rights. It was the then Commissioner for Freedom, Security and Justice, Franco Frattini, who was strategically positioned to employ an EU enlargement issue—the Romanian children's case—as a window of opportunity to introduce children's rights as an overarching EU policy issue (Iusmen 2013, 2014). Frattini took advantage of the political momentum provided by the Romanian children's case, on the one hand, and the broad contention that more concerted effort is needed at the EU level to address fundamental rights, on the other. To this end, DG Justice (then DG JLS-Justice, Freedom and Security) took the lead in developing an overarching EU action plan and policy aimed at upholding the protection of children's rights at the EU level (Iusmen 2014). This was a quantum leap initiative, given that till the mid-2000s there were limited EU actions targeting the protection of children's rights as part of the EU's internal policy dimension.

The 2006 Communication attempted to bring together all European Commission policies affecting children into an integrated, rights-based framework which drew on the CRC principles (European Commission 2006). The Communication established the protection of children's rights as an EU policy objective, while committing EU institutions to employing the CRC as the main international instrument informing EU action in this area. The 2006 Communication, setting out the development of an EU child's rights policy, included two kinds of objectives in relation to this policy sector: actions *targeting* specific violations of children's rights and actions *mainstreaming* children's rights into EU policies and legislation. The EU's overarching aim was to bring added value in the field of children's rights both in its external relations and within the EU. The content and focus of the 2006 Communication reflected the children's rights narrative as transpiring from the CRC.

Prior to the 2006 Communication, there were no EU provisions—with the exception of the then non-binding EU Charter of Fundamental Rights—that addressed children's rights matters in a manner that was consistent with the CRC. The Treaty of Amsterdam (1997) included the first significant provisions relevant to children at the Treaty level. For instance, Article 29 TEU provided for intergovernmental cooperation to tackle 'offences against children'—which is the first ever mention of children at the Treaty level—while Article 13 TEU included a 'non-discrimination' clause enabling the Union to take action on equality grounds, particularly age. Additionally, Article 137 TEU provided a legal basis for combating social exclusion and thus tackling child poverty. It was the adoption of the EU Charter of Fundamental Rights (2000) that mentioned for the first time children's rights as part of the EU's broader endeavour to advance human rights. The Charter refers specifically to the child's right to protection and participation in Article 24, which draws on the CRC's key principles such as 'best interests of the child' (Article 3 CRC) and 'child participation' (Article 12 CRC). By embracing the promotion of children's rights in line with the CRC principles, therefore, the EU is bound to face important challenges due to the complexities characterising the CRC and the EU's competence limitations with respect to children's rights matters. However, economic integration and the operation of the EU law impinge significantly on the protection of children's rights at the national level, although the EU is not a State Party to the CRC. As shown above, both the EU Charter and the 2006 Communication signal the EU's, particularly the Commission's, endorsement of the children's rights narrative—as enshrined in the CRC—and therefore, reinforce the EU institutions' commitment to advancing this narrative in practice.

The 2006 Communication, followed by another one—'An EU Agenda for the Rights of the Child'—in 2010, reinforced the Commission's commitment to advance children's rights in line with the CRC principles. To this end, the vast majority of child-relevant Commission policy documents and measures mention the CRC as the main guiding framework for Commission actions. For instance, some of the key principles of the CRC, such as the 'best interest of the child' (Article 3 CRC) and child participation (Article 12 CRC), have been included in EU policy documents and measures as key standards underpinning EU actions relevant to children.[1] Therefore, in theory, the Commission has fully endorsed the children's rights narrative given the amount of references and mentions that the Commission, and the EU more generally, makes to the CRC and its principles in official policy and legal documents.

The children's rights narrative, which amounts to the promotion of child rights measures in line with the CRC, entails a focus on children as independent, autonomous subjects of rights, i.e. a rights-based approach. Indeed, in theory, the European Commission has embraced the employment of a rights-based approach in all its actions and measures relevant to children. In practice, a rights-based approach means that human rights principles should guide all processes of planning, including the initial assessments and analyses identifying the underlying and structural causes of the child rights' non-realisation (UN 2003). Therefore, by advancing child rights measures in line with the CRC principles, the

Commission indirectly promotes the compliance with CRC via a rights-based approach. Furthermore, this rights-based commitment endorsed by the EU institutions also gives rise, in practice, to the need of ensuring that Commission child-related actions apply key CRC principles, such as the best interests of the child and child participation.

The entry into force of the Treaty of Lisbon in 2009 amounted to major EU constitutional and legislative change relevant for the protection of the rights of the child. The Lisbon Treaty reinforces the EU's commitment to fundamental rights as integral principles of EU law and provides enhanced visibility and status to fundamental rights within the EU's constitutional framework. There are two components that enhance the EU's fundamental rights regime in relation to children's rights: the binding nature of the EU Charter of Fundamental Rights and the inclusion of children's rights at Treaty level. The inclusion of children's rights among the EU's objectives (Article 3 TEU) ensures that EU laws and policies are child proofed and that they contribute to the promotion of children's rights and well-being. The Charter includes Article 24 specifically focusing on the rights of the child. This article refers specifically to the CRC principles such as the 'best interests of the child' and the 'child participation'. A number of other Charter articles are relevant to children's rights, including Article 33 on children and their families right to legal, economic and social protection (reflecting Article 8 CRC) or Article 32 on the prohibition of child labour (based on Article 32 CRC). The Charter does not extend the EU's powers in children's rights: the Charter applies primarily to EU institutions in relation to their legislative and decision-making processes. The explicit inclusion of child rights protection in the Charter provides a more visible benchmark by which to monitor the development and application of EU policies vis-a-vis children. However, the binding nature of the Charter at the EU level means that EU institutions have an obligation to respect the rights, freedoms and principles set out in the Charter. It is the Commission's role to oversee that the Charter provisions in relation to children's rights are respected both during policy-making and policy implementation processes. These Treaty provisions provide a solid constitutional basis for the promotion of EU measures and policies to protect children's rights in line with the CRC principles.

The sections above illustrate that the protection of children's rights informed by the CRC, as a Commission policy objective, has become more visible and frequently referred to across key EU legal and policy documents.

At least on paper, the EU institutions are committed to upholding the CRC principles and to adopting child-related policies and measures that would respect these principles. By embracing the role of a 'global children's rights actor' (Iusmen and Stalford 2016), along with the challenges that come with it, the European Commission—steered by DG Justice in particular—developed a policy narrative about the scope and importance of children's rights norms and principles for the EU. However, as shown in the sections below, the effective transposition of this children's rights narrative into practice amounted to a wide range of interpretations and misinterpretations of the CRC principles. I argue that this institutional narrative has a dual function: on the one hand, it establishes a proactive role that the Commission embraces vis-à-vis the CRC and children's rights more generally, as it transpires from the key EU legal and policy documents. On the other hand, however, it can act as a defensive narrative, whereby the narrow and limited interpretation and implementation of child rights principles can protect the EU against the allegations of the Member States that it acts outside its legal remit.[2] As shown below, there is a disjuncture between the Commission's official commitment to advancing the CRC-inspired children's rights narrative, and how this narrative is pursued in practice. In other words, there is a significant gap between the theoretical, i.e. on paper, and practical dimensions of the Commission's, and broadly the EU's, children's rights narrative.

Policy Narratives and Policy-Making

Policy narratives play a crucial role in justifying and legitimising the actions taken by policy-makers and politicians more generally. Their action-sanctioning role is even more pertinent at the EU level, where EU intervention in policy sectors is confined to the availability of EU legal mandate to act. According to the literature, the concept of a policy narrative can refer to 'attempts by actors to develop plausible interpretations of complex phenomena or events' (Boswell et al. 2011: 4). Policy narratives become important in situations of uncertainty and of complex policy matters. In essence, the role of a narrative is to provide a storyline 'about who should do what, and how, when and why they should do it in order to address policy dilemmas' (Kaplan 1986: 770). Policy narratives are created and promoted by various policy actors (McBeth and Shanahan 2004; Shanahan et al. 2008) with the intention of providing a legitimising narrative for a certain course of action. These policy actors can sometimes act as an advocacy coalition (Sabatier and Jenkins-Smith 1993) underpinned by shared policy beliefs, coordination and desired policy output. Mark Bevir and Rod Rhodes' (2006) research on Whitehall shows, the pattern of governance changed leading to the emergence of a new governance narrative, which is a story that emphasises the role of networks, in particular, in exploring how government decision-making processes occur (Rhodes 2000).

Narratives are essential to the policy-making process (Jones and McBeth 2010) as they are strategically constructed by policy-makers (McBeth and Shanahan 2004) in order to achieve specific policy outcomes. Narratives also 'distil and reflect a particular understanding of social and political relations' (Feldman et al. 2004: 148). Furthermore, a policy narrative provides a simplified version of policy issues or controversies which are 'put together into a plot in which there are causal relations between actions' (Banerjee 1998: 193). Indeed, as Boswell et al. (2011: 4–5) clearly state it, a policy narrative consists of three interrelated components: firstly, a set of claims about the *policy problem*; secondly, claims about the *causes* of the problem; and thirdly, claims about *policy interventions* to address the policy problem. Policy narratives contain some key policy beliefs, shaped by the political and sociocultural contexts in which the policy issue occurs (McBeth et al. 2005). But the key elements of these narratives are strategically constructed stories as they are intended to persuade the public and stakeholders about the need to take a certain course of action to address a policy problem. All policy narratives make some key assumptions (cf. Shanahan et al. 2011), such as their centrality in the policy process, the broad set of actors that can generate policy narratives, or that policies constitute translations of beliefs that are conveyed through policy narratives.

The policy narrative framework is a useful heuristic device that can help explain the story that the Commission, under the leadership of DG Justice, tells about its role vis-a-vis children's rights protection and how this narrative takes shape in practice, where child rights norms and principles are interpreted and applied. More specifically, the question rises as to what extent the child rights narrative endorsed by the Commission in official documents is also upheld consistently in practice, via concrete actions and measures. As shown below, the policy narrative of the Commission's commitment to CRC principles constitutes a window-dressing exercise in practice, whereby the Commission pays lip service to the Convention principles and children's rights on paper, in the main EU documents; nevertheless, in practice, it fails to provide a meaningful and coherent interpretation of these rights and principles. Policy narratives, in this context taking the shape of institutional narratives—i.e. how the Commission[3] envisages its child rights role—are important as they provide a story for the Commission's involvement with a complex and non-traditional EU policy sector. The policy narrative embraced by the Commission consists of the Commission's commitment to children's rights and the CRC, the added value that EU action can bring to address the violations of child rights and finally, the broader legal and constitutional relevance of children's rights for the European project, in line with the 'normative power' (Manners 2002) description that the EU has in international politics. However, how this policy narrative takes concrete shape and how the CRC principles are operationalised becomes challenging, and the Commission has been widely criticised by children's rights stakeholders for failing to uphold children's rights principles in a coherent and comprehensive manner (Grugel and Iusmen 2013).

The policy narrative can provide a justifying storyline if the Commission is perceived by the Member States or other political actors that it is overstepping its legal mandate. The core aspect of this policy narrative is that the EU institutions have a normative and political role to play to address child rights violations. This role is enshrined in key EU legal and policy documents, and this constitutes the children's rights narrative that the Commission has embraced since 2006 in particular. Nevertheless, translating this narrative in practice successfully has proved to be challenging, particularly when it came to the operationalisation of CRC principles, such as child participation and best interests of the child. The positive dimension of the narrative is that the Commission is an international actor committed to upholding child rights and the CRC principles in all its child-related actions, while the negative dimension signals that the narrow and tokenistic interpretations and misinterpretations of these rights and principles can be deployed to legitimise Commission, and more broadly EU, actions in relation to the Member States. In essence, what is argued here is that the children's rights narrative endorsed by the Commission on paper failed to materialise in practice in a manner consistent with the spirit and letter of the CRC particularly in relation to two core CRC principles, child participation and the best interest of the child, as the discussion below demonstrates.

Interpretation and Implementation of Child Participation

The Commission's lack of expertise in children's rights matters has been reflected in its inconsistent approach to child rights provisions and principles. This has particularly been evident in the way in which the Commission interpreted and applied the child participation principle in practice. Child participation is one of the fundamental principles of the CRC (Article 12), and it establishes that children and young people have the right to freely express their views in all matters affecting them within the family, schools, local communities, public services, institutions, government policy and judicial procedures. To this end, duty bearers, such as the state, have an obligation to listen to children's views and to facilitate their participation in processes where they can freely express their views. The child participation principle states that children are full-fledged persons, and in line with a rights-based approach, it requires that those views be heard and given due weight in accordance with the child's age and maturity. Furthermore, this core CRC principle recognises the potential of children to influence decision-making processes, to share perspectives and to participate as citizens and actors of change. Child participation is envisaged both as a process—a key means of helping to fulfil all child rights—as well as an outcome, namely as a set of rights to be fulfilled as such. One of the key upshots of implementing this principle in practice is the empowerment of children via their participation in decision-making settings (Simmons and Birchall 2005; Percy-Smith and Thomas 2009, Beazley et al. 2011).

Child participation studies (Tisdall 2013; Westwood et al. 2014; Tisdall et al. 2009; Lundy and McEvoy 2009; Thomas 2014) have shown that there is a gap between the 'rhetoric of participation' (Badham 2004: 153)—endorsed by European and national policy-makers—and the implementation of inclusive and effective child participatory practices on the ground. Most often, policy-makers fail to develop and apply genuine and meaningful child participation instruments: to this end, they deploy in practice non-genuine 'participation' mechanisms, which disguise what is actually the manipulation of children, or tokenism. This is consistent with the emergent discrepancy—observed at the level of the Commission as well—between the endorsement of children's rights narrative in theory and its pursuit in practice.

As part of the 2006 Communication initiatives, the Commission set up a European Forum on the Rights of the Child, which aimed to bring together the leading child rights stakeholders[4] with the goal of feeding into the policy-making process (European Commission 2008: 3). Including the participation of all key children's rights organisations and transnational networks, the Forum on the Rights of the Child was intended to play an advisory role to the Commission services (DGs) on specific child rights policy matters that the Commission intended to tackle. The Forum was expected to provide a space to exchange knowledge and examples of best practice among stakeholders, which would feed into the policy process (European Commission 2006: 1). Furthermore, the Forum aimed to engage children in its meetings—by implementing child participation in practice—in order to feed children's views and ideas into the EU policy process. Although the Forum was intended to provide a participatory setting for all key civil society actors, the institutional design of the Forum obstructed the emergence of a genuinely open and inclusive environment whereby child rights stakeholders could feed into the policy process (Grugel and Iusmen 2013). This was particularly the case when it came to the effective and meaningful implementation of child participation mechanisms within the Forum context.

The direct participation of children was seen as the most significant issue to address in terms of stakeholder representation during the Forum meetings. Indeed, the direct involvement of children along with the increased awareness of child participation and representation in EU policy processes were key priorities for the Forum. This is important because surveys and studies of children and young people showed that they have limited input into decisions that affect them and the vast majority feels that what is missing is being heard on the 'important topics' which influence their lives (Eurobarometer 2010). Often young people report that the lack of information regarding procedures, competent authorities and their rights themselves as the major obstacles that they encounter when they need help to defend their rights (Eurobarometer 2009). Surveys have confirmed the importance that young people themselves attach to child rights initiatives taken at EU/European levels, as an overwhelming majority of respondents think that the EU should strive to provide more information to children about their rights as well as support to child rights organisations (Eurobarometer 2009).

Over the years, the Commission used child participation in tokenistic and unrepresentative manners. For instance, in the context of the Forum, small groups of children from Brussels-based schools were invited to present drawings, sing, plant trees or merely take part in photo sessions at the end of the Forum discussions. To this end, children's participation remained at an elementary level (Grugel and Iusmen 2013). It lacked meaningful and genuine content so children's views could not be taken into account. In other instances, children were invited to share their views and opinions on issues of importance to them. However, the policy matters discussed during the Forum meetings were not presented in a child-friendly format. What emerged from the Forum meetings was that the Commission employed a tokenistic approach to child participation. Indeed, on paper, the Commission consulted with children and young people, yet in practice, the participatory mechanisms employed did not amount to meaningful child participation. Having children invited to take part in the Forum meetings, yet without giving them a real opportunity to voice their views on the matters discussed means, that in practice, there was no input from children into the EU policy process relevant to children themselves.

Child rights stakeholders argue that a more appropriate way of representing children in EU processes is by their being represented by NGOs, Ombudspersons and other organisations. However, given its commitment to uphold and pursue the CRC principles, the Commission is expected to provide its own meaningful and effective application of these principles. Nevertheless, the recent child participation examples such as the Forum demonstrate that the approach to participation and consultation endorsed by the Commission is not consistent with the CRC view on both the participation and the empowerment of children. In the same vein, the Commission conducted a public consultation with the key stakeholders, including children, on the adoption of the EU's 'Guidelines on Child Protection Systems' in 2011. The consultation took place over the summer when most children were on holiday and, therefore, could not take part in it. Therefore, this consultation was another missed opportunity to implement genuine child participation mechanisms.

The Commission's failure to implement meaningfully the child participation principle at the EU level shows that it only pays lip service to the core CRC principles. This tokenistic approach to child participation can be explained as an upshot of the Commission's lack of expertise and experience in engaging with the CRC and children's rights matters (Iusmen 2013, 2014; Grugel and Iusmen 2013). This criticism has been levelled particularly at DG Justice, which is responsible for organising and running the Forum annually. However, there could also be a more cynical explanation for the Commission's misinterpretation of the CRC principles. While child rights stakeholders and experts often offered their know-how and practical knowledge to assist the Commission services in interpreting the complex provisions of the CRC, DG Justice jealously guarded both the agenda and the format of the Forum (Grugel and Iusmen 2013). It allowed little external input into how this consultation mechanism, i.e. the Forum, ran in practice. Regardless of the Commission's reasons for the failure to implement child participation in a meaningful manner, what transpires from this case is the Commission's attachment to a box-ticking role regarding the CRC principles: they are included in the official documents earmarked for child-related matters, and in practice, window-dressing activities take place that, in the view of the EU institutions, are in line with the CRC previsions, at least according to the Commission's interpretation of them.

Interpretation and Implementation of Best Interests of the Child

The 'best interests of the child' is another CRC core principle that has been endorsed by the EU as part of its commitment to protect children's rights, and hence part of its policy narrative according to EU legal and policy documents. The 'best interests of the child' principle is laid down in Article 3(1) CRC:

> [I]n all actions concerning children, whether undertaken by public or private social welfare institutions, courts of law, administrative authorities or legislative bodies, the best interests of the child shall be a primary consideration.

The concept of the child's best interests is complex, and its content has to be determined on a case-by-case basis. For instance, according to the General Comment 14 of the Committee on the Rights of the Child the 'best interests of the child' concept 'should be adjusted and defined on an individual basis, according to the specific situation of the child or children concerned, taking into consideration their personal context, situation and needs' (para 32). The Committee on the Rights of the Child recommends that:

> [T]he best interests of the child is understood, appropriately integrated and implemented in all legal provisions as well as in judicial and administrative decisions [...] that have direct and indirect impact on children. (Committee on the Rights of the Children 2013)

Article 24(2) the EU Charter of Fundamental Rights codifies the best interests of the child concept as enshrined in Article 3(1) CRC in EU law. The text of the Charter provides that:

> In all actions relating to children, whether taken by public authorities or private institutions, the child's best interests must be a primary consideration.

According to the Explanation relating to the Charter, Article 24 is based on the following CRC articles: Articles 3 (best interests), 9 (unity of family), 12 (participation) and 13 (expression) of the CRC. In Article 24 of the Charter, the child participation principle is also mentioned: namely children have the right that their views are taken into consideration. This is particularly important as often in practice, the best interests of the child are interpreted in conjunction with child participation. More specifically, it is crucial that the child's best interests' assessment should take full account of the views of the child concerned. In brief, according to child-relevant EU official documents the 'best interests of the child' should be considered when decisions are taken concerning children.

When it comes to the interpretation of the meaning of the 'best interests' principle, two main conceptualisations have been developed in the literature (Moloney 2008). The first one endorses a 'welfarist' approach by outlining the importance of 'best interests' assessments of the extent to which particular decisions serve the welfare of the child. This approach is reflective of a 'needs-based' understanding of children's rights. However, this interpretation has been criticised by child rights stakeholders for contradicting the nature and scope of the CRC, which makes children subjects of rights. A second interpretation of the 'best interests' principle follows the approach of the General Recommendation 14 of the Committee on the Rights of the Children which embraces a rights-based approach, in tune with the spirit and letter of the CRC. In this case, when determining the 'best interests of a child', the focus should be placed on the child's agency and the decisions taken in line with the 'best interests principle' should reflect this agency dimension of the children's rights.

Apart from the EU Charter, the 'best interests of the child' principle is mentioned in a wide range of EU policy documents and legislation.[5] For instance, in EU Family Reunification law, the best interests of the child are mentioned in Directive 2003/86/EC on the right to family reunification, and most of the legislation making up the Common European Asylum System (CEAS) includes references to it. While most of the EU legislation has to be first transposed into national law, and then implemented on the ground, which makes the national authorities responsible for interpreting the meaning of 'best interests of the child' in practice, the EU uses no clear guidance as to how the principle should be assessed in specific situations or whether particular aspects should be considered during assessment. However, at the European level 'there is too little standardisation of what [the principle] means in practice' (House of Lords 2016: 32), and generally, despite the multitude of vague references to the best interests of the child in EU law and policy, there is little done about its application in practice both at national and EU levels. Indeed, according to leading child rights stakeholders 'while lip service is already paid to the best interests principle, it is not currently being implemented effectively' (child rights NGO cited in House of Lords 2016: 67) by the EU institutions. The effective operationalisation of the best interests of the child principle is particularly important with respect to unaccompanied minors, when decisions taken at national and EU levels have to reflect their best interests and therefore uphold their human rights as children. The Commission has not provided any guidelines as to how the 'best interests' principle should be interpreted in specific situations or policy areas. The EU institutions should endeavour to ensure that, indeed, the best interests principle is not merely referred to in various EU documents, but that it is being 'dealt with substantively in all decisions, with clear reference to an assessment being carried out as to a child's best interests, and what, if anything, justified the departure from that position' (Coram Children's Legal Centre cited in House of Lords 2016: 67).

When it comes to EU asylum law and policy, it has been shown that the EU tends to prioritise stability, border control and security at the expense of human rights protection (Koenig 2016). This is particularly the case when the protection of children's rights is juxtaposed with the EU's broader security and migration control objectives. Child immigrants and asylum-seekers do not fit neatly within the existing EU legal structures covering these policy areas as children's needs and rights are not 'commensurate with those of adults with a similar immigration status, on the one hand, or with those of the wider group of host-state national children, on the other' (Drywood 2011: 408). It is contended that, in general, immigration laws and policies are notoriously age and gender skewed (Bhabha 2004), based on the presumption that the category of asylum seekers usually consists of politically active men. A specific category of children, i.e. unaccompanied minors, falls between the cracks of EU legislation. The Commission adopted an 'Action Plan on Unaccompanied Minors' (2010) aimed at addressing the situation of children from third countries arriving into the EU unaccompanied. Despite focusing on the promotion of the child's best interests when decisions are reached on the situation of unaccompanied minors, not all pieces of EU legislation in this area provide for the protection of children's rights. For instance, only the Return Directive provides safeguards for children, while the Temporary Protection Directive and the Directive on Victims of Trafficking leave a wide margin of interpretation—for national authorities—with respect to their application in relation to children in the Member States. Indeed, it has been claimed that 'among refugees and asylum-seekers, children are one of the most vulnerable groups' (Spindler 2001). Therefore, it is not surprising that immigrant children face the 'double jeopardy' of their status as both migrants and children (Bhabha 2001), particularly as this is reflected in the Commission's limited involvement with the operationalisation of the 'best interests' principle, apart from its mere mention in the official documents.

The Commission's and more broadly the EU's formal references to the 'best interests' principle in the key EU legal and policy documents lacks teeth as it cannot be operationalised without clear and coherent guidance. In order to substantiate the meanings and implications of this principle in practice, the Commission should aim to adopt minimum standards for 'best interests' assessments. These assessments should reflect the provisions in the General Comment 14 of the UN Committee on the Rights of the Child and should act as guidance to EU institutions and national authorities when implementing the relevant EU legislation and policies that include the best interests of the child application in practice. Indeed, the Commission is well-positioned within the EU's institutional architecture—as the Union's agenda-setter and the guardian of the Treaties—to take action to clarify how the 'best interests' principle should be applied in concrete terms. This lack of teeth vis-à-vis Commission's endorsement of the best interests principle is also reflective of the broader EU lack of genuine allegiance to the CRC principles, which has often been criticised (Stalford and Drywood 2011) as this should imply more than passing references to the CRC in formal texts: the entire process, investment and ideology surrounding the CRC also needs to be embraced (Stalford and Drywood 2011: 214). Similar to the child participation case, the Commission's commitment to promoting the 'best interests of the child' principle only exists on paper as no concrete measures were taken to apply it in practice, via concrete legal and policy measures.

What transpires from the above is that rather than misinterpreting the 'best interests of the child' principle, as it occurs in the case of the 'child participation' principle, the Commission merely lacks an interpretation of it altogether. The 'best interests of the child' narrative exists only on paper, although child rights stakeholders have often demanded the EU institutions to adopt specific guidelines about the transposition of this CRC principle in practice, whenever EU laws and policies relevant to children are implemented. Indeed, national authorities carry out their own 'best interests' assessments when enforcing EU legislation, however, in practice it is clear that the standards underpinning these assessments vary across the Member States (UNHCR and UNICEF 2014) and therefore what occurs on the ground, in terms of actual protection of children's best interests, is also significantly diverse and often to the detriment of children's rights protection (UNHCR and UNICEF 2014). This is particularly the case in the area of refugee and asylum law and procedures. By playing a more active role in upholding the children's best interests principle via the provision of minimum standards and benchmarks that Member States should follow when implementing EU laws relevant to children, the Commission could indeed pay allegiance to the CRC principles, rather than paying lip service, as it currently does.

Conclusion

The analysis above has shown that the Commission has adopted a tokenistic, at times cautious, interpretation of the two key children's rights principles, namely child participation and best interests of the child. The Commission's policy narrative regarding CRC principles, therefore, materialised only on paper: in practice, the EU institutions were less successful in implementing the children's rights principles in a genuine and meaningful manner. On the contrary, the Commission paid only lip service to the CRC principles by creating a policy narrative about the EU's endorsement of these principles in the official EU documents, which was further bolstered by the EU's new legal and constitutional provisions enshrined in the Lisbon Treaty.

Nevertheless, in practice, this commitment failed to have a positive impact. Examples of the Commission's tokenistic interpretation and misinterpretation of children's rights principles examined here could be explained as an upshot of its lack of expertise and experience of engaging with child rights matters. However, these also point to a more deliberate and pragmatic decision whereby the Commission, specifically DG Justice, refrains from an outright and bold involvement in children's rights matters, including in the application of CRC principles, as these are deemed to be the purview of the Member States. From a child rights perspective, this amounted to the Commission's advance of a primarily a 'needs-based' approach rather than a 'rights-based' approach to child rights at the EU level. This 'needs-based' approach to children entails the depiction of 'children as passive victims who are psychologically scarred and vulnerable' (Hinton 2008: 288), rather than the view that children are autonomous individuals and fully fledged beneficiaries of human rights. This is consistent with how the child rights narrative in relation to child participation was translated into practice by the Commission. A limited application of the rights-based narrative in practice was an approach that appealed to the Member States, as it demonstrated that the Commission had not overstepped its mark vis-a-vis the protection of children's rights, particularly as this policy area is politically sensitive at the domestic level.

The emphasis on needs and protection is perhaps not surprising, given that it reflects the Commission's standard approach taken to children's rights in EU internal action (Stalford and Drywood 2009: 171) in general. For instance, according to one of the leading child rights umbrella organisations, Eurochild, the emphasis on protection ignores the fact that 'it is investment in prevention and children's empowerment that will have the longest term benefits for society as at a time of enormous pressure on budgets, we believe this [focus on protection] is short-sighted and sends the wrong signal' (Euractiv 2011). A focus on a needs-based approach highlights the marginalisation of children's voice, which then becomes subject to interpretation by EU policy-makers. To sum up, the emergence of a Commission-driven EU policy narrative regarding its allegiance to the CRC principles justifies the adoption of a wide range of EU policy documents and measures that focus on the protection of children's rights. However, the skewed interpretation, or in some cases, a lack of interpretation altogether, of the CRC principles as part of the pursuit in practice of this policy narrative, diminished its power of persuasion among children's rights stakeholders and activists.

Notes

1. The Council adopted the *EU Guidelines for the Promotion and Protection of the Rights of the Child* (2007) and, in so far as children's rights in zones of conflict are concerned, the Council issued *EU Guidelines on Children and Armed Conflict* (2003, 2008). The Commission developed an action for EU external policies by adopting the Communication *A Special Place for Children in EU External Action* (2008). Child rights are also promoted via the EU's thematic programmes in EU development and cooperation policy, primarily via the Investing in People and the European Instrument for Democracy and Human Rights (EIDHR). For a full list of all the EU-relevant legislation and measures related or impacting on children's rights see European Commission (2016) *EU acquis and policy documents on the rights of the child*, JUST.C2/MT-TC, November 2016.
2. For instance, Iusmen and Boswell (2017) discuss how the Commission's development of participation and engagement mechanisms with leading child rights NGOs and networks was intended, among others, to elicit legitimacy for the Commission's child rights initiatives in relation to the Member States, who were unsupportive and suspicious of the Commission's new role in advancing children's rights matters in the EU.
3. The main focus in this chapter is on the European Commission and its engagement with children's rights. As the EU's main agenda-setter and policy initiator, the Commission is well-placed to provide an outlook into the EU's overall involvement with this human rights sector.
4. According to the Forum's 'Terms of Reference' (2008), it was supposed to achieve two objectives: 'advise and assist the Commission and other European Institutions, in particular as regards mainstreaming of children's rights in EU legislation, policies, and programmes; exchange information and good practice between stakeholders […]' (European Commission 2008: 3).
5. An important number of EU directives and regulations include references to children and to the best interests of the child principle. In chronological order, these include the Family Reunification Directive, the Directive on residence permits for victims of human trafficking, the Returns Directive, the Anti-trafficking Directive, the EU Long-term Residence Directive, the Schengen Border Code and the recast five legal instruments making up the Common European Asylum System (CEAS).

References

Badham, B. (2004). Participation—For a Change: Disabled Young People Lead the Way. *Children and Society, 18,* 143–154.

Banerjee, S. (1998). Narratives and Interaction: A Constitutive Theory of Interaction and the Case of the All-India Muslim League. *European Journal of International Relations, 4,* 178–203.

Beazley, H., Bessell, S., Ennew, J., & Waterson, R. (2011). How Are the Human Rights of Children Related to Research Methodology. *The Human Rights of Children: From Visions to Implementation.* (pp. 159–178). Ashgate: Ashgate Publishing Company.

Bevir, M., & Rhodes, R. A. W. (2006). *Governance Stories.* Oxon: Routledge.

Bhabha, J. (2001). Minors or Aliens? Inconsistent State Intervention and Separated Child Asylum-Seekers. *European Journal of Migration and the Law, 32,* 283–314.

Bhabha, J. (2004). Demography and Rights: Women, Children and Access to Asylum. *International Journal of Refugee Law, 2,* 227–243.

Boswell, C., Geddes, A., & Scholten, P. (2011). The Role of Narratives in Migration Policy-Making: A Research Framework. *The British Journal of Politics and International Relations, 13,* 1–11.

Committee on the Rights of the Children. (2013, May 29). General Comment No. 14 (2013) on the Right of the Child to Have His or Her Best Interests Taken as a Primary Consideration (Art. 3, Para. 1), CRC/C/GC/14.

Cordero Arce, M. (2012). Towards an Emancipatory Discourse of Children's Rights. *The International Journal of Children's Rights, 20,* 365–421.

Drywood, E. (2011). Child-Proofing' EU Law and Policy: Interrogating the Law-Making Processes Behind European Asylum and Immigration Provision. *The International Journal of Children's Rights, 19,* 405–428.

Euractiv. (2011, 16 February). *Brussels Adopts Agenda to Improve Children's Rights.* Available at: https://www.euractiv.com/section/justice-home-affairs/news/brussels-adopts-agenda-to-improve-children-s-rights/.

Eurobarometer. (2009, May). *The Rights of the Child.* Analytical Report.

Eurobarometer. (2010). *The Rights of the Child.* Aggregate Report October 2010. Qualitative Study. Available at: http://ec.europa.eu/commfrontoffice/publicopinion/archives/quali/ql_right_child_sum_en.pdf.

European Commission. (2006, July 4). *Communication from the Commission: Towards an EU Strategy on the Rights of the Child,* COM (2006) 367 final, Brussels.

European Commission. (2008). *12th Meeting of the Commissioners Group on Fundamental Rights, Anti-Discrimination and Equal Opportunities. Rights of the Child,* CG4, 3/2.

Feldman, M. S., Sköldberg, K., Brown, R. N., & Horner, D. (2004). Making Sense of Stories: A Rhetorical Approach to Narrative Analysis. *Journal of Public Administration Research and Theory, 14*, 147–170.

Freeman, M. (2000). The Future of Children's Rights. *Children and Society, 14*, 277–293.

Gareth, A. (2005). Children and Development: Rights, Globalization and Poverty. *Progress in Development Studies, 5*, 336–342.

Grugel, J., & Iusmen, I. (2013). The European Commission as Guardian Angel: Agenda-Setting for Children's Rights. *Journal of European Public Policy, 20*, 77–94.

House of Lords. (2016). *Children in Crisis: Unaccompanied Migrant Children in the EU*, HL Paper. Available at: https://publications.parliament.uk/pa/ld201617/ldselect/ldeucom/34/34.pdf.

Iusmen, I. (2012). Civil Society Participation and EU Children's Rights Policy. *Journal of Civil Society, 8*, 137–154.

Iusmen, I. (2013). Policy Entrepreneurship and Eastern Enlargement: The Case of EU Children's Rights Policy. *Comparative European Politics, 11*, 511–529.

Iusmen, I. (2014). *Children's Rights Eastern Enlargement and the EU Human Rights Regime*. Manchester: Manchester University Press.

Iusmen, I., & Boswell, J. (2017). The Dilemmas of Pursuing 'Throughput Legitimacy' Through Participatory Mechanisms. *West European Politics, 40*, 459–478.

Iusmen, I., & Stalford, H. (2016). *The EU as a Children's Rights Actor: Law Policy and Structural Dimensions*. London: Budrich Academic Publishers.

Jacoby, W., Lataianu, G., & Lataianu, C. M. (2009). Success in Slow Motion: The Europeanization of Romanian Child Protection Policy. *The Review of International Organizations, 4*, 111–133.

Jones, M. D., & McBeth, M. K. (2010). A Narrative Policy Framework: Clear Enough to Be Wrong? *Policy Studies Journal, 38*, 329–353.

Kaplan, T. J. (1986). The Narrative Structure of Policy Analysis. *Journal of Policy Analysis and Management, 5*, 761–778.

Kilkelly, U., & Lundy, L. (2006). The Convention on the Rights of the Child: Its Use as an Auditing Tool. *Child and Family Law Quarterly, 18*, 331–350.

Koenig, N. (2016). *EU Security Policy and Crisis Management: A Quest for Coherence*. Abingdon, Oxon: Routledge.

Lansdown, G. (2005). *The Evolving Capacity of the Child*. Florence: UNICEF Innocenti Research Centre.

Lundy, L., & McEvoy, L. (2009). Developing Outcomes for Educational Services: A Children's Rights-Based Approach. *Effective Education, 1*, 43–60.

Manners, I. (2002). Normative Power Europe: A Contradiction in Terms? *Journal of Common Market Studies, 40*, 235–258.

McBeth, M. K., & Shanahan, E. A. (2004). Public Opinion for Sale: The Role of Policy Marketers in Greater Yellowstone Policy Conflict. *Policy Sciences, 37*, 319–338.

McBeth, M. K., Shanahan, E. A., & Jones, M. D. (2005). The Science of Storytelling: Measuring Policy Beliefs in Greater Yellowstone. *Society and Natural Resources, 18*, 413–429.

Melton, G. B. (2008). Beyond Balancing: Toward an Integrated Approach to Children's Rights. *Journal of Social Issues, 64*, 903–920.

Moloney, L. (2008). The Elusive Pursuit of Soloman: Faltering Steps Toward the Rights of the Child. *Family Court Review, 46*, 39–52.

Percy-Smith, B., & Thomas, N. (Eds.). (2009). *A Handbook of Children and Young People's Participation: Perspectives from Theory and Practice*. London: Routledge.

Rhodes, R. A. W. (2000). The Governance Narrative: Key Findings and Lessons from the ERC's Whitehall Programme. *Public Administration, 78*, 345–363.

Sabatier, P. A., & Jenkins-Smith, H. C. (Eds.). (1993). *Policy Change and Learning: An Advocacy Coalition Approach*. Boulder, CO: Westview Press.

Shanahan, E. A., McBeth, M. K., Arnell, R. J., & Hathaway, P. L. (2008). Conduit or Contributor? The Role of Media in Policy Change Theory. *Policy Sciences, 41*, 115–138.

Shanahan, E. A., Jones, M. D., & McBeth, M. K. (2011). Policy Narratives and Policy Processes. *The Policy Studies Journal, 39*, 535–561.

Simmons, R., & Birchall, J. (2005). A Joined-Up Approach to User Participation in Public Services: Strengthening the "Participation Chain". *Social Policy and Administration, 39*, 260–283.

Spindler, W. (2001). *The Situation of Separated Children in Central Europe and the Baltic States*. Denmark: Separated Children in Europe Program.

Stalford, H. (2012). *Children and the European Union: Rights Welfare and Accountability*. Oxford: Hart.

Stalford, H., & Drywood, E. (2009). Coming of age? Children's rights in the European Union. *Common Market Law Review, 46*(1), 143–172.

Stalford, H., & Drywood, E. (2011). Using the CRC to Inform EU Law and Policy-Making. In A. Invernizzi & J. Williams (Eds.), *The Human Rights of Children. From Visions to Implementation* (pp. 199–218). Aldershot: Ashgate.

Thomas, N. (2014). Children's Rights and the Law. In S. Powell & K. Smith (Eds.), *An Introduction to Early Childhood Studies* (3rd ed., pp. 141–152). London: Sage.

Tisdall, E. K. M. (2013). The Transformation of Participation? Exploring the Potential of 'Transformative Participation' for Theory and Practice Around Children and Young People's Participation. *Global Studies of Childhood, 3*, 183–193.

Tisdall, E. K. M., Davis, J. M., & Gallagher, M. (2009). *Research with Children and Young People: Research Design, Methods and Analysis*. London: Sage.

Tomás, C. (2002). Infância como um campo de estudo multi e interdisciplinar, algumas relexões. *Revista Psicologia e Educação, 1,* 131–146.

UN. (2003). *Statement of Common Understanding on a Human Rights-Based Approach to Development Co-operation.* Geneva: United Nations.

UNHCR & UNICEF. (2014). *Safe and Sound. What States Can Do to Ensure Respect for the Best Interests of Unaccompanied and Separated Children in Europe,* Available at: http://www.refworld.org/pdfid/5423da264.pdf.

Van Bueren, G. (1998). Children's Rights: Balancing Traditional Values and Cultural Plurality. In G. Douglas & L. Sebba (Eds.), *Children's Rights and Traditional Values.* Hants: Dartmouth.

Westwood, J., Larkins, C., Moxon, D., Perry, Y., & Thomas, N. (Eds.). (2014). *Participation, Citizenship and Intergenerational Relations in Children and Young People's Lives: Children and Adults in Conversation.* New York: Springer.

Woodhouse, B. (2000). '*Children's Rights*', University of Pennsylvania Law School. Public and Legal Theory Research Papers, No. 1–6.

CHAPTER 6

How Do You Go From Demonising Adversaries to Deliberating with Them?

John Boswell

INTRODUCTION

Theories of policy advocacy typically present the actors involved as calculating automatons. Prevailing models turn on the belief that such actors are always capable of rationally advancing their claims across settings and stages of policy work (see, e.g., Sabatier 1988; Potters and Sloof 1996; Baumgartner and Leech 1998). Yet important interpretive work sheds doubt on this parsimonious assumption, revealing that 'organized interests' are seldom very organised and often do not share coherent interests (e.g. Hajer 1995; Lejano et al. 2013). This chapter builds on this decentred alternative of complex governance networks. It sheds light especially on the *human* side of policy advocacy. To complicate further the parsimonious orthodoxy of myopic utility maximisation, I explore the dilemmas and anxieties, challenges and frustrations, of advocacy work within such networks.

J. Boswell (✉)
Department of Politics and International Relations,
University of Southampton, Southampton, UK
e-mail: j.c.boswell@soton.ac.uk

This perspective is especially important because contemporary governance arrangements typically comprise a growing range of different settings, each of which features different norms of engagement and rewards different practices of advocacy (see Warren 2009). Some, like the media, thrive on confrontation and bold assertions. Others, like expert committees, reward sober analysis and technical mastery. Some, like crisis meetings or innovative participatory exercises, are new or one-off occasions without any clear script. Others, like legislative processes, are steeped in tacit assumptions and hidden customs. Often it is the same actors who are expected to perform equally well across all these sites. And often these actors know one another—allies *and* adversaries—well, on the back of long professional associations and inevitable personal ties. How do actors negotiate divergent settings and complex networks to best promote their policy claims? How do they go from demonising adversaries in one space to deliberating with them in another? These human challenges of doing advocacy work remain largely unasked in policy studies.

In this chapter, I seek to explore these questions by decentring the networks that govern obesity in Australia and the UK. I focus on the beliefs and practices of prominent advocates engaged in political debate and policy work in this area. My analysis centres around three prominent metaphors about the work of advocacy that participants either stated or invoked. The first metaphor sees advocacy practices as a 'war' pitted largely between a (courageous/zealous) public health lobby and a (cynical/pragmatic) food industry lobby, in which actors reflect on policy debate on this issue as *inflaming conflict*. The second metaphor sees advocacy practices as a 'game' played out by savvy insiders, in which actors reflect on different venues of debate and policy work as helping *orchestrate conflict*. The third metaphor sees advocacy practices as a 'club' with strange rituals and steep barriers—one that renders outsiders to the club vulnerable and naïve and has the overall effect of *masking conflict*. Through this analysis, I show that some actors, especially those with significant experience who have a central and confident role in the governance network, are able to push skilfully for their desired ends in a manner that aligns with prevailing theories of policy advocacy. But I show that others, especially those newest and least established, struggle to navigate the advocacy world. They typically either remain adversarial and thus peripheral to settings of network influence, or else they risk conceding too much ground. These differential experiences, I will conclude, create dilemmas for the moves to open up practices of networked governance.

DEBATING OBESITY

The analysis that follows is based on an in-depth, qualitative case study of deliberation on obesity across a range of democratic sites in Australia and Britain.[1] Obesity provides an especially interesting topic for an analysis of advocacy beliefs and practices for a number of reasons.

One, it is a relatively new issue on the agenda. Defined officially as a body mass index of 30 or higher, obesity has emerged as an important issue in public health policymaking only over the last three decades (see WHO 2000; Wang et al. 2011). It is thought by most experts to have increased around fivefold increase in prevalence in Australia and Britain over this period, with most experts linking this so-called epidemic to major spikes in the rates of expensive, debilitating and deadly chronic diseases such as diabetes and heart disease. Because of this relative novelty, many of the advocates engaged in settings of political debate and policy work are new to the political arena. Others, in the powerful medical profession and food industries, are much more experienced advocates. This discrepancy provides a broader range of reflections and diversity of experiences to draw on in the analysis.

Two, it is recognised as a 'wicked problem' (see Rittel and Weber 1973). Though there is broad agreement that obesity is a problem, there is little consensus among experts, politicians, lobbyists and NGOs, among others, about obesity's nature, its causes and the appropriate public policy response. It is, firstly, an issue of considerable contestation, both on ideological and material grounds (Broom and Dixon 2007). There are clashing philosophies about the role of the state; there are also a multitude of interests involved, including the powerful food and pharmaceutical industries, competing expert and professional groups, patient activists and so on. Obesity is, secondly, an issue of great scientific uncertainty. Little is known about the relationship of obesity to health outcomes and even less known about the capacity of government to intervene (Botterill 2006; Botterill and Hindmoor 2012). And, finally, obesity is an issue of immense complexity (Foresight 2007). It cuts across a range of different specialties, both within health and beyond, and involves an array of interrelated factors (Lang and Rayner 2007). These 'wicked' characteristics make obesity—and the advocacy surrounding it—informative for how we think about the thorniest and most interesting governance challenges facing policymakers today.

Three, and perhaps most important of all for the aims of this chapter, obesity typifies the complex range of interconnected and differentiated settings through which political debate and policy work are channelled. Understanding advocacy on obesity requires taking into account different settings with different remits and purposes, different traditions and norms of engagement, and different but frequently overlapping memberships and audiences. Below, I set out the key sites of advocacy on obesity in both countries during the time period under examination (2007–2013). This volume and variety raises pertinent questions about how advocates practise and reflect on their work.

Drawing on over 1000 documents, 25 hours of video footage and 36 semi-structured interviews (see Table 6.1 for a breakdown), I set about determining how actors engaged in this policymaking network experienced and perceived the process and their role in it (see Boswell 2016a). The approach was, in this sense, interpretive. Though typically associated with an effort to bring to light the views and experiences of the marginalised (see Schwartz-Shea 2006), interpretive research is equally valuable as an approach for 'studying up', shedding new light on the beliefs and practices of elites, too (see Rhodes 2011). The theme of advocacy, and its challenges, was something which interview participants were particularly keen to reflect and dwell on.

The analysis then focuses on understanding the different metaphors that actors either stated or invoked in their reflections on this work and in their practice of advocacy. A focus on metaphors is a common strategy in interpretive policy research (see also Dryzek 2013; Barry et al. 2009). Such metaphors operate as shorthand for the contending narratives that policy actors tell to understand their world and the dilemmas they confront within it (see Bevir and Rhodes 2006). Its particular use is that it can capture in stark, authentic and creative ways the manner in which actors make sense of their experiences.

Inflaming Conflict: Advocacy as a War

> In this space, there's the black hats and the white hats. We don't have all of de Bono's hats. We only have the black one and the white one. The good guys are the people in public health and research and the bad guys are the guys in industry. It's really simple. (Interview with Australian food industry representative, May 2011)

Table 6.1 Sites of policy advocacy on obesity

Australian sites	British sites
Mass media —News articles, opinion pieces and letters to the editor from a sample of major tabloid and broadsheet publications with progressive and conservative editorial reputations *Data*: approx. 500 articles, interviews with 1 journalist and 14 public advocates *2020 Summit* —Australia's 'best and brightest' discuss critical issues, including a health stream (86 members) with particular focus on obesity *Data*: Report and government response, notes and 3 hour of video footage (via Freedom of Information Act), interviews with 2 participants *Parliamentary Inquiries* —One lengthy House of Representatives' (HoR) Inquiry into Obesity; a shorter Senate Inquiry into Protecting Children from Junk Food Advertising *Data*: Reports and government response, submissions, Hansard, 8 hours of video footage (Senate), interviews with 3 MPs (2 HoR and 1 Senate) and 8 witnesses (7 HoR and 2 Senate) *Preventative Health Taskforce (2009)* —An expert-driven discussion and assessment of evidence around the causes of obesity and the possible solutions *Data*: Reports and government response, submissions, consultation notes, interviews with 3 taskforce members *Food and Health Dialogue* —A collaborative body of government, food industry and public health representatives working mainly on food reformulation targets *Data*: Communiques, website, interviews with 3 Dialogue members	*Mass media* —News articles, opinion pieces and letters to the editor from sample of major tabloid and broadsheet publications with progressive and conservative editorial reputations *Data*: approx. 250 articles, interviews with 7 public advocates *Foresight (2007)* —An expert-driven assessment of obesity rates, its causes, its future costs, and the regulatory and non-regulatory options for government *Data*: Report and related documentation, interviews with 2 participants, interview with 1 member of expert advisory committee *Food Standards Agency (FSA) Board* —The FSA Board discusses key policy issues at 10 'open' meetings every year broadcast live on television and archived online—4 meetings in this timeframe had obesity and related sub-issues (e.g. food labelling) as a major focus *Data*: Meeting agendas and minutes, full video footage (12 hours analysed) *Public Health Responsibility Deals* —A collaborative body with government, the food industry and public health experts to develop non-regulatory, voluntary industry directives and policy solutions to obesity *Data*: Website, interview with 1 Responsibility Deal member

The competing narratives that actors adhere to and promote contribute on obesity to a pronounced us-versus-them, binary conception of debate (Chilton 2004: 202). Though my full analysis (see Boswell 2016a) uncovers 6 key narratives—each of which depicts a distinctive 'us' and 'them'—my focus here is on the highest profile contest, between an assorted coalition of Big Food, advertisers, mainstream political parties and local health campaigners, on the one hand, and a public health lobby of experts, clinicians and NGOs, on the other. I will from this point on refer to the 'status quo coalition' and the 'public health lobby' as shorthand. The public depiction and private conviction of an 'us' versus a 'them' represent this contest not as a dialogue among parties committed to give and listen to reasons behind claims, but as an adversarial one of public debate as a war played out between sworn enemies.

Those in the status quo coalition are dismissive of the public health lobby's attempt to 'paint targets' on food companies and oversimplify the nature of the issue and the debate. One senior bureaucrat, for example, reflected:

> There's been a tendency to try to model it on the tobacco debate and make fast food restaurants the enemy, make the food industry the enemy, make the sugar producers the enemy, and that's just not going to work. (Interview with senior Australian bureaucrat, July 2011)

The objection in either case is not so much that these experts are completely wrong-headed, but that in their approach they inflame a sense of crisis and obstruct reasonable progress. As such, frequent sarcastic or concerned reference is made to the so-called 'war on obesity' and the alleged threat posed by the 'fat bomb'—as it is represented by some of the more radical public health campaigners in Australia. These tropes become targets of derision or concern. For instance, MP Mark Coulton of the Australian House of Representatives (HoR) Inquiry committee thanked an expert witness who had performed Moral Panic (and thus downplayed the threat posed by obesity):

> Thank you for your submission. I find it quite refreshing because unfortunately we seem to get run over with what is sensational. The day we had our inquiry in Melbourne the entire front page of the newspaper down there was 'Australia's fat bomb'. Something I have been grappling with: if we are having a war on obesity and you are obese, does that mean we are having a war on you? (HoR Inquiry, September 11, 2008: 39)

In contrast, most public health advocates in Australia especially are convinced that it is the damaging image of the 'nanny state' which stops them from mobilising public opinion effectively. They therefore make frequent and scathing reference to this trope. One, for example, reflected ruefully on the shallow arguments mounted against the banning of junk food advertising on children's television: 'Aren't nannies meant to protect children anyway?' (Olver 2008). In the UK, in contrast, it is the notion of 'nudge theory' that is seen as most problematic. 'Nudge' is drawn on scornfully by members of the public health lobby to embody the perceived failings of the government's 'soft' approach to the issue. In an interview, one dismissed 'nudge theory' witheringly as 'soft pop psychology seen through the filter of economics' (Interview with British public health researcher, April 2011).

The metaphor that predominates in private reflections and the most public performances of advocacy (especially in the media) is of political debate as a 'war'. This sort of language even seeps into the reflections of some of my interview participants. One noted:

> Kate Carnell sort of speaks about it like it's a war. She said to someone at a party the other day who's related to someone I work with that 'they're winning'. It's not about health. It's a war and it's about who's winning. It's really strange how these...I think the words sort of say a lot. And that's how they fight it. It's not like it's about public health, or doing the right thing. (Interview with Australian public health advocate, June 2011)

Kate Carnell was, during the period under examination, the chief executive officer of the Australian Food and Grocery Council (AFGC), the peak lobby group for the processed food industry in Australia. She is a well-known political figure in Canberra, having served as Chief Minister of the ACT Government for several years, and having worked as a lobbyist for other high-profile national organisations. She represented, as this quote would suggest, a central figure in the debate in Australia. She was feared, loathed and begrudgingly admired by public health advocates, and her name cropped up repeatedly in interviews. The public health lobby were especially aggrieved at her refusal to recuse herself from the Preventative Health Taskforce, the single setting that they pinpointed as the most important in influencing policy. Carnell had initially been appointed to the taskforce as head of the GP Network, but was headhunted by the AFGC prior to the taskforce commencing its work. She remained on the taskforce on the new basis that she could represent the industry voice. For much of the public health lobby, this was like an infidel sneaking into their high temple under cover of disguise; having to deliberate with her in such a setting was like having to deliberate with 'the devil' (for detail on this episode, see Boswell 2016b).

A number of actors—either in interviews or in their public statements—reflected on polarisation and its implications for the possibility of collaborative policy engagement on obesity. A British food industry representative noted with frustration that the prevailing antipathy towards industry meant they were 'damned if they did and damned if they didn't' participate in collaborative policymaking processes like the Public Health Responsibility Deals:

> There is also a feeling of well, we're engaging in these processes. Either we don't engage in which case the health charity NGO lobby will react negatively, because you can find that on the public list. It's all mailed out. So you'd get slammed by the charities. If you do sign up, the press will say: 'Look, isn't this ridiculous?' (Interview with British food industry representative, March 2012)

Colin Segelov, executive director of the Australasian Association of National Advertisers, echoed much the same point about the attitude to his particular industry:

> They do not want to engage with us. They are on a mission from God or from somewhere where they want to engage with [politicians] and do not want to engage with the food industry. That is of concern to me because, as long as we have the us and them mentality, I do not think we are going to see very much progress at all. I have been hearing the same arguments for eight years and I have been giving the same or similar responses for most of that time. We have not advanced very far in all of the time that obesity has been on the table. (HoR Inquiry, October 1, 2008: 52)

Meanwhile, an Australian NGO representative in the public health lobby joked about the prospect of genuine engagement with adversaries so devoted to their own self-interest:

> And we do talk to industry. You know, Coke comes in their limo, and pops in, has a chat, and drives away in their limo. (Interview with Australian public health advocate, June 2011)

A British counterpart was equally cynical, dismissing industry claims to being a 'part of the solution':

Technically speaking they have public health messages saying: 'Don't eat too many cheeseburgers. This message is sponsored by McDonald's.' There's no way…those of us involved in it are extremely cynical that the food industry is going to talk themselves out of business. (Interview with British clinician, April 2012)

This pervasive antagonism led a politician, in discussing the different advocacy campaigns, to reflect on the debate as a whole:

[Actors across all sides] are completely consumed by their argument. It actually means that rather than having open discussion people go into camps. (Interview with Australian Senator, May 2011)

Orchestrating Conflict: Advocacy as a Game

She got a foothold in [an important committee]. She continually leaked information to her side. It made it very difficult. She's been a good player for her side alright. But unfortunately she's playing on the wrong side as far as I'm concerned. (Interview with Australian public health expert, June 2011)

Scratching beneath the surface revealed that not everyone buys into the hostility associated with publicly locking horns. In particular, many of the more experienced advocates—those who had been around politics for a long time, or who were employed as professional interest group representatives—saw the hostility as a performance, rather than a core aspect of their identity. As the quote above indicates, they may have retained a sense of grievance or animosity. Yet, on reflection, several interview participants talked about the personal conflict and adversarialism as simply being part of the way politics is always done, making parallels to established rituals of political institutions more broadly. For example, referring more broadly beyond the obesity debate to his experiences in Parliament, one interview participant echoed a sentiment also expressed in richly qualitative empirical work on deliberation within legislative assemblies (see Bessette 1997):

I think that it's not that unusual because a lot of the things that we do in this place are of a collegial nature. Quite often we're judged on the hour and half of Question Time every day, which is not how things operate. (Interview with Australian MP, May 2011)

The implication is that the dramatised performances in public spaces are replaced by more sober and generous accounts in expert or elite-dominated sites like the taskforce and the Dialogue in Australia, and the open board meetings of the FSA and the deliberations associated with Foresight and its aftermath, as well as in informal negotiations among parties outside of institutionalised settings. As such, an industry representative reflected on the noticeable change in how public health campaigners interact with him in different contexts with a degree of cynicism:

> A time when we have experienced healthy debate is when we have reached out in these types of outreach stakeholder engagement programs, and there are no cameras there, no one is looking to get their sound bite on the 6 o'clock news, no one's looking to advance in their various industry associations by the boss seeing that they've taken a swipe at the horrible beverage manufacturers. (Interview with Australian food industry representative, June 2011)

One interpretation of this is that the actors involved are being disingenuous in their more public performances of the narratives they subscribe to. Certainly, this is the way some of my interview participants perceived things (in relation to their adversaries, not themselves or their allies). In discussing the advocacy efforts of one of the best known and most outspoken members of the public health lobby in Australia, one interview participant suggested:

> He also understands debate very well and understands that fundamentally in most of these things where you're going to end up is somewhere in the middle, so you've got to take a position a long way over towards the side. (Interview with Australian industry representative, May 2011)

Yet in my interview with the advocate in question, I got the impression he was restraining his public claims in order to appear more mainstream and reasonable. Moreover, as I alluded to above, many of my interview participants reserved their most dramatic accounts, and with them scathing attacks on their enemies, for our private, anonymous interviews. In response to the age-old dilemma of political influence, many had opted to ameliorate their claims to exert pragmatic influence for change as insiders rather than demand radical change as outsiders.

An alternative and in my view, more convincing way of interpreting this state of affairs, then, is through the logic of performativity (see Hajer 2009). In other words, that performances of narratives are sometimes, and in some places, more reasonable and respectful reflects the fact that 'bashing each other over the heads' can be inappropriate and counter-productive in certain circumstances (Interview with Australian industry representative, May 2011). The prevailing norms and the social, historical and institutional ties binding the participants necessitate a different way of going about debate. Whether an instinctive communicative response or a calculated advocacy strategy (or more likely a bit of both), the result is that more public sites facilitate more adversarial, dramatising performances and more closed-off sites facilitate more consensual performances. Neither should be seen as a more authentic performance than the other.

Indeed, rather than debate being a war, it is perhaps more useful to think of it, as some of my interview participants said and many more intimated, as akin to 'a game'. A member of the British public health lobby justified her continued participation in the Public Health Responsibility Deals—which most advocates of the public health lobby in Britain are hugely sceptical about—in these terms:

> We publish reports criticising practices and trying to highlight the need for change. But we also work within the system where it's useful to do that as well. (Interview with British public health advocate, April 2012)

A counterpart in Australia made the point more starkly:

> There will still need to be the screamers on the outside chucking bricks to keep the pressure up. If we all said yep, we want to work with industry, and we'll all be on advisory boards, and we'll all take funding for research and for conferences and stuff, then we're all going to be in the pocket of industry and there won't be enough independent people keeping things honest. (Interview with Australian researcher, June 2011)

This perspective was perhaps best summed up by Public Health Association of Australia (PHAA) CEO, Michael Moore.[2] Moore explained how he went about locking horns with Kate Carnell over public health on the back of years of similar experience serving as an independent Health Minister in the Liberal ACT government which she led:

I've had this ongoing relationship with Kate for 20 years, where actually we've always both understood that conflict is part of getting our message through. And because we actually understand that, sometimes it's actually quite useful. And in fact we've had in the past within the political sphere, when I was a Minister in her government but I was opposing something… we would actually discuss beforehand the way this sort of conflict was going to go. Generally, it went the way we had expected it to. So as far as the general public was concerned, there we were, having a very significant debate—and we did, we had a genuine difference of opinion. We may have looked like we were cross at each other or something but in fact it was quite orchestrated. (Interview with Michael Moore, April 2011)

In this way, adherents to the competing narratives have a capacity to put these differences aside to some extent—or at least to be represented by others who are capable of that—and participate in less adversarially scripted sites of policy work and deliberation. The conflict engendered in the different narratives they subscribe to does not lead to paralysis; though magnified in public settings, it does not foreclose the possibility of pragmatic engagement in more closed-off or elite sites. Certainly, even the engagement within these more cosseted sites is not as open-minded and typified by deep mutual respect as some (especially most early) accounts of deliberative democracy would have it—actors do not, for instance, cast off their pre-commitments. Indeed, none of the actors I spoke to believed their opinion had been changed at all during the course of their participation in sites of deliberation, and nor did they believe it should have. For the most part, these experienced campaigners arrived committed to a cause and saw their role as representing that to the best of their abilities in each particular site. They were happy to play their part in the advocacy 'game'.

Masking Conflict: Advocacy as a Club

If advocacy is a 'game' for some of the most experienced and central members of the governance network surrounding obesity in both countries, then it is more commonly thought of as a 'club' by those more peripheral to policy work on the issue. These are often actors who are new to advocacy, and who engage only in some settings of policy work (typically those further removed from the corridors of power). These actors sometimes speak of a 'culture shock' in becoming engaged in policy advocacy and reflect on the strange norms and rituals and exclusionary practices of those they perceive as being in the 'club'.

Of course, the 'dark side of networks' and the dominance of a cosy club of lobbyists—especially career lobbyists on the payroll of corporate interests—are a well-worn theme in politics and policy scholarship (see, e.g., Schattschneider 1960; O'Toole and Meier 2004; O'Toole 2015). Many in the public health lobby reflected on this at length. One complained:

> The stuff I do in advocacy is not my day job. This is all done kind of as an addition. So, my day job is in research. The role I have taken since I've been involved in this is one of the advocate–and hopefully evidence-based-with-sufficient-credibility-type-advocate-position—calling for change. We don't have that many levers being public interest advocates. We have tiny bits of money. We have tiny bits of time. We have no open doors to go knocking on.

Yet this actor was among the best known public health advocates in Australia, one that peers would namecheck and express admiration for regularly. What I am driving at here is not so much this long-standing theme of corporate capture in the policy and politics literature (though of course I acknowledge its presence—see Baker et al. (2017) for more detail). Instead, what interests me are the advocates whose status in the debate is much more unsure and tentative: they perceive *both* Big Food *and* key public health advocates as being in the 'club', and themselves as being out of it.

Perhaps the best example through which to illustrate this belief is from a peripheral member of the public health lobby in Australia. She repeatedly made reference to being made to feel 'outside' the mainstream and to having been excluded from professional and personal networks. This frustration especially boiled over in our interview in discussion of the Preventative Health Taskforce. As I have already intimated, the taskforce was perhaps the high-water mark of expert influence on obesity policy in Australia. Its members and collaborators make a veritable *Who's Who* of public health in Australia. So, her exclusion was baffling and painful:

> I found it pretty strange that I wasn't invited considering I've got the best dataset in Australia together with [another researcher] to show what's happening, and I've written extensively about what you should and what you shouldn't do in [a particular area]. I was fairly flabbergasted that I wasn't invited…. I'm an expert about what should be done in [a particular area] and I didn't get invited to the Preventative Health Taskforce. So I don't know why.

Later on, however, she spoke with great satisfaction and warmth at being able to bypass professional gatekeepers and address policymakers directly in the *Weighing it Up Inquiry* at Parliament. She explained:

> And I can remember just being so grateful for having the opportunity to say in my opening statement, which I didn't read, I didn't prepare, I just said it, that the government needs to understand that there's a lot of money to be made out of the idea that every child woman, man, dog in Australia could lose some weight. You know what a little marketing goldmine it would have been for a lot of people. And the day I was at the parliamentary inquiry, there were presentations by weightwatchers, the bariatric surgery people, people who were running obesity clinics, McDonalds. It was just an interesting day. But it was a great pleasure to say, hang on a minute, there are a lot of vested interests in this debate, and you government folks have got to understand that. And the reply from the Chair was, yes, yes, we understand that. And that was a Labour Government, wasn't it? Georganas? I said that that was one of the best days of my life, and my teenage daughter said. 'Mum!' 'Of course the day I gave birth to you...' But seriously professionally it was one of the best days of my life. It was like: 'Now I'm saying this. Now I'm showing you this graph. Now I'm showing you this data. Here's this evidence—good, hard, cold evidence.

On the one hand, this sense of gratitude contrasted sharply with many of my other interview participants—specifically those in the 'club'. They typically either had no memory of their engagement in the inquiry (or similar set-piece arrangements), because they perform this ritual all the time, or joked that they no longer bother to take part in such events. One pair of advocates that I interviewed together explained that they had not bothered with *Weighing it Up* and began joking about the submissions to the inquiry gathering dust on a shelf in the 'vault' under Parliament—recounting a (probably) apocryphal story about an enormous repository for useless documents hidden under the hill where Australia's Parliament is situated. The discussion ended with one remarking acerbically: 'The last place you go if you actually want to influence policy is a Parliamentary Inquiry' (Interview with Australian professional association representative, August 2011).

But, on the other, this sense of gratitude at being 'listened to' or given a platform to speak also spilled over into a tentativeness in advocacy, even a potential for co-optation. The advocate peripheral to the public health lobby quoted above, for instance, revealed her delight at having her ideas picked up by the national press. She explained:

You might have seen the article on the front page of [an Australian broadsheet]. And I wasn't fiddling with anything. I wasn't manoeuvring. I wasn't meddling. I was simply reporting the data. And I think prior to that there was a lot of media that was very light on scientific information and very emotionally charged.

Yet my reading of that same media coverage suggests that her research and ideas were significantly distorted. Indeed, claims about her research were made in editorial content that sought to affirm obesity as an issue of personal rather than collective responsibility. It painted public health researchers as proponents of the Nanny State—a perspective that she had expressly and harshly criticised in the course of our interview. The point was that she was so delighted to have been noticed—to have felt affirmed as a member of the 'club'—that she was unable or unwilling to aggressively pursue her personal beliefs through the process.

What this example speaks to is the difficulty for newcomers with a precarious place in the network. Many fail to grasp the tacit assumptions and ingrained practices that those in the 'club' take for granted. They bump up against adversaries, unwilling to play the 'game' or unable even to understand the rules. A food industry representative explained:

[The personal stuff] doesn't worry me. I think it's harder for [public health advocates]. I think the trick here is actually to—from my perspective—is always to keep the level of respect. Put aside the debate, shall we say. Because people are just pushing and pushing a barrow. That's okay. But I think that's actually tougher for others. Especially academics. So when…because they tend –sorry, you guys—can tend to be a bit holier-than-thou at times. I got over being holier-than-thou a very long time ago. I know that when the stoush over [an academic paper questioning the 'obesity epidemic'] happened and some of the people who were pushing the 'Big Food is the new Big Tobacco' space, it was really quite bloodthirsty and people took it incredibly personally, because they were academics.... But it's 'the game'. [Laughs]. Well, you know, it's not a game. But you have to accept that people all come from different positions. (Interview with author, May 2011)

The alternative is that these newcomers risk conceding too much ground. The apparent 'war' on obesity peters out as many advocates allow debate to settle around apparently conciliatory ground. The most prevalent and pertinent example is around the 'complexity' of the issue and the need for an 'integrated' or 'holistic' response (see Boswell 2016b). Within the public health lobby especially, peripheral actors outside the 'club' typically deem policymakers' gradual acceptance of 'complexity' to be a mini-victory. Yet those in the 'club' remain deeply frustrated that this shift is too gradual and too hollow—that their efforts are undermined by a lack of cohesion and focus within the public health lobby, and that the concessions towards accepting 'complexity' and the need for an 'holistic' response represent empty signifiers. The effect is to mask conflict. These apparent concessions allow government to get away with doing nothing while making the right sorts of sounds. One British public health advocate explained in relation to the much maligned Responsibility Deals, for instance:

> The result is lots of vague statements of intent with unclear limits and timelines. There is no threat of what will happen if nothing actually is done. (Interview with author, July 2012)

Conclusion

By decentring the networks that govern obesity in Australia and Britain, I have shown here that the work of policy advocacy is demanding. I presented three metaphors of the work that advocacy involves: one as a war, one as a game and one as a club. The most experienced advocates—either professional lobbyists or those with the longest history of policy engagement—are typically willing to engage in advocacy as a 'game'. Some, but not all, still view it privately as a 'war'. But they still understand the importance of carefully orchestrating conflict in order to push for the ends that they see as being best or in their best interests. However, those most peripheral to settings of policy influence—the skilled amateurs, in this case often expert academic and physicians, who come in and out of policy work—are less able to play or even understand it as a game. To them, it either remains a 'war' or else it represents a mysterious 'club' to which they do not really belong. These actors struggle to navigate the terrain of policy work because they either rock the boat too much, or concede too much ground. This account has important implications conceptually and pragmatically.

For theories of policy advocacy, it presents a decentred account of how individuals act in a network and how they experience this work in different ways. It shows that all actors are not equally capable of advancing their cause across policy debate. In particular, it shows that the most inexperienced and peripheral actors—mostly in the public health lobby in this case—can be naïve, and that their naivety can be exploited to mask conflict. Looking at the human side of advocacy reveals yet another way in which the 'dark side' of networked governance can work to exacerbate further asymmetries in terms of access and influence.

Pragmatically, these insights should prompt a rethink of continual efforts to open up policymaking to a broader range of skilled amateurs. Efforts towards greater inclusion are of course well meaning. However, greater thought needs to go into how settings of greater inclusion are scripted and enacted in order to counter these pervasive asymmetries (see also Boswell 2016c). Knowing more about the human side of advocacy can only help in that regard.

Notes

1. My analysis of Australia and Britain was initially intended to be comparative in nature. In practice, however, the differences between the two were minimal and the commonalities overwhelming, and so functionally they operate as a single case. This evolution aligns with best practice in interpretive research, whereby preconceived analytical categories often dissolve upon immersion in the empirical data (Flyvbjerg 2006).
2. I am extremely grateful to Michael Moore for allowing me to quote him by name, as his identity would have been obvious otherwise, and I would not have been able to use these valuable insights in writing up my findings.

References

Baker, P., Gill, T., Friel, S., Carey, G., & Kay, A. (2017). Generating Political Priority for Regulatory Interventions Targeting Obesity Prevention: An Australian Case Study. *Social Science and Medicine, 177,* 141–149.

Barry, C. L., Brescoll, V. L., Brownell, K. D., & Schlesinger, M. (2009). Obesity Metaphors: How Beliefs About the Causes of Obesity Affect Support for Public Policy. *Milbank Quarterly, 87,* 7–47.

Baumgartner, F. R., & Leech, B. L. (1998). *Basic Interests: The Importance of Groups in Politics and in Political Science.* Princeton, NJ: Princeton University Press.

Bessette, J. M. (1997). *The Mild Voice of Reason: Deliberative Democracy and American National Government.* Chicago: University of Chicago Press.

Bevir, M., & Rhodes, R. A. W. (2006). Interpretive Approaches to British Government and Politics. *British Politics, 1,* 84–112.

Boswell, J. (2016a). *The Real War on Obesity: Contesting Knowledge and Meaning in a Public Health Crisis*. Basingstoke: Springer.

Boswell, J. (2016b). The Performance of Political Narratives: How Australia and Britain's 'Fat Bombs' Fizzled Out. *The British Journal of Politics and International Relations, 18,* 724–739.

Boswell, J. (2016c). Deliberating Downstream: Countering Democratic Distortions in the Policy Process. *Perspectives on Politics, 4,* 724–737.

Botterill, L. C. (2006). Leaps of Faith in the Obesity Debate: A Cautionary Note for Policy Note for Policy-Makers. *The Political Quarterly, 77,* 493–500.

Botterill, L. C., & Hindmoor, A. (2012). Turtles all the Way Down: Bounded Rationality in an Evidence-Based Age. *Policy Studies, 33,* 367–379.

Broom, D., & Dixon, J. (2007). Introduction: Seven Modern Environmental Sins of Obesity. In D. Broom & J. Dixon (Eds.), *The Seven Deadly Sins of Obesity: How the Modern World Is Making Us Fat*. Sydney: UNSW Press.

Chilton, P. (2004). *Analysing Political Discourse: Theory and Practice*. London: Routledge.

Dryzek, J. S. (2013). *The Politics of the Earth: Environmental Discourses*. Oxford: Oxford University Press.

Flyvbjerg, B. (2006). Five Misunderstandings About Case-Study Research. *Qualitative Inquiry, 12,* 219–245.

Hajer, M. A. (1995). *The Politics of Environmental Discourse: Ecological Modernization and the Policy Process*. Oxford: Clarendon Press.

Hajer, M. A. (2009). *Authoritative Governance: Policy Making in the Age of Mediatization*. Oxford: Oxford University Press.

House of Representatives (HoR) Standing Committee on Health and Ageing. (2008). *Inquiry into Obesity in Australia*. Hansard, Australian Government, Sydney, September 11.

House of Representatives (HoR) Standing Committee on Health and Ageing. (2008). *Inquiry into Obesity in Australia*. Hansard, Australian Government, Brisbane, October 1.

Lang, T., & Rayner, G. (2007). Overcoming Policy Cacophony on Obesity: An Ecological Public Health Framework for Policymakers. *Obesity Reviews,* (s1), 165–181.

Lejano, R., Ingram, M., & Ingram, H. (2013). *The Power of Narrative in Environmental Networks*. Cambridge, MA: MIT Press.

Olver, I. (2008, September 6). Curbing Advertising Will Cut Obesity. *The Australian*. Available at http://www.theaustralian.com.au/news/health-science/curbing-advertising-will-cut-obesity/story-e6frg8y6-1111117397209. Accessed January 22, 2013.

O'Toole, L. J. (2015). Networks and Networking: The Public Administrative Agendas. *Public Administration Review, 75,* 361–371.

O'Toole, L. J., & Meier, K. J. (2004). Desperately Seeking Selznick: Co-optation and the Dark Side of Public Management in Networks. *Public Administration Review, 64,* 681–693.

Potters, J., & Sloof, R. (1996). Interest Groups: A Survey of Empirical Models That Try to Assess Their Influence. *European Journal of Political Economy, 12,* 403–442.

Preventative Health Taskforce. (2009). *Australia: The Healthiest Country by 2020.* Canberra: Australian Government, Department of Health and Ageing. Available at http://www.preventativehealth.org.au/internet/preventativehealth/publishing.nsf/Content/AEC223A781D64FF0CA2575FD00075DD0/$File/nphs-overview.pdf. Accessed January 18, 2013.

Rhodes, R. A. W. (2011). *Everyday Life in British Government.* Oxford: Oxford University Press.

Rittel, H. W. J., & Webber, M. (1973). Dilemmas in a General Theory of Planning. *Policy Sciences, 4,* 155–169.

Sabatier, P. A. (1988). An Advocacy Coalition Framework of Policy Change and the Role of Policy-Oriented Learning Therein. *Policy Sciences, 21*(2), 129–168.

Schattschneider, E. (1975[1960]). *The Semi-Sovereign People.* New York: Holt, Rinehart and Winston.

Schwartz-Shea, P. (2006). Judging Quality. In D. Yanow & P. Schwartz-Shea (Eds.), *Interpretation and Method: Empirical Research Methods and the Interpretative Turn* (pp. 89–113). New York: M. E. Sharpe.

Wang, Y. C., McPherson, K., Marsh, T., Gortmaker, S. L., & Brown, M. (2011). Health and Economic Burden of the Projected Obesity Trends in the USA and the UK. *Lancet, 378,* 815–825.

Warren, M. E. (2009). Governance-Driven Democratization. *Critical Policy Studies, 3,* 3–13.

World Health Organization (WHO). (2000). *Obesity: Preventing and Managing the Global Epidemic.* Report of a WHO Consultation (WHO Technical Report Series No. 894). Geneva.

CHAPTER 7

How Have Narratives, Beliefs and Practices Shaped Pension Reform in Sweden?

Karen Anderson

Existing accounts of pension reform in Europe emphasize the impact of political partisanship, institutional constraints and problem pressure (demographic and economic pressures) in shaping the direction of policy change (see, e.g., Bonoli 2000; Immergut et al. 2017; Schludi 2005). The general orientation of this body of scholarship is (boundedly) rationalist in the sense that political actors respond to the constraints and opportunities created by formal and informal political institutions in responding to pressures for policy change. Above all, it is the desire of elected politicians to be re-elected that drives the political calculations and behaviours that result in policy reform. This chapter adopts a different analytical perspective by investigating how narratives, beliefs and practices have shaped pension reform processes. In doing so, the analysis challenges the rationality assumption explicit or implicit in much of the literature on pension reform.

The chapter analyses the development of pension policy in two major reform episodes in Sweden, the 1959 ATP reform and the 1994/1998

K. Anderson (✉)
Department of Sociology, Social Policy and Criminology,
University of Southampton, Southampton, UK
e-mail: k.m.anderson@soton.ac.uk

© The Author(s) 2018
R. A. W. Rhodes (ed.), *Narrative Policy Analysis*, Understanding Governance, https://doi.org/10.1007/978-3-319-76635-5_7

reform of that system. The chapter shows how important pension reform struggles in the past shaped policy-makers' beliefs and shared institutional narratives concerning the appropriate design and role of the pension system. The failure of collective bargaining to produce supplementary pension coverage for blue-collar workers in the two decades prior to the 1959 ATP reform generated grass-roots pressure for union leaders and eventually, the Social Democratic Party, to pursue a legislative solution. The emergence of widespread belief in the virtues of expertise-based socio-economic planning intersected with growing Social Democratic influence in politics to create a centre-left world view that saw major pension reform as desirable, achievable and just. In the 1990s, the intense political conflict associated with the 1959 ATP pension reform helped to generate a shared narrative in which political conflict was to be avoided at all cost in negotiating the parameters of a reformed pension system in the 1990s. Indeed, one of the most important features of the 1994/1998 Swedish pension reform is the broad parliamentary alliance behind it.

Decentring Pension Reform

One of the most important tasks of democratic governments is to promote the welfare of their residents. Public expenditure on social protection tops 25% of GDP in most European countries (the OECD average is 21% in 2016), with pensions accounting for the largest share, at 9% of GDP for the OECD in 2010–2015 (OECD 2015, 182). Because of these high financial and social stakes, policy-makers keep a close eye on the development of pension policy, especially since the maturation of many public schemes in the 1980s and 1990s. The importance of this policy field has inspired a large literature in political science, public administration, history and sociology that attempts to explain cross-national differences in the origins of pension systems (Heclo 1974; Baldwin 1990; Orloff 1993) and the scope and content of reforms of mature pension systems (Pierson 1994; Bonoli 2000; Schludi 2005; Immergut et al. 2017).

Much of the pension reform literature emphasizes the electoral dynamics surrounding pension reform. According to influential accounts, pension reform reaches the political agenda because powerful political actors wish to challenge the policy status quo, either for electoral (to gain or keep voters) reasons or to respond to financial and or demographic pressures such as an increase in the old-age dependency ratio. Either way, pension reform processes are typically explained as the outcome of a political bargaining process in which elected politicians try to mobilize support for their reform plans within specific institutional contexts. The motivations for the behaviour of politicians, voters and affected interests are assumed to be rational and material in the sense that individuals understand how they benefit (or not) from existing pension provision and how reform plans will affect this calculation (see, e.g., Pierson 1994; Bonoli 2000; Schludi 2005).

The analysis presented here attempts to decentre pension reform processes by focusing on how the beliefs and practices of policy-makers in specific historical contexts shaped policy-making. I focus on two extremely important episodes in the development of the Swedish welfare state: the adoption of the statutory earnings-related pension system (*Allmänna tilläggspension, ATP*) in 1959 and the reform of this pension system in the 1990s. In the narratives that follow, I emphasize how beliefs, informed by tradition, shaped the actions associated with pension reform and the reform packages that resulted. I highlight how the 'contingent actions and beliefs of particular individuals' are necessary for understanding how and why pension reform processes unfolded as they did (Bevir and Rhodes 2010). In particular, I emphasize the reasons that motivated the actions of policy actors in reform processes (Bevir and Needham 2017). The analysis is based on documentary sources and six semi-structured interviews with relevant policy-makers undertaken in May 1994, March 1995 and February 2000. I rely on memoirs, published interviews and official documents to capture the motivations and world views of key actors involved in the 1959 ATP reform. I draw on the same kinds of documentary sources for my analysis of the 1994/1998 pension reform, supplemented by interviews with important policy-makers.

Pension Reform in Sweden

The narratives that follow first show how policy-makers' traditions, beliefs and practices shaped the foundational 1959 ATP pension reform. The narrative charts how the tradition of the 'strong society', Social Democratic 'Harvest Time' and 'universal social protection' influenced how policy actors, especially on the centre-left, viewed the pension policy area. The narrative emphasizes the norms and understandings that influenced this interpretation, and how the beliefs and practices associated with these traditions shaped how actors defined their interests (Bevir and Needham 2017). This is followed by a second narrative that charts the ways in which policy-makers adapted their beliefs and practices to respond to dilemmas associated with the maturation of the ATP system. This process of adaptation and reinterpretation culminated in a major pension reform in 1994/1998. The meanings associated with the ATP systems also shaped the 1990s reform process in important ways. By the 1990s, the ATP reform had taken on a symbolic significance that extended far beyond its role as an instrument for providing retirement income. Indeed, policy-makers (and elites) in Sweden viewed the ATP reform as the crown jewel of social democratic reformism, and this shared meaning had to be redefined in the reform processes of the 1990s and 2000s. A second meaning associated with the ATP reform also influenced the renegotiation of beliefs and practices: the process that culminated in the 1959 ATP legislation was marked by protracted, intense and bitter partisan conflict. Voters went to the polls four times in four years to vote on pension issues (3 parliamentary elections in 1956, 1958 and 1960 and one referendum, in 1957), and the final legislation passed by a razor-thin margin. The legacy of this long and conflictual process was a widespread understanding in the 1990s that political conflict on pensions was to be avoided at all cost, and this view was shared by both the centre-left and the centre-right.

The Struggle for Supplementary Pensions

What were the world views that shaped actors' beliefs and actions as they contemplated pension reform in the 1950s? How did these world views shape their definition of the pension problem and their own interests? In other words, what were the narratives that actors constructed about pension reform, their own role in the process, and their own interests and values? The discussion that follows centres on the key political and economic actors in the reform process.

Harvest Time, the Strong Society and Universal Social Protection

Understanding the traditions that informed political and economic actors' beliefs and actions requires placing them in historical context. In the second half of the 1940s, the Social Democratic Party (SAP) and the Union Confederation (*Landsorganisationen*—LO) inherited a social policy tradition based on three central ideas: 'Harvest Time', the 'strong society' and universal social rights. I will discuss each in turn.

By the end of World War II, the Social Democratic Party had established itself as the largest party in Parliament, governing alone or coalition since 1932. In the late 1940s, the SAP embarked on its so-called Harvest Time (*skördetiden*) during which the major programmes of the post-war welfare state were introduced. In coalition with the Agrarian Party, the Social Democrats embarked on an ambitious programme to expand the housing stock and improve cash benefit programmes like unemployment insurance, sickness insurance and old-age pensions. Organized labour also began to flex their muscles, as union membership grew from 67.3% of workers in 1950 to 69.2% in 1955, one of the highest rates in Western Europe (Waddington 2004, p. 33). The SAP relied on the cooperation and support of the powerful union movement, led by the LO, which organized blue-collar unions.

The SAP and their union allies were strongly influenced by the development in the 1930s and 1940s of a perspective known as the 'strong society' ('*starka samhället*'). The key ideas underlying the strong society were a very strong belief in rationalism, planning and central steering. Political actors across the partisan spectrum came to believe that societal change could be achieved through democratic institutions based on rationalism and democratic legitimacy (Rothstein and Westerhåll 2005).

The central elements of this perspective were that modern science could generate the knowledge necessary for identifying, explaining and responding to social problems. Once modern science had identified the causes and remedies, democratic institutions would generate ideologically motivated but legitimate priorities about how to deal with social problems. Scientific knowledge and ideological priorities would thus be integrated to form a national reform programme. Once science and democratic institutions had done their part, the state would use its administrative economic and judicial instruments to implement reforms. In short, modern science and the modern democratic state could try to change society for the better. A key element in this vision of policy-making was the Official Commission of Inquiry (OCI; *Statens Offentliga Utredning*, SOU) which was based on expert knowledge and consensus building between different ideological groups and interests (Rothstein and Westerhåll 2005; see also Heclo 1974).

The early post-war period also marked a shift in social democratic thinking concerning the basis for social entitlements. Prior to this, most social insurance and other benefits were income-tested or means-tested. The 1930s and 1940s were marked by internal disagreement among key social democratic figures on this issue. The view of Gustav Möller, the Minister of Social Affairs from 1932–1951, prevailed: all citizens should have the right to uniform, tax-financed social provision. The 1946 basic pension law reflects this perspective and the defeat of social democratic voices (the Prime Minister, Tage Erlander and the Finance Minister, Ernst Wigforss) who advocated income-tested pensions for budgetary reasons (Lindberg 1999).

The 1959 ATP Reform

The idea of the 'strong state' and universal social rights profoundly influenced how SAP and LO elites and their members approached social policy reform during 'Harvest Time'. One of the SAP's priorities was the improvement of public pensions. Legislation adopted in the early 1950s had increased the level of the universal basic pensions (it equalled about 30% of average industrial wages; Ackerby 1992). Political actors soon turned their attention to earnings-related pensions in the 1950s, ushering in the greatest political conflict of the post-war period: the 'ATP Struggle' (*ATP-striden*). In the early post-war period, public employees and white-collar workers enjoyed generous occupational pensions while the majority of workers, mainly in industry, only had access to the flat-rate basic pension. Metalworkers, later supported by LO, were the first blue-collar group to demand earnings-related pensions on equal terms with white-collar workers (Molin 1965; Heclo 1974).

With blue-collar workers agitating for a legislative solution to the supplementary pensions question, the Social Democratic-Agrarian Party coalition government appointed several commissions of inquiry to study the issue. The first commission, appointed in 1947, issued its findings in 1950. Its proposal was based on pay-as-you-go pensions that would maintain their value over time. Any necessary savings (to fund future pensions as the system matured) would be achieved by setting contribution rates somewhat higher during the initial phases of the programme in order to cover the first pension payments (SOU No. 33, 1950). The proposal was highly controversial so the government appointed a new commission in 1951. The Social Democratic Minister of Social Affairs held out hope that supplementary pensions could be negotiated in the wage bargaining sphere, but LO voiced its scepticism (Erlander 1976).

At this point, the issue of equality between white-collar and blue-collar workers emerged as a key issue, especially for LO. Even if collective bargaining resulted in supplementary pensions for all blue-collar workers (which the centre-right parties and employers preferred), these would be fragmented and probably not as generous as those that already existed for white-collar workers and public sector employees. Consensus was emerging on the centre-left that pay-as-you-go financing should be combined with a collective pension fund as the basis for a universal, obligatory system. The SAP leadership and LO agreed to this solution in talks at Harpsund in 1955 (Erlander 1976).

In September 1955, the second pension commission proposal was issued (SOU No. 32, 1955). The proposal built on earlier commissions' work, proposing an obligatory system of earnings-related pensions with a central pension fund. A majority in the commission favoured this approach. By now, however, the lines of conflict were even clearer than in previous discussions: the centre-right parties, backed by the employers, preferred to improve basic pensions and leave earnings-related pensions to collective bargaining (Erlander 1976, pp. 126–139). Given the level of disagreement, the government appointed another commission of inquiry to respond to the most important criticisms as it formulated its legislative proposal (Molin 1965).

Elections to the Second Chamber were held in September 1956, further delaying the pension legislation. The pension issue and taxes dominated the campaign, with the SAP absorbing slight losses. The SAP-Agrarian Party government remained in power, however. The government continued its preparations for pension legislation, with the commission appointed the previous year issuing its report in February 1957 (SOU 1957a: 7). Again, the Social Democrats and LO supported the proposal for obligatory supplementary pensions. The Agrarian Party advocated a higher basic pension with voluntary top-ups, while the Liberals and Conservatives (backed by employers) pushed for collectively agreed pensions. Given this level of disagreement, the SAP could not be sure of legislative passage, especially without the support of its coalition partner, the Agrarian Party.

The centre-right parties now pushed for an advisory referendum, despite SAP opposition, hoping to mobilize support for a voluntary system. In October 1957, voters could choose between three 'lines':

> Line 1) the SAP proposal to include all wage earners in a pay-as-you-go (PAYGO) system with collectively managed pension funds to finance future pensions;
>
> Line 2) the Agrarian Party's proposal for a voluntary system; or
>
> Line 3) a system based on collectively negotiated occupational pensions advocated by the Liberals, Conservatives and employers. (Molin 1965)

The result of the referendum did not settle the issue because none of the alternatives received a majority of votes. The Social Democratic proposal (Line 1) received a plurality (45.8%), followed by the Liberal-Conservative proposal (Line 3, 35.3%) and the Agrarians' proposal (Line 2, 15%).

Both the SAP and centre-right claimed victory: the SAP argued that its alternative received the most votes, while the centre-right claimed that there was a majority in favour of voluntary provision. The referendum prompted the break-up of SAP-Agrarian coalition and a cabinet reshuffle. The SAP government invited the centre-right parties for talks to come to a common position on the pension issue, but these efforts failed. The SAP went ahead with its legislation, which then failed to pass in April 1958. The government had no choice but to call new elections, which were held in June 1958. The SAP gained slightly in the election and continued in government, but it did not have a majority in the Second Chamber. After a dramatic debate and vote in the Second Chamber, the legislation passed by one vote in April 1959 when a Liberal MP abstained (Molin 1965). The Conservative Party vowed to overturn the reform if it returned to power, but the Liberals soon accepted the reform, prompting the other parties to follow.

The ATP system was introduced in 1960. Employers paid 12% of payroll into the system, and wage earners earned pension rights based on the best 15 of 30 years of labour market participation. Contributions were set higher than pension costs, and the surplus capital accumulated in the state-run AP Funds. The ATP pension and the basic pension together paid about 65% of average wages for the typical wage earner.

Decentring the ATP Reform

Existing explanations of the ATP reform process highlight the political mobilization and superior power resources of the SAP and LO in determining the outcome (see, e.g., Esping-Andersen 1985). However, this explanation assumes that labour's superior numbers would have more or less automatically resulted in the introduction of a universal, PAYGO earnings-related pension scheme with collectively managed pension funds. It is equally plausible that labour would have chosen some other pension blueprint. In other words, existing accounts do not adequately explain how the shared meanings and beliefs of key actors guided their actions in the policy-making process shaped the ATP reform. Moreover, existing analyses of the ATP reform in particular and pension reform in general downplay or exclude the role of historical contingency. The ATP reform is a strong example of the importance of contingency: the reform passed because a single member of the opposition, despite strong pressure not to do so, abstained. Were it not for this abstention, the ATP reform as envisioned in the 1959 legislation would probably not have been introduced.

A decentred approach illuminates many of the lacunae in the ATP reform process. I focus on three of them here:

- the SAP's reform blueprint;
- the policy blueprints of the centre-right parties; and
- the decision of one Liberal MP to abstain in the final parliamentary vote.

The excellent secondary literature concerning the ATP reform (Molin 1965; Heclo 1974), as well as primary sources like memoirs and parliamentary documents, permits an analysis of the motivations, beliefs and reasoning of key participants in the reform process. As the next sections show, the ATP reform is rooted in the contingent beliefs of union members, union functionaries, pension experts and Social Democratic Party politicians. The centre-right parties were slower to form their own countervailing vision of what the supplementary pension should look like, and it was likewise shaped by the beliefs and experiences of both company directors, employers' representatives and key figures in the Liberal and Conservative parties. Finally, role of the Liberal MP who abstained in the 1959 parliamentary vote cannot be underestimated. Tore Königson broke with the leadership of his party because of his strongly held beliefs about democracy and fairness.

The Social Democratic Blueprint

Why did the leadership of the LO and SAP support an obligatory, universal system of supplementary pensions with publicly controlled pension funds? Labour parties have chosen different pension policy designs in other countries, so it was by no means foreordained that the SAP and LO would settle on this particular policy blueprint. The SAP's adoption of the LO's policy blueprint was also not foreordained. Indeed, the SAP leadership was sceptical of the LO blueprint because of its projected effect on public finances. This section discusses the development of two opposing narratives concerning how the supplementary pension issue should be solved, providing detail about the traditions, beliefs and practices that drove the legislative policy-making process sketched in the previous section.

Over two decades, a joint SAP-LO perspective emerged from the bottom-up actions of union members, SAP members of parliament and SAP/LO elites. This perspective relied on the norms of the 'strong society' and the belief in a Social Democratic 'Harvest Time' in the pursuit of universal, obligatory supplementary pensions where all wage earners enjoyed the same conditions. Moreover, the accumulation of capital in a state-run pension fund would create the conditions for democratic influence over investment.

The idea of obligatory, universal, earnings-related pensions originated in the union movement in the 1940s amid collective bargaining conflict. In the 1940s, local branches of the Metalworkers Union began to demand the same pension rights as those enjoyed by salaried employees and blue-collar workers with more negotiating power. Workers voiced their demands in local and regional union forums, and these demands eventually reached the national leadership. Grass-roots union demands for statutory supplementary pensions soon reached parliament and national trade union meetings. A Social Democratic MP with a union background (Åkerström) took up the issue in 1944, introducing a parliamentary motion to study the feasibility of introducing earnings-related pensions that would cover all employees. Progress was slow, but grass-roots pressure on the LO leadership continued at the 1946 LO conference. By now, the Metalworkers Union had settled on a position that favoured an obligatory and universal statutory supplementary pension scheme (Heclo 1974, pp. 232–234; Molin 1965).

The Metalworkers' perspective was met with some scepticism, both among other blue-collar unions and the SAP. By 1947, as noted above, the issue had garnered sufficient attention that the Social Democratic government established a commission of inquiry to study the issue. In keeping with the tradition of the 'strong state', the government appointed experts and members of affected interests (three from the employers' side and three from the union side) with the intention of forging a workable, expertise-based compromise. As Heclo (1974, p. 234) notes, the government viewed the issue as 'non-political' and 'semi-technical' because it was delegated to the Ministry of Commerce and handled by experts and representatives of unions and employers. The Metalworkers' perspective met with serious opposition, not only from employers who opposed the establishment of a state-run pension fund, but also from white-collar workers who already had their own occupational pensions and feared that a statutory system would result in losses for them. The representatives from the Metalworkers Union concluded that employers would block any effort to negotiate occupational pensions, and this added to their resolve in pursuing a legislative solution (SOU No. 33, 1950). The situation came to a head at the 1950 LO Congress. By this time, several of the local union representatives who had agitated for occupational pensions in the 1940s had achieved important positions within the LO, and they pressed for a legislative solution. A total of nine important motions were introduced at the Congress, all arguing for a legislative approach. In particular, the motions argued that the new system should abolish unfair differences between workers and salaried employees. The LO Congress declared its support for a legislative solution to the supplementary pensions issue (Heclo 1974, p. 235).

The commission of inquiry appointed by the SAP minority government in 1951 now included representatives from the main parties, the unions (including a member from the Metalworkers Union, Paul Steen, who had been influential in pushing the issue in the 1940s) and the Employers. As the commission started its work, Social Democratic MPs with union background continued to push the issue in parliament by introducing motions calling for legislative action on supplementary pensions, but the party leadership was wary of the legislative route.

Union functionaries, led by representatives of the Metalworkers, continued to refine their blueprint for obligatory supplementary pensions as the commission worked, even as the SAP leadership remained hesitant to push for a legislative solution. The commission established in 1951 was, like the previous one, under the supervision of the Ministry of Commerce, and it included several of the same members. Even though the commission failed to produce a consensus on reform, the unions' position, backed by an increasing number of SAP rank and file, had hardened, and the SAP leadership began to take notice. It was now clear that key voices within LO, pushed by its most powerful union, the Metalworkers, believed strongly that collective bargaining would never produce supplementary pensions for all workers under equal conditions. In 1953, the Minister of Social Affairs (Gunnar Sträng) consulted with Axel Strand and Arne Geijer about the feasibility of collectively bargained pensions. Strand pointed out that large firms preferred collectively negotiated pensions because they could accumulate capital within the firm to fund pensions, and this capital could finance their operations (Erlander 1976, p. 133). Both expressed their conviction that it would not work (Erlander 1976, p. 132).

At this point, the equality between white-collar and blue-collar workers emerged as a key issue. Even if collective bargaining resulted in supplementary pensions for blue-collar workers, these would be fragmented and probably not as generous as those that already existed for white-collar workers and public sector employees. Consensus was emerging that pay-as-you-go should be combined with funding, and funding should be social rather than company based. The SAP met with representatives from the unions at Harpsund in June 1955. The LO representative argued that collectively negotiated pensions would lead to inequalities and hinder labour market mobility. A key Social Democrat, John Ericsson i Kinna (later Minister of Social Affairs), argued that equality between blue-collar and white-collar workers was of crucial importance. Other central Social Democrats weighed in with their support for an obligatory system with funding. Per Edwin Sköld argued for funding so that the government could steer investment. Gustav Cederwall agreed. As Erlander notes, promoting a uniform system based on both PAYGO and funding would achieve both social policy goals and consolidate the support of the labour movement for such a solution. As Erlander states:

> We were convinced that Kinna was right. It would be possible to gain the labour movement's support for a radical proposal. This would also decrease the popularity of the non-socialist parties. It would be difficult for them to oppose the demand that manual workers should have occupational pensions on equal terms with salaried personnel. (Erlander 1976, p. 137)

The SAP and LO began to converge around a common line. However, when the commission released its findings in September 1955, it was clear that there was no consensus, however. Even if the SAP leadership was wary of the fiscal implications of a major pension reform and its implications for the coalition with the Agrarian Party, they began to take the union position more seriously.

The SAP-Agrarian Party government (in coalition since 1951) responded by appointing a new commission in 1956, this time including all of the political parties. Now the political parties could not ignore the issue, which created a dilemma for the SAP because it feared losing white-collar votes and undermining their coalition with the Agrarian Party. By September 1956, however, the Social Democratic Prime Minister Erlander was fully in support of a legislative solution (Erlander 1976). The next commission was largely an exercise in formulating the basis for legislation. When the commission released its report in February 1957, the SAP and LO were on the same line.

The Non-socialist Blueprint

The positions of the non-socialist parties/organized business developed more slowly and were often at odds with each other. By 1955, however, the non-socialists, backed by the Employers Organization (*Svenska arbetsgivareföreningen*, SAF), had formed a loose alliance around the belief that improved basic pensions combined with voluntary earnings-related pensions were the best solution to the problem of expanding coverage to blue-collar workers. They vehemently opposed the establishment of a large, state-controlled fund because they claimed it would choke investment and lead to a state monopoly of the credit market. SAF was slow to formulate a detailed position; with legislation looming, however, they set up a committee to formulate their position. SAF had already signalled their willingness to take action on supplementary pensions, but they were alarmed by proposals to locate supplementary pensions in the state sphere and to create a large, state-run pension fund (Heclo 1974, p. 235; Molin 1965).

How did SAF counter the narrative supplied by LO and SAF? SAF constructed a narrative in which only the private sector could provide the economic growth and resources that could be used to finance improved old-age provision. A key precondition was that the private business sector be allowed to 'develop freely' and this precluded both the nationalization of supplementary provision and the build-up of large, state-controlled pension funds (SOU No. 16, 1957b, p. 230).

SAF made three central points. The first was that supplementary pensions were not a 'social issue' which the state should address. Earnings-related pensions were instead an issue to be solved by employers and unions. The second issue was that obligatory pensions would deprive citizens of freedom of choice in terms of how they wanted to organize their own supplementary retirement position. Third, the employer's completely rejected a centralized pension fund because they claimed it would completely dominate the capital market.

Sven Hydén, the SAF member of the commission, emphasized SAF's interest in solving the pension problem, citing its previous initiatives in this area. Hydén repeated SAF's position that collective agreements were the best solution to the pension problem.

> In recent decades, employers in Sweden have shown their interest in solving the pension problem. The number of employers participating in SPP [a pension scheme] and other insurance-based arrangements for salaried employees has increased. Direct provision for manual workers has increased both quantitatively and qualitatively. SAF presented a proposal in 1954 to solve the pension problem for manual workers based on the idea of collectively agreed pensions. (SOU No. 7, 1957a, p. 161)

SAF supported improvements in the universal basic pension, but they drew the line at expanding the role of the state in supplementary pensions (SOU No. 16, 1957b, p. 231). Employers accepted that it was the state's responsibility to provide reasonable basic old-age pension provision, but it vehemently opposed any attempt by the state to provide earnings-related pensions. The employers argued that earnings-related pensions were not a 'social issue' (*social angelägenhet*), but rather, something that should be decided between employers and unions. In short, earnings-related pensions belonged in the realm of collective bargaining.

SAF were even more critical of the idea to establish a state-run pension fund, warning that such a fund over time would equal one-third of privately owned national wealth and would cover two-thirds of the credit market at the time and would eventually dominate the credit market. SAF argued that interest rates and lending conditions would largely be decided by the policies of the pension fund. Mortgage institutions would run the risk of being transformed into branch offices of the pension fund. If the central fund would be involved, as was envisaged, in providing credit to the economy, individual companies would become strongly dependent on the central fund. In other words, the central fund of the size planned in the proposal would become a 'powerful instrument for long-term state control of the economy' (SOU No. 16, 1957b, pp. 233–243).

Other business groups echoed this position. The Organization for Retail Employers (*Handelns Arbetsgivarorganisation*) pointed to the 'enormous concentration of resources that would mean that the state would completely control the capital market' (SOU No. 16, 1957b, p. 249). Small business owners (*Sveriges hantverks- och småindustriorganisation*) also vehemently opposed the establishment of the central fund. Even though the fund would be administered by representatives for the state, wage earners and employers, small business owners argued that the central fund would pose a serious threat to small business owners because it would create a de facto state monopoly of the capital market (SOU No. 16, 1957b, p. 255). The central fund would also prevent small business owners from relying on their regular sources of credit: small banks, business banks, etc. This would mean that small business owners would have to contribute to the growth of this central fund, but the state and large companies would decide how the capital in the fund would be invested. The organization thus vigorously opposed the establishment of the giant fund which would give the state 'total control over the private sector and a monopoly position in the capital markets' (SOU No. 16, 1957b, p. 256).

The Contingency of the Parliamentary Vote

One of the key details concerning the passage of the 1959 ATP reform legislation concerns the role of a single Liberal member of the Second Chamber in Parlia As discussed, the SAP picked up seats in the June 1958 election, but it did not have a majority in the Second Chamber (the SAP had a clear majority in the First Chamber). Even with the support of the Communist Party, the SAP was one vote short of a majority. It was by no means clear that the government could count on a majority when it presented its legislative proposal. Uncertainty reigned until January 1959, when Ture Königson, a Liberal member of the Second Chamber, announced that he would not vote against the government's ATP legislation. Königson had a working class background and was an

LO member. This did not mean he wholeheartedly favoured the ATP reform; Königson had worked closed with his Liberal colleagues in formulating the Liberal pension position. However, Königson justified his vote by arguing that the electorate had rejected his own party's proposal, and it was important to reach some kind of solution. Königson's thinking was that even though the Liberal pension blueprint was better, the Social Democratic plan was better than no plan at all. According to Königson, the June election meant that the voters

> rejected our proposal....it is especially significant that those who are directly affected by the proposal chose the system favoured by the social democrats....A clear majority of wage-earners has said that they want a pay-as-you-go system, and I thus yield solidaristically to this....a 'no' would mean that my fellow wage-earners would be able to call me a traitor to our common purpose, and rightly so. (*Dagens Nyheter*, 23 January 1959)

Königsson also complained that his own party was not willing to compromise on the issue of funding, whereas the Social Democrats were willing to make concessions.

> The reason that there was no agreement (between the social democrats and the non socialists) has less to do with the social democrats than the non-socialists' belief that there will always be a social democratic government in this country. I would like to say that now, the chance of this is great because of the way the Liberal Party is now behaving. (*Dagens Nyheter*, 23 January 1959)

Königson was unanimously and strongly criticized by his party colleagues and expelled from the Liberal Party (Heclo 1974, pp. 245–246). The ATP legislation passed both chambers in May 1959.

Pension Reform in the 1990s

The 1994/98 reform of the ATP pension system has been extensively studied (Anderson 2001; Lundberg 2003; Anderson and Immergut 2007) and need not be rehearsed in detail here. The goal of this section is to decentre the reform of ATP in the 1990s by highlighting how dilemmas associated with the maturation of the ATP system, as well as the beliefs and practices associated with ATP, explain the 1994/1998 legislation.

The ATP system was established in 1960 and quickly formed the backbone of old-age provision. Together with the basic pension, a full ATP pension would provide 65% of previous income (the best 15 of 30 years) up to the ATP ceiling (equal to average earnings). According to the generous transition rules, the system would approach maturity by the early 1990s. The AP Funds also grew quickly; by 1992, these funds stood at SEK 512 billion, or 35% of GDP.

By the 1980s, however, economists and actuaries pointed to growing weaknesses in the ATP system. Two things worried the experts: the growing costs of benefits relative to income from contributions, and the increasing number of wage earners with earnings above the ATP ceiling (the ceiling was equal to average wages). In the late 1980s, rising expenditures for ATP pensions dramatically reduced the strength of the AP Funds as the Funds began to finance a growing share of pension benefits. This development triggered an intense policy debate among experts (mainly economists) about how to reform the system (Anderson 2001).

Expert criticism of the ATP system created a dilemma for the SAP. The ATP system had not been designed for a context of low economic growth and increasing life expectancy. If the ATP system could not provide adequate old-age provision for the working and middle classes, its legitimacy would be doubted. In 1985, the SAP government set up a commission to study reform of the ATP system. In keeping with the norms of the 'strong society', the commission included representatives from the political parties and affected interests. After five years of work, the commission largely agreed on a common definition of what the ATP's weaknesses were, but it could not agree on a reform proposal. The Federation of White-Collar Unions (TCO) opposed any departure from the 15/30 rule for benefit calculation (SOU No. 76, 1990). Many TCO functionaries and members considered the 1959 ATP reform to have been disadvantageous for white-collar workers, and they resolved to not make the same mistake again (Lundberg 2003; Interview with Sigge Goodin, May 1994).

The issue lay dormant until a non-socialist coalition led by the Conservative Party took office after a close election in 1991. The 1991 election loss was symptomatic of the SAP's waning parliamentary dominance; Harvest Time was definitely over. The SAP leadership thus agreed to cooperate with the four governing parties on a comprehensive pension reform. The government and SAP formed a parliamentary group in 1991; the SAP got two members, and other parties got one member each. The Liberal Minister of Social Affairs, Bo Könberg, chaired the group.

The five-party group (representing 80% of Parliament) agreed on the principles for the reformed pension system in June 1994. Supplementary pensions would remain obligatory and universal, but the benefit formula changed significantly: a defined contribution lifetime earnings formula replaced ATP's defined benefits based on the best 15 of 30 years of labour market participation. Payroll contribution levels remained stable, but would now be shared by employers and employees. An important novelty was the introduction of mandatory individual investment accounts (the premium reserve): 2.5 percentage points of contributions flow into individual accounts that allow pension savers to choose their own investments from a range of approved options. A state agency would administer the individual investment accounts. 1998 legislation adopted under an SAP minority government provided the detailed rules for the premium reserve and the transition to the new system.

All participants agreed that avoidance of political conflict was essential. This shared understanding meant that the five parties were committed to finding common ground that would allow all parties to claim some sort of victory: the SAP could claim that the reform stabilized the ATP system to make it fit for the future, and the four non-socialist parties could claim important gains (see Anderson and Immergut 2007 for details). All four parties wanted to reduce the size and influence of the AP Funds, introduce some sort of individual premium reserve, replace the 15/30 rule with a lifetime earnings benefit formula and switch from DB to DC. The SAP had to compromise on the premium reserve and the reduced role of the AP Funds. Framework legislation on the principles of the new pension system was adopted in June 1994.

The reduced role of the AP Funds reflects the waning of the 'strong society' perspective. The norm of rational, expertise-based planning certainly continued, but this was not coupled with the idea that the state should steer society as it had in the past. By the 1990s, the AP Funds had ceased to finance large-scale public projects like the expansion of social housing in the 1960s and 1970s (the 'Million Program'). Instead, the AP Funds functioned more as passive buffer bunds than tools for an active investment policy.

Existing explanations of this far-reaching reform emphasize the role of party politics and path dependence in shaping the 1994/98 pension reform. The declining political power of the SAP provided an opportunity for the non-socialist parties to pursue substantial reform, but the latter's efforts were constrained by the sheer weight of existing pension promises. Elected politicians worried about re-election thus had to pursue a reform that minimized electoral retribution at the hand of voters who stood to lose in the reformed system (Schudi 2005; Lundberg 2003; Anderson and Immergut 2007). This type of argument obscures the role of actors' world views and beliefs, however, and it ignores the importance of contingency. Decentring the reform process allows us to see how actors' contingent actions and beliefs explain the form and content of the reform.

One of the keys to the passage of the 1994/1998 reform was the role of the parliamentary group that negotiated the initial reform blueprint and its subsequent implementation. The choice for a parliamentarian-only commission in 1991 was followed by the establishment of a parliamentary implementation group with members of the five parties backing the reform. Why was this procedural approach chosen? Interviews with key participants in the policy-making process emphasize that the choice was part of a strategy to de-politicize the reform process and facilitate a compromise. As Bo Könberg put it, 'both sides wanted to reach agreement' (Interview, February 2000). The specific nature of the pension policy area was one of the reasons to do this. For example, when asked whether it was more important to reach cross-party agreement on ATP than in other areas of social policy the SAP Parliamentary Group Leader at the time, Jan Bergqvist, put it this way:

> Yes, because pensions are different from other kinds of social policy in that changes will affect people for 20 years into the future.

Bergqvist justified the choice for a parliamentary group as follows:

> The reality is that there was a commission in the 1980s, but it proposed nothing. And this (policy area) is very sensitive. And so they did not dare propose anything. …it was just too hard. There was no awareness of crisis. There was a sense that all were disappointed, and there was a recognition that the pension system had to change.

Bergqvist also pointed to the advantage of the parliamentary group for depoliticizing the issue:

> We could have exploited this as an election issue. And we were concerned with keeping the basics of the ATP system… If the SAP had waited until

it had a majority, we would only have a slim majority, and this would not be a stable system. And so with broad agreement, it's more stable, even if everyone is not happy with everything. Everyone accepts the main principles.' (Interview, March 1995)

The Conservative Party (Margit Gennser) member of the parliamentary group expressed similar beliefs and experiences.

I have never been part of a commission that has had such a positive cooperative climate. It has functioned more as an academic seminar than a political gathering. ... 'You can't make short term savings in a long-term pension system. Otherwise you don't have credibility....I think one should stick to an agreement. (Interview, May 1994)

A Social Democratic member of the Parliamentary Standing Committee for Social Insurance, Margareta Israelsson, also expressed a belief in the importance of creating a stable agreement that all could support in order to minimize politicization:

There has been an agreement among five parties...and we will keep our word on what we agree on. The reason for this is the unstable political situation that there are not clear majorities, and the other is that a change in the pension system affects so incredibly many people, for such a long time, so that it would be very stupid if we made a decision now, and then if a new government comes in the Autumn, then there would be a new proposal, and then if that government falls....and we can't have this. So we are trying to come to an agreement. (Interview, May 1994)

Israelsson acknowledged that some aspects of the reform were difficult for the SAP to accept, but concessions were made in order to reach a stable compromise:

So when everyone began to examine how we could get this through, there was give and take, and I would think that when one comes so far, that one could be less strict about some things....and it's clear that it has been difficult for us to let go of some things, but otherwise maybe it would not have worked.

Israelsson's reasoning was typical of the approach of leading Social Democrats: supporting a compromise that would preserve core SAP principles, especially universal, obligatory supplementary pensions:

When one tries to find a way to agree when there are always different standpoints, because my party, SAP, we want to have a universal system, a system for everyone. An obligatory system. This is our basic principle. And of course this will be related to what one has paid in. There are changes, but it is still a universal system. (Interview, May 1994)

This reasoning is based on the belief that the ATP reform was one of the crowning achievements of social democratic social policy reformism. The SAP owned the ATP reform; it was a central part of the SAP's identity, and probably the most important example of the SAP's ability to shape society.

A Liberal Party member of the same standing committee, Sigge Goodin, expressed similar views concerning the urgency of reaching a stable agreement across the blocs:

We have discussed the pension issue back and forth for ten years. This particular proposal is a compromise which is far-reaching for all parties. One has given up on many principles because one sees now that the money is starting to run out. Something has to be done in good time.

In this case, one realized that we have a minority government and we don't know what the election (in September 1994) will bring. We usually joke and say that we can't trust the voters, and in cases like this where it is so important, we have to make the kind of decision so that we know that it will hold after the Autumn if we have a change in government. (Interview, May 1994)

Conclusion

This analysis presented in this chapter decentres two important pension reform processes in Sweden: the 1959 adoption of the ATP reform and the reform of this system in 1994/1998. By highlighting how individual actors' beliefs, practices and worldviews shaped the final reform package in each case, the analysis explains several of the lacunae present in existing explanations of both reforms. Existing scholarship on the political-economic drivers of pension reform depicts boundedly rational political actors making intentional choices in the context of identifiable partisan, institutional and demographic constraints. The two case studies analysed here—the 1959 adoption of the far-reaching ATP reform and the 1994/1998 revision of the ATP system—demonstrate that outcomes in both cases are much more open and contingent that existing research allows.

In both cases, the beliefs and practices of both elite and grass-roots actors shaped the content and direction of reform. The 1959 ATP reform was the result of at least two decades of bottom-up mobilization by union members and functionaries who sought a legislative solution to the inequalities between occupational pension provision for manual workers and salaried employees. Union and Social Democratic Party leaders were slow to embrace this position because of fiscal concerns. Ultimately, however, beliefs about equality, the growing influence of social democracy and confidence in a 'strong state' capable of mobilizing public resources for social policy goals persuaded key actors to pursue a legislative solution to occupational pension provision. The 1959 ATP reform is also a spectacular case of belief-based contingency: the reform passed by one vote in the Second Chamber because a Liberal MP abstained for reasons for democratic process.

The beliefs and practices of key policy-makers also shaped the 994/998 revision of the ATP system. Five parties representing 90% of voters agreed on the reform, and all key plays agreed that wide consensus was essential because of the long-term nature of pension policy. Perhaps even more important was the widespread desire to avoid conflict and prevent pension reform from becoming an election campaign issue. Memories of the bitter conflict surrounding the 1959 ATP reform were still important three decades later, especially after the failure to forge a reform compromise in the 1980s. The legacy of conflict shaped participants' world views concerning the importance of compromise.

References

Ackerby, S. (1992). *Pensionsfrågan. Bilaga 12 till La 'ngtidsutredningen 1992.* Stockholm: Ministry of Finance.

Anderson, K. M. (2001). The Politics of Retrenchment in a Social Democratic Welfare State. *Comparative Political Studies, 34*(9), 1063–1091.

Anderson, K. M., & Immergut, E. M. (2007). Sweden: After Social Democratic Hegemony. In E. M. Immergut, K. M. Anderson, & I. Schultze (Eds.), *The Handbook of Pension Politics in Western Europe*. Oxford: Oxford University Press.

Baldwin, P. (1990). *The Politics of Social Solidarity: Class Bases of the European Welfare State 1875–1975.* Cambridge: Cambridge University Press.

Bevir, M., & Needham, C. (2017). Decentering Social Policy: Narratives, Resitance, and Practices. *International Journal of Sociology and Social Policy*, 2–19.

Bevir, M., & Rhodes, R. A. W. (2010). *The State as Cultural Practice*. Oxford: Oxford University Press.
Bonoli, G. (2000). *The Politics of Pension Reform. Institutions and Policy Change in Western Europe*. Cambridge: Cambridge University Press.
Erlander, T. (1976). *Tage Erlander. 1955–1960*. Stockholm: Tidens Förlag.
Esping-Andersen, G. (1985). *Politics Against Markets. The Social Democratic Road to Power*. Princeton: Princeton University Press.
Heclo, H. (1974). *Modern Social Politics in Britain and Sweden*. New Haven, CT: Yale University Press.
Immergut, E. M., Anderson, K. M., & Schultze, I. (Eds.). (2017). *The Handbook of Pension Politics in Western Europe*. Oxford: Oxford University Press.
Lindberg, I. (1999). *Välfärdens idéer*. Stockholm: Atlas.
Lundberg, U. (2003). *Juvelen i kronan. Socialdemokraterna och den allmänna pensionen*. Stockholm: Hjalmarsson and Högberg.
Molin, B. (1965). *Tjänstepensionsfrågan. En studie i svensk partipolitik*. Göteborg: Scandinavian University Books.
OECD. (2015). *Pensions at a Glance*. Paris: OECD.
Orloff, A. S. (1993). *The Politics of Pensions. A Comparative Analysis of Britain, Canada, and the United States, 1880–1940*. Madison: University of Wisconsin Press.
Pierson, P. (1994). *Dismantling the Welfare State*. Cambridge: Cambridge University Press.
Rothstein, B., & Westerhål, L. V. (Eds.). (2005). *Bortom den starka statens politik?* Stockholm: SNS Foerlag.
Schludi, M. (2005). *The Reform of Bismarckian Pension Systems. A Comparison of Pension Politics in Austria, France, Germany, Italy and Sweden*. Amsterdam: Amsterdam University Press.
Statens Offentliga Utredninar. (1950). *Allmän pensionsförsäkring. Undersökningar och förslag av Pensionsutredningen. Principbetänkande*. SOU 1950: 33.
Statens Offentliga Utredninar. (1955). *Allmän pensionsförsäkring. Förslaget avgivet av pensionsutredningen*. SOU 1955: 32.
Statens Offentliga Utredninar. (1957a). *Förbättrad pensionering. Betänkande av allmänna pensionsberedningen*. SOU 1957: 7.
Statens Offentliga Utredningar. (1957b). *Remissyttranden över allmänna pensionsberedningens betänkande om förbättrad pensionering*. SOU 1957: 16.
Statens Offentliga Utredningar. (1990). *Allmän pension*. SOU 1990: 76.
Waddington, J. (2004). Charing the Dimensions of the Merger Process. In J. Waddington (Ed.), *Restructuring Representation: The Merger Process and trade Union Structural Development in Ten Countries*. Brussels: Peter Lang.

CHAPTER 8

What Are the Consequences of Incessant Reform? Losing Trust, Policy Capacity and Institutional Memory in the Queensland Core Executive

Anne Tiernan

INTRODUCTION

As anyone who has ever visited or lived in Australia knows, the Christmas–New Year holidays are sacrosanct. Australians may work some of the longest hours in the developed world, but they remain seriously committed to their summer ritual of rest and relaxation. So Campbell Newman's announcement on 5 January 2015 of an early Queensland state election—to be held on 31 January—carried an inherent risk for a Premier whose approval ratings among constituents had dived.

Just three years previously, Newman had led the Liberal National Party (LNP) to an historic victory over the deeply unpopular Labor government of Anna Bligh (Rhodes and Tiernan 2016). Despite not holding a seat in Queensland's legislative assembly at the time, the former Lord Mayor of Brisbane won the inner-city electorate of Ashgrove from

A. Tiernan (✉)
Griffith University, Brisbane, QLD, Australia

a popular incumbent Labor member by a margin of 5.7%. Although his party secured seventy-eight seats in the eighty-nine seat unicameral parliament, and Labor just seven, Newman's electorate would again be in contention at the 2015 poll.

As family and friends swam, read novels and flicked between channels to watch the cricket and tennis, I spent my summer holidays closely observing and providing regular media commentary on Queensland politics for the Australian Broadcasting Corporation (ABC). A substantial correction was expected following Labor's landslide defeat in 2012. Most analysts predicted Premier Newman's pugnacious style and unfortunate tendency to 'pick fights' with key constituencies (Borbidge and Sheldon 2015) were likely to hinder his prospects of being returned in Ashgrove. This outcome became more likely when the former Labor member Kate Jones announced she would recontest, challenging Newman for the seat. But virtually no one—including (despite their protests to the contrary) the Labor Party,[1] predicted the extent of the voter backlash against the LNP. For the second time in three years, Queenslanders delivered a resounding rebuke to a sitting government, electing a hung parliament—leaving the LNP with forty-two seats and Labor with forty-four (a net gain of thirty-six seats). Newman lost Ashgrove and subsequently resigned as Leader of the LNP. After more than ten days of negotiation with three independents, Labor leader Annastacia Palaszczuk emerged with the support necessary to form minority government. She was sworn in as Queensland's thirty-ninth Premier on 14 February 2015.

From my vantage point outside government, the interregnum between polling day and the Premier's swearing-in revealed much that I want to reflect on in this chapter. The public service, which had been dramatically reshaped by Newman (including wholesale replacement of the senior leadership cadre; a net reduction of 14,000 public service positions; and sweeping machinery of government and policy changes embracing contestability and marketisation), appeared frozen. Its senior leaders—few of whom had prior experience of state government (or, it has to be said, a shared narrative of Westminster governance)—seemed uncertain about how to navigate the caretaker period and the ambiguities of the electoral result. It seemed to me that few preparations had been made for a potential change of government. As I reassured journalists and ABC listeners that Queensland's Westminster-style system had conventions to cope with the prevailing uncertainties, I became concerned those conventions might not be fully understood at the most senior levels of government. This chapter documents the decades of disruption and 'reform' that provided the context for my concerns. It attempts to understand how this came to be so and to explain why, when I was invited to give a dinner address to the newly appointed Queensland Director-Generals (DGs) in November 2015, I described myself—an academic—as the institutional memory of the Queensland Public Service.

The chapter is structured as follows. This introduction is followed by a discussion of the decentred research method used to develop the Queensland case. The third section presents an overview that covers the period from 1987 to 2005—including from my own perspective of returning to work in the Queensland Public Service in 1994. I show how this historical context shaped the beliefs and practices of political-administrator actors in more recent administrations. I trace my journey from official to participant-observer of governance in Queensland, focussing on stories about the business of government during the final term of the Beattie government, the Bligh years, and under Campbell Newman. The chapter concludes by considering the dilemmas revealed by a decentred perspective and reflects on some of the challenges inherent to being an 'active member researcher' (Adler and Adler 1987).

This chapter is not an exercise in narrow parochialism. The Queensland experience provides an opportunity to explore the cumulative effects of machinery of government change and successive waves of public-sector 'reform' on the capacity and institutional memory of a Westminster-style core executive. I review how the traditions, beliefs and practices of the central networks that comprise executive government in Queensland were affected by four changes of Premier, a slew of administrative reforms, and one largely anticipated (2012) and another largely unexpected (2015) change of government. The Queensland case is a microcosm in which to consider the medium-term implications and impact of frequent, discontinuous change and the dilemmas posed by contending traditions on the capacity for executive governance.

THEORY AND METHOD

This chapter presents a decentred analysis of reform and change in the central courts that surround political leaders in Queensland. I construct a first-person account from notebooks, personal observations and stories that key core executive actors—senior officials, ministerial advisers and ministers—have told me about the Cabinet process, about the role of the public service and about relationships between ministers and officials. I present a story about the cumulative impact that a period of turbulence and instability has wrought on the composition, capacity and performance of the state's central core executive networks. It is difficult to overstate the extent of the changes: wholesale turnover of successive leadership cadres of government departments; the steadily decreasing tenure of political leaders, ministers and their private office staff; the making and remaking of the machinery of government; and the sometimes-wanton destruction of the 'storage locations' of institutional memory. The resulting portrait is one of professional disorientation and bewilderment, of sadness and disappointment at how practices and conventions have deteriorated and how the 'rules of the game' became unclear and contested—creating uncertainty and a pervasive discourse of anxiety and 'fear'.

The ethnographic method used to develop my decentred account of reform and change in Queensland derives from Adler and Adler's (1987) analysis of membership roles in field research. I draw on their concept of the 'active member researcher'—who 'does more than participate in the social activities of the group; they take part in the core activities of the group… Instead of merely sharing the status of insiders, they interact as colleagues: co-participants in a joint endeavour' (Adler and Adler 1987: 50). I have been an 'active member researcher' who has worked closely with the political-administrative networks at the centre of Queensland government (see Fig. 8.1) for the past twenty years in roles that have included: as a colleague; four years as a member of the Board of the Queensland Public Service Commission; a consultant; a professional educator; a researcher; a confidante; and now a 'critical friend'.[2]

My range of roles has spanned six governments: Goss, Borbidge, Bligh, Beattie, Newman and now Palaszczuk (see Fig. 8.2). My 'insider affiliation' (Adler and Adler 1987: 3) differentiates my approach from more observational forms of field research and administrative ethnography. To the extent possible in such a fraught operating environment, I am a trusted member of the cohort of individuals that has passed through Queensland's central core executive networks—the continuity amidst ceaseless change.

That I have served in these different roles is itself a local tradition. Griffith University was an active participant in the reforms that helped to modernise politics and public administration in Queensland from the

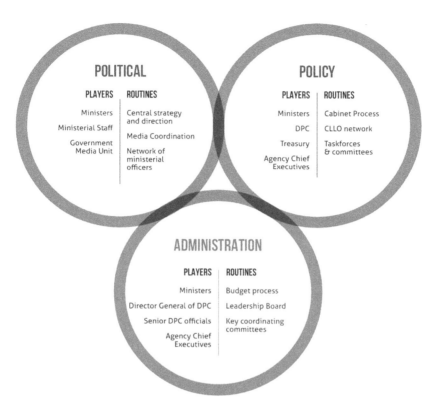

Fig. 8.1 The central networks of Queensland's core executive

late 1980s (see, e.g., Hogan 2016). I am heir to a tradition of engaged scholarship that derives from the practices of a cohort of academics who had played active roles in reforming Commonwealth administration in the late 1970s and who were attracted to Queensland in the early 1980s (see Davis and Rhodes 2014: 22–24). These researchers became part of political-administrative networks, and grew a generation of scholars who were comfortable, and indeed expected to span the boundaries of research and practice. The chapter draws on documentary and interview data collected in the course of my evolving affiliation with the networks under study. It presents an 'insider's story'—comparable to Norell's (2007) account of governance in the Swedish city of Karlstad.

Ministry	Party	Period
Goss	Labor	7 December 1989 – 19 February 1996
Borbidge	National-Liberal Coalition	19 February 1996 – 26 June 1998
Beattie	Labor	26 June 1998 – 13 September 2007
Bligh	Labor	13 September 2007 – 26 March 2012
Newman	Liberal National Party	26 March 2012 – 14 February 2015
Palaszczuk	Labor	14 February 2015 – present

Fig. 8.2 Queensland governments—1989 to present

Decentred analysis produces detailed accounts of the beliefs and practices of key actors—the stories they tell and the meanings they make from their everyday work (Bevir and Rhodes 2016; and Chapter 1 above). It seeks to understand and explain evolving patterns of policy and decision-making by focusing on people's interpretations of events and interactions—recognising their beliefs and actions are informed by traditions: inherited beliefs and practices received during socialisation about 'how things work around here'. Decentred analysis proceeds from the understanding that people's actions arise from and are informed by their beliefs, which themselves derive from the narratives and traditions that shape those beliefs (Bevir and Rhodes 2016). I am especially interested in the forms of knowledge that actors use to interpret and create governance practices and in how they respond when confronted by 'dilemmas'—new ideas, information or experience that challenge existing beliefs, forcing them to reflect on, reinterpret and adapt their beliefs and related traditions.

The dataset used to construct my account of reform in Queensland comprises interviews, participant observation and other data collected over the course of my career in government and at the University. It includes documentary sources to which I had access during my various roles.[3] I cannot offer a complete chronology, but personal notebooks that capture meetings and discussions with key actors, projects and events that I have worked on with them over the period, enable me to produce 'scenes' from key events. I develop a 'collective portrait' of how these shaped beliefs and practices (Corbett 2014). They help to explain how we got to now.

Although many of my dealings have been with governing elites—ministers, their senior staff and agency heads—my teaching, consultancy and 'critical friend' work brings me into contact with a wide range of officials, staffers, parliamentarians and others. My dataset includes documentary sources, biography, memoir and the first-hand accounts of key protagonists—whether in parliament, media interviews, public speeches, etc. Where appropriate, I include links to interviews publicly available on the 'Queensland Speaks'[4] website.

I joined the Queensland Public Service from a post in the Commonwealth government in September 1994. A Queenslander, I was thrilled to be returning home after years in Canberra. My path back home had been circuitous. In 1988, I was a first-year teacher at a state secondary school in Central Queensland. My petit-bourgeois upbringing—my girls-only Catholic school and matriarchal family—proved poor preparation for what then was mandatory 'country service' for graduate teachers. I would have gone anywhere rather than a mining town. But when I graduated in 1987 there were, quite simply, no jobs. You took what you were offered, because 'there wouldn't be another chance', as the Regional Director of Education in Central Queensland told me over the phone.

First Encounters

Queensland's Department of Education was my first brush with bureaucracy, and they fit the stereotype: paternal, rule-bound and perpetually ominous. I was determined to escape its power to determine where I would live and work. Opportunity presented when I spied an ad for the Commonwealth public service graduate programme in one of the newspapers that I rushed to purchase every Saturday from the town's newsagent. A posse of fellow teachers joined me to travel to Rockhampton to sit the entrance examination. Incredibly, I received offers of employment from two federal departments: Attorney-General's and Finance. I chose Finance on the advice of a friend of my sister, who had gone to Canberra five years earlier.

I had no understanding of, or background in, government or public policy processes—or anything really, looking back. I did not appreciate that Finance was then the epicentre of the Hawke–Keating government's reform agenda: I was just exhilarated to have escaped another three years in a mining town that every single day had been an intolerable assault on my nineteen-year-old sensibilities—which, I will concede, were easily offended. I still cannot account for why I was selected, other than perhaps having blitzed the test. Peers in my graduate cohort were infinitely better qualified; more serious; and career-focussed. Most had double degrees from Australia's elite universities and a number had graduate qualifications. I had not set foot in a university, although the Brisbane College of Advanced Education (BCAE) where I had studied teaching was in the process of being incorporated into the Queensland University of Technology under the Dawkins reforms to higher education.

From my perspective, Finance was boring; the people were formal, humourless and badly dressed (neither then, nor since had I seen such an array of brown cardigans). My socialisation to the work of assembling the federal budget, overseeing and reporting online departments' expenditure was abrupt and bewildering. Little of what was required was explained. The predominant teaching and learning styles were, it seemed to me at least, osmosis, imitation and avoiding the disapproving glares of more senior officers. Later, as I gained confidence and promotion in a line agency, I realised that those two years had been invaluable experience. I had learnt the fundamental tradecrafts of public administration: how to write a brief and a note for file; the importance of hierarchy and control in ensuring ministers received accurate advice (that one hurt); and a litany of other lessons, both positive and negative about what to do and what not to do. Slowly, over six years through a succession of jobs, I discerned that the tacit knowledge needed to survive and thrive was held by my elders and betters. This group of talented officials would later rise to leadership roles across the Australian Public Service (APS).

But, the Canberra winters seemed endless, and I was desperate to go home. By chance, I found a job in Queensland that looked a fit for my skills and experience (and at around the pay-grade needed to justify my return) in the Department of Housing, Local Government and Planning (DHLGP). Serendipitously, since it coincided with a friend's wedding in Brisbane, I was able to attend my interview in person. I loved the sound of it and hardly slept for fear I might miss the chance to work with people who seemed enthusiastic and friendly and who were engaged in major reforms. When I was offered the job, I scarcely pondered the advice of the Deputy Secretary of the department I was leaving that I was making 'a huge mistake' and would find myself 'a small cog in a big wheel' of state government. I scoffed mentally out of ignorance and youthful bravado, but accepted without question his offer that I could take 'leave without pay' and return if I found it as menial and unrewarding as they expected. It was kind of them, because they had been generous in supporting my career and they must have been stung by what appeared as my flagrant ingratitude. I am shamed by it, of course, but I can honestly say that the pull of the sun and the salty smell of the Brisbane River were my singular focus.

I am fond of telling my postgraduate students that I returned to Queensland at what was purportedly the zenith of the reform era. Growing up, my impression of the Queensland Public Service was that it was the pathway for school-leavers of average achievement who were unsure about their career direction, but seeking security. The rest of us (especially girls) went into nursing or secretarial work, or to teachers' college; the more adventurous went to the police service or the banks. Rates of graduate employment in the public sector were low; it was a 'career service' primarily oriented towards administration—to implementing and delivering the government's agenda, which under the National Party was focused on capital works and development. I know this to be fact because I am from around here, unlike so many members of the political and administrative elites who have come to Queensland from elsewhere. Orienting newcomers to local traditions and norms—to how we do things around here and why—has been part of my work with successive cohorts of senior officials over the past two decades.

Queensland and Its Traditions

Since Labor's Wayne Goss ended the thirty-two-year reign of the National Party government of Sir Joh Bjelke-Petersen in 1989, Queensland has had six Premiers. Labor has held office for twenty-three years; the LNP just five—on both occasions (1996–1998 and 2012–2015), for just a single term. Media commentators describe the past decade of Queensland politics as especially volatile, but a decentred view helps to demonstrate that, in fact, turbulence has been a constant in Queensland politics for more than thirty years. The final four years of the Bjelke-Petersen government may have set the benchmark for intrigue and political drama, but the Fitzgerald Inquiry, and the modernisation and reforms that followed, saw a decisive reshaping of governance beliefs and practices. This section provides background to my developing role as participant-observer. It surveys Queensland's recent political history, highlighting 'critical moments' from my involvement that I consider significant in shaping shared traditions about the practice of executive government that have been progressively weakened under more recent Queensland governments.

An understanding of the governance traditions that have shaped the beliefs and practices of key actor cohorts is essential background to my insider's account of disruption and change. The state traditions reflect its geography—vast and decentralised, spanning 1.853 million square kilometres—its demography and its history. Uniquely among Australian jurisdictions, as many Queenslanders live outside the capital as reside in the state's more populous south-east. These factors account for the first and most enduring tradition: the need to deliver public services to a dispersed and spatially differentiated population, including in rural and remote areas. This tradition also explains fierce resistance to outsourcing, privatisation and other forms of marketisation of the public sector adopted in other parts of Australia during the 1990s. Regional Queensland perceives such changes will have negative impacts on local economies through losses of public service jobs and will reduce their access to quality services. These political realities help to explain why the Queensland Public Service remains comparatively large and why governments are beset by service delivery challenges that in other jurisdictions have long been put at arms-length from ministers.

Other traditions are associated with Queensland's unicameral parliament,[5] which provides relatively few checks to the power of the executive. For decades, long-term majoritarian governments faced weak oppositions, fostering a political culture that favoured 'strong leaders' (Wanna and Arklay 2010; Davis 1995). Arguably, this exceptionalism enabled systemic corruption in Queensland's public institutions that culminated in the Fitzgerald Inquiry. Fitzgerald's final report, delivered in July 1989, provided a blueprint for reforming the police, the conduct of politicians, crime and law enforcement, administration of the political system, the media, electoral laws and official misconduct.

The public service that I joined in late 1994 was learning—slowly and often painfully—to serve the Labor government of Premier Wayne Goss. After three decades in opposition, the incoming government was suspicious of the public service, perceiving it as having helped maintain the National Party's vice-like grip on power. Labor's public service reform agenda was bold and wide-ranging. Machinery of government changes reduced the number of departments from 27 to 18; it established a Senior Executive Service (SES) for senior officers below the Chief Executive level, who were appointed on contracts. Three years before I returned from Canberra where such practices were well entrenched, Chairman of the Public Sector Management Commission (PSMC) Peter Coaldrake (1991) acknowledged some 'digestive difficulties' associated with the scope and pace of the reforms initiated under Goss.

A key point of contention concerned the 'brutal' treatment of DGs and senior officials seen as overtly loyal to the National Party. Many were replaced, or assigned to 'the gulag'—an office away from the central business district, where distrusted, with little work to do and deprived of information, it was hoped they would 'move on' (see, e.g., Borbidge 2011; Head 2009). A public servant perceived by some as aligned with conservative governments, described the consequence of Goss's sackings on the morale, experience and institutional memory of departments, citing his own experience aged 32, as being left the most senior officer in the then Attorney-General's department (Sosso 2011).

A key criticism of the Bjelke-Petersen regime was that decision-making was centralised around a dominant and increasingly erratic Premier (see, e.g., Davis 1995: 65–66; and for primary evidence, Queensland State Archives (QSA) 2017).[6] A succession of inquiries found that a lack of rigour and discipline in Cabinet processes had enabled corruption to flourish. Cabinet processes became an instrument for reform. Goss adopted a set of operating principles aimed at ensuring Cabinet deliberations were well informed, that policies were coordinated and that there was a whole of government perspective. These were formalised in a Cabinet Handbook, adopted as the first decision of the newly elected Goss Cabinet in December 1989. Davis (1995: 63–72) describes the institutions and 'rules' that Premier, Wayne Goss, created to ensure the 'orderly flow of government business'. The Goss government's insistence on 'routines' to ensure coordination and policy coherence across government ushered in a narrative that became widely shared across the central courts of executive government in Queensland.

In 1991, consistent with Queensland's 'strong premier' tradition, Goss established a politically appointed Office of Cabinet with its own DG Kevin Rudd, later Australia's 26th Prime Minister. Though initially welcomed, the Cabinet Office came to be associated with a 'Praetorian Guard' that surrounded the Premier. It was seen as an arrogant, domineering and politicised outfit that discomforted ministers and agencies alike. I heard this story countless times when I returned to Queensland government. I was told how agencies had struggled with the unrelenting demands of the political centre, while ministers bridled at the Premier's controlling style. The culture of 'ambush' and 'intimidation' pursued by Goss and his Cabinet Office bred resentment that would shape beliefs and practices when Peter Beattie became Premier in 1998.

The Goss government lost its majority at the 1995 election—ostensibly because it lost support in the regions, but also because its commitment to National Competition Policy reforms antagonised the public service and its unions. A by-election in the North Queensland seat of Mundingburra in late January 1996 was won by the Coalition. That victory enabled Rob Borbidge to form a minority government with support from independent Liz Cunningham.

I was on maternity leave, so I spent much of the Borbidge government's first year watching from the outside, although I was in frequent contact with departmental colleagues. From where I stood, the fragility of Labor's public-sector reforms quickly became apparent. Determined to drive its own agenda, the new government dismantled many of Labor's innovations, including the more directive role played by the Premier's Department. The Office of Cabinet was abolished, as was Goss' PSMC, established to conduct reviews to improve the organisational efficiency and effectiveness of Queensland public-sector agencies. Across the public service, policy units were disbanded and the coordinating routines that the Department of the Premier and Cabinet (DPC) had enforced in the Goss years were downplayed. However, poor advice, ministerial inexperience and its lack of investment in routines made the government 'prone to undisciplined and sometimes eccentric, decision-making' (Glyn Davis, quoted in Menzies 2005: 11). Poor coordination, communication and discipline problems across the ministry cost it dearly (Borbidge 2011; Sosso 2011).

The Borbidge government continued the practice of terminating agency heads that had begun with Goss. It was rumoured that in opposition the Coalition had prepared a public service 'hit list'—claims that were later investigated by the Criminal Justice Commission (CJC). Rob Borbidge (2011) denied personal involvement in preparing a 'hit list', but acknowledged that people in the Coalition's parliamentary and organisational wings considered it unlikely that Goss' recruits would be 'comfortable' working for them. The new government was convinced that the public service was full of political appointees determined to entrench Labor policies.

In a portent of the 'night of the long knives' to follow in Canberra when John Howard sacked six departmental secretaries on taking office in March 1996, Borbidge terminated DGs seen as having been too close to Goss government ministers, or too enthusiastic in supporting Labor's agenda. This cemented what has become an unfortunate fact of administrative life in Queensland since 1989—the inclination of incoming governments to summarily dismiss agency heads. The DG of DPC and the Head of Treasury (known as the Under-Treasurer) are usually the first to go—generally on the Sunday immediately after the Saturday poll. They tend to be replaced by someone known (and presumed to be sympathetic) to the incoming government. I have worked with them all—that's my job—but the implications for the tradition of a career public service are clear. The talent pool is not deep enough to withstand that kind of loss of specialist knowledge and expertise, particularly given the complex service delivery systems that in Queensland still remain largely the province of state government.

I was there. I know the atmosphere created in departments, particularly when former Bjelke-Petersen era agency heads were reappointed en masse. This 'Dad's Army' approach was widely criticised and fed perceptions the Coalition was shackled to its dark past. My discussions with members of the cohort of supplanted senior officials both then and since suggest that the experience of not being offered the opportunity to demonstrate loyalty to the new government shocked and in some ways radicalised them. Confronted by this dilemma, they learned that they needed to pick sides. The cycle of reprisal became strongly entrenched from one administration to another. No matter what they did, they would be perceived as loyal to and aligned with one side of politics or the other.

Other Westminster norms fared little better. I recall arguing with a senior officer in the department where I was then working, who refused to endorse a briefing note that I had prepared for the minister. He explained the minister 'wouldn't want to know' about the issue my briefing note addressed; that such advice would not be welcomed. I was appalled. My eyes wide, my mouth agape, I insisted that as public servants, we had a professional obligation to tell the minister what he needed to know, without fear or favour. Whether he took our advice was the minister's prerogative entirely. My manager, recently promoted to our policy unit from a financial area, eyed me wearily—much as I might regard an annoying toddler. He didn't study 'Government 101 at university', he told me, and he disagreed the briefing should go to the minister's office. I replied that his lack of governance expertise was self-evident. Since my professional values had been affronted and the system debased, I resolved to look elsewhere for work. I learned there's little satisfaction in having the last word. That individual's career prospered, while mine languished.

Twenty years on, I still maintain that my response was the appropriate one for a career public servant. I mention this not to imply I had a superior command of key tenets of Westminster, but to illustrate that uncertainty about what constituted the professional obligations of career officials was already evident in Queensland. I attribute this to the incoming government's disrespect for the work of policy and contending partisan traditions over the role of the public service.

Approaching the 1998 election, high unemployment in the regions, Rob Borbidge's principled support for John Howard's gun control laws and the emergence of the populist right-wing One Nation party split the conservative vote. One Nation won eleven seats in the legislative assembly, mostly from the LNP after the Premier refused to do a preference swap. This gave Labor leader Peter Beattie the opportunity to form minority government with support from independent Peter Wellington.

Participant-Observer

I left Queensland government to return to university in 1999. I worked with academics while at DHLGP and for them during my maternity leave. I wrote curriculum materials for a professor of housing studies, familiar with my background as a teacher. He encouraged me to pursue further study, recommending Griffith University as the obvious choice for someone interested in the potential for research to influence policy reform. The decision was as much personal as professional. Balancing two little boys and a busy job as head of policy in a statutory authority was proving tough. I was leading the implementation of a package of legislative reforms that had survived the change from the Borbidge to Beattie governments mostly intact. There was so much to do and a new minister and her office were demanding a lot of support. I was exhausted. My plans to work flexibly were thwarted by the volume of work. Something needed to change. Once again, I took leave without pay and enrolled in an Honours programme in politics at Griffith. My choice of thesis topic reflected my efforts to grapple with the dilemmas presented by some of the Borbidge government's policy decisions.

I was surprised how much of my experience in government in both Canberra and Brisbane could be explained by literature and theory. Griffith researchers were intensely interested in the work of governing and the problems of public administration. There was healthy respect for theoretical and applied research, and a strong commitment to teaching and what might now be called 'engagement' with practitioners was expected, not abhorred. Senior officials and expert scholars from all over the world wandered the hallways and participated in conferences and seminars; they authored book chapters and journal articles individually and collaboratively with students and academic staff. I loved it. I accepted a scholarship to complete my doctoral studies, and so, without much planning, but with plenty of relevant experience and topics I wanted to pursue, suddenly I was an academic.

The combination of positional credibility afforded by Griffith, my research interest in policy advising and the fact that several of my former departmental contemporaries had moved into leadership roles, perhaps explains how I came to be drawn into the central core executive networks of Queensland government. From 2005 onwards, I became in Adler and Adler's words, a 'participant-observer'; an outsider whose interest in the quality of government and understanding that trust is hard-won but fragile was judged sufficient to warrant admission to the nexus of power.

Peter Beattie

Rob Borbidge's decision to appoint agency heads for the term of the government (a position the former Premier continues to advocate) gave Premier Peter Beattie significant scope to reshape the public service's senior leadership when he took office in 1998. Several who were sacked in 1996 were reinstated—returning to their former posts from positions interstate, in local government and elsewhere. Beattie rejected a return to Goss' centralised approach, opting for a more collaborative style. He was cognisant of the need for coordination and coherence, but sought to make Cabinet a more collegiate forum. Beattie insisted on accurate, succinct, well-informed and timely advice. The language of 'routines' remained central, but instead of using his department to police line agencies, the routines coordinated through DPC aimed to ensure Cabinet dealt at the level of strategy; that its time was not wasted contesting details or facts. Much of this was cultivated through the Policy Division of DPC under the leadership of then DG Dr. Glyn Davis, an academic from Griffith University, who served in the Goss government and had studied its lessons. Later in Beattie's tenure, coordinating arrangements began to fray, but his commitment to 'transparent briefings' and to strong coordination remained.

Over subsequent terms, however, and especially after his landslide election victories in 2001 and 2004, Beattie pursued a more directive approach, centralising power and decision-making within DPC and increasing reporting obligations on ministers. The latter period was marred by policy failures and scandals that claimed several ministerial scalps. The Premier identified implementation as one of his government's weaknesses. Though generally disinterested in the 'nitty gritty' of administration, Beattie indicated to senior DPC officials that he wanted changes to ensure Cabinet decisions were being implemented in a timely manner and that election commitments were being acted upon. An Implementation Unit was duly established within DPC, but it could do little to prevent escalating delivery problems. From 2004, the government was besieged by failures in child protection, electricity supply, roads and, most damagingly, the state's public hospital system.

As Labor's fortunes faltered in its third term, Beattie scapegoated the public service, blaming 'unacceptable failures' in the state bureaucracy for his government's troubles. Despite lambasting its deficiencies, the Premier resisted wide-ranging reforms, making only incremental changes, usually in response to political pressure. In June 2005, he complained that the public service's poor performance was putting the future of his government at risk. He foreshadowed an overhaul of some departments, warning senior bureaucrats he expected them to 'lift their game'.

Beattie's response to the Bundaberg Hospital controversy—the most damaging of the problems besetting his government—set the template for what would follow. I witnessed the impact on the public service at close hand, since I was completing a consultancy for Queensland Health as what at first appeared to be an issue of clinical governance in a regional hospital, morphed into an all-encompassing political crisis.

For many years, Queensland's health system had struggled to attract and retain appropriately qualified medical staff to regional areas.

In 2005, claims emerged that overseas-trained surgeon, Dr. Jayant Patel, was being investigated over the deaths of 87 patients. Patel, who had been recruited from the USA two years earlier, left Queensland on a one-way business class flight approved by a local health service manager. A Google search by a Brisbane-based newspaper journalist revealed that Patel had been struck off in the state of New York and found guilty of gross negligence in Oregon. After enduring months of scandal that revealed hospital administrators had ignored, or sought to silence, complaints raised by medical staff about Patel's incompetence, Beattie established a Commission of Inquiry (the Davis Inquiry). Its findings were damning. The Commissioner described a culture characterised by 'calculated concealment' of facts; inadequate risk identification; and untimely advice to ministers. It was not the first, nor would it be the last review to draw similar conclusions about briefing practices in Queensland's health system.

From my perspective, the Premier's handling of the scandal marked a turning point for political-administrative relationships in Queensland. By July 2005, the two most senior executives of Queensland Health were sacked along with their minister, Gordon Nuttall.[7] By November, all but one member of the department's leadership team had been replaced. There were flow-on consequences for DPC. Trusted senior officers—policy generalists with limited experience of service delivery—were sent to 'fix' problems in health. Reflecting the Premier's penchant for personalised and hastily concocted governance arrangements, a new DG was appointed, and a new independent statutory authority responsible for 'performance' was created—thickening and confusing arrangements at the centre of Queensland's core executive networks. DPC was robbed of valuable institutional memory and experience, while agency heads noted the Premier seemed distant and increasingly difficult to engage.

At around the same time, Beattie affected a major reshuffle of his ministry to accommodate the sacking of the health minister, the resignation of the speaker and the unexpected retirement of treasurer and Deputy Premier, Labor powerbroker, Terry Mackenroth. Reflecting a lack of confidence in the talent of the ministry more generally, Beattie appointed himself treasurer. But this was short-lived. In February 2006, he relinquished the Treasury portfolio to concentrate on 'the basics' of health, water, education and transport. In just a few months, many of the traditions that had informed the work of the core executive were broken—supplanted by symbolic politics and expectations of responsiveness less characteristic of a 'government of routines' than of a government under siege. I heard stories of centralisation; that little policy was being driven out of departments; instead, it was initiated in DPC or the Premier's office. According to one agency head:

> In the last throes of the [Beattie] Labor Government in Queensland, I can't actually think of too many examples where a policy was driven by the Minister ... which seemed to me to be a quite perverse way of actually managing the policy debate for government. But as I've said frequently, the Ministers I had had much less influence over the outcomes than I did as a Director-General. There would be often occasions when we'd talk with the head of Premier's and you'd then have to go back and tell the Minister what the outcome would be. In the end they all almost always copped it...

> My view is that at least the Ministers I had were never influential enough to take on the Premier anyway. So, who my contract was with was not the critical factor. The fact was that the Premier was effectively insisting that Directors-General call or convince the Ministers to toe what was the government's position.

Beattie retired in September 2007, gifting the premiership to his anointed successor, Deputy Premier Anna Bligh. I distinctly remember the change of leadership because as Beattie was advising Cabinet of his decision, I was next door in a meeting of senior ministerial staff (a weekly meeting known colloquially since the Goss days as 'Prayers'), conducting the third session of a four-part professional development programme with senior policy and media advisers.

I was present at the request of Beattie's long-serving Chief of Staff. My notebook recalls his concerns that Labor's long stint in government had diminished both departments' and political offices' awareness of what constituted an appropriate 'line' between politics and administration. He observed that relationships between some ministers' offices and departments were 'too close'; while in others, the dynamic was 'them and us'. He was keen to restore the collaborative model reflected in the relationship between Beattie's office and DPC under Glyn Davis' leadership. He was of the view ministerial staff positions should be time-limited, not a career, and noted the tensions caused by a changing media environment and new communications technologies as demands for immediate decisions brought media advisers into areas of policy that were not their expertise. I played an active part in developing the framework for ministerial staff under Queensland's next Premier.

Anna Bligh

Beattie's staff departed with their leader. I completed the fourth session of the programme with Anna Bligh's (former and strictly interim) Chief of Staff (now Senator) Murray Watt. At the DG's request, I facilitated a strategic planning process to help DPC to align its agenda with that of Bligh as incoming Premier. I was involved in these processes between 2007 and 2010; I also moderated Chief Executive Officer (CEO) retreats and planning sessions. I was in sessions where the Premier explained that her government would not be 'business as usual'; that some things would remain consistent, but others would have to change. Bligh committed to restoring Cabinet and policy routines. She had clear ideas about her policy priorities and declared herself open to robust debate in Cabinet. Bligh told public service leaders she expected them to 'stay ahead of problems', 'to know what is coming' and to be 'looking out for opportunities and challenges'. Agency heads should be prepared to provide coordinated leadership in key priority areas. CEO Committees would be the primary mechanism for driving this, reporting to twice-yearly Strategic Cabinet meetings.

Within months of assuming the premiership, Bligh announced a suite of reforms intended, my notebooks recall, to 'commence a period of major renewal of the public sector'. Key among these was her decision to establish the Public Service Commission (PSC) to be responsible for 'modernising' and 'renewing' the public sector, including 'providing focused programmatic reviews to support the government's efficiency agenda'. I was appointed to the new entity's Board of Commissioners in March 2008. Chaired by prominent business leader Ann Sherry, AO, our role was to provide independent advice to the Premier about public service matters. Our appointment letters stressed Anna Bligh's hope the Board would bring 'fresh thinking and new ideas to our management of the public service and our consideration of service delivery in Queensland'. Board members were drawn from key sectors of Queensland's economy: financial services, retail and tourism and in my own case, higher education. They included the late James Strong, AO, (then) Chair of Woolworths, who had previously been both CEO and Chair of Qantas.

Such developments seemed promising. Board members were keen to share the benefit of their experience to support agency Chief Executives. Their overtures—to work with CEOs; to host them on tours of own their operations, for example—were seldom embraced. There was no discourtesy as such—just determined and ultimately intractable resistance. I remember being perplexed by this. Had I been a serving official, I would have jumped at the opportunity to learn from successful business leaders, whose commitment derived from having grown up here and wanting to see their home state successfully navigating a darkening economic outlook.

As so often happens to political leaders, Bligh's ambitions were mugged by the realities of governing. Political circumstances, not least that her Cabinet was full of critics and factional rivals, constrained Bligh's potential to undertake the reforms she considered necessary to present a renewed, reinvigorated Labor Party to voters at the next election. Unable to stamp her personal authority on her government, and still managing legacy issues from her predecessor, Bligh faced the Global Financial Crisis. This forced her to confront Queensland's deteriorating economy—the state's prized AAA credit rating was downgraded. The pressure was on to find significant savings to reduce government debt. Aware of the political backlash such a decision would precipitate, notably from Labor's trade union base, the central court surrounding Bligh began to contemplate the privatisation of public assets.

Labor won the 2009 election, but without securing a majority of the popular vote. The public service, still accommodating the turnover and churn of the Beattie era, was further disrupted by sweeping machinery of government changes that reduced the number of departments from 22 to 13. A commensurate number of serving DGs were displaced, many of whom were designated as 'deputies' in new mega-departments. Most heeded the message and chose to leave. The changes also introduced new complexities for agency heads by creating matrix relationships that required them to report to multiple ministers. There was significant turnover within DPC. Several experienced hands from its Policy Division were promoted to senior line agency roles. The crucial position of Deputy DG Policy changed hands several times in quick succession. The department struggled under political pressure and beset by internal tensions. The Premier's commitment to DPC operating as a 'traditional central agency whose core business is coordination' gave way to small group decision-making within a small, personalised and increasingly insular inner court.

Sometimes the court performed admirably, such as during Queensland's 'Summer of disasters' in 2010–2011. The unprecedented crisis, which affected 80% of the state's landmass, demonstrated Bligh's leadership under pressure. It was the high-point of her premiership. Her government's effective response was enabled by relationships of confidence and trust between ministers and the streamlined DG cohort and was underpinned by policy and funding arrangements predicated on local disaster management networks coordinated from the bottom-up.

If her management of natural disasters was the highlight of Bligh's premiership, her government's handling of yet another implementation failure—the Health payroll debacle—was the nadir. An information technology (IT) project failure that resulted in thousands of health and public hospital workers being either not paid, or incorrectly paid became a potent symbol that the government's political capital was spent. Like Beattie's experience of the Bundaberg Hospital controversy eight years earlier, Bligh's powerlessness to address the crisis was demonstrated fortnightly for more than two years. Failures persisted despite enormous effort and huge resources being devoted to attempting to solve them. Nor did the ritual sacrifice of a succession of Health Department officials provide a circuit breaker. Those left behind noted that the assortment of private-sector consultants and contractors was also involved in the project emerged largely unscathed.

In the prevailing political context, it is unsurprising that my contacts described the last 18 months of Bligh's tenure to me as 'awful'—a 'terrible time'. It was indeed diabolical. I know; I observed the toll it took on ministers, their staff and officials—particularly DGs. Significantly, for the purposes of my account, it was period when many of the traditions and beliefs that had guided governance in Queensland were further challenged. Key among these were the traditions and beliefs in respect of Cabinet routines and Cabinet government. Although the language of 'routines' maintained its normative status amongst public servants, in practice Cabinet processes were fractured. Recognition and respect for their importance were diminished by court politics, centralisation and short-term, often crisis-driven responses.

The central leadership group disputed this—arguing criticisms came from 'disgruntled' or 'underperforming' ministers, staffers and officials who 'weren't up' to the challenges of reform and change that Bligh initiated. In this environment, the already tenuous 'line' between politics and administration became even more blurred, as ministers and senior officials alike encountered a more confrontational, directive and media-focussed Premier's office. Agency heads and staffers alike explained that 'it [government] became all about issues management'. Their days were 'ruled by what was in *The Courier Mail* [newspaper]'. The need to be vigilant and to 'push back' against unreasonable demands for public service responsiveness from ministerial offices has been a constant since Queensland followed other Australian jurisdictions in developing larger, more activist partisan private offices. But experienced ministerial staff and public servants described the period from 2006 on as especially challenging and from 2009 to 2012 as unprecedented.

Campbell Newman

Like Queensland voters, the public service was ready for a change of government. Outraged by the Bligh government's asset sales, its cap on public service wages and planned redundancies, the public service union pledged it would support the LNP at the 2012 poll. In early 2011, Lord Mayor of Brisbane, Campbell Newman resigned his post in an effort to become the first political party leader to become Premier from outside the parliament. From a military and business background, but with parents who had each served as Cabinet ministers in Federal Coalition governments, Newman had been Lord Mayor for eight years. The LNP won in an historic landslide that left Labor with just seven of the 89 seats in the Queensland parliament. After 14 years and five election defeats, the newly merged LNP was back in office and determined to put its stamp on the business of government in Queensland.

Repeating the practice of predecessors stretching back to Wayne Goss, the incoming government immediately sacked the DG of DPC and the Under-Treasurer; other agency heads and senior DPC officials soon followed. After the turmoil of the previous seven years, it was a significant loss of administrative, policy and delivery experience. As well as striking fear into the hearts of public servants, it hampered an inexperienced government, whose leadership, according to officials close to the transition, was 'pretty green'—especially about government processes. Their appointees, personal loyalists often drawn from local government, knew little about state government and certainly did not know what to expect of the jobs to which they found themselves drafted. The appointment of Liberal powerbroker, former Brisbane City Councillor Michael Caltabiano as DG of the Department of Transport and Main Roads, was seen as an egregious example of the government's apparent disrespect for Westminster principles of merit-based senior appointments. It was one of numerous controversies over appointments that would combine to drain the Newman government's political capital. Within six months, Caltabiano was forced to resign for misleading a parliamentary estimates committee.

The LNP concedes the damage wrought by the inexperience of the central courts that comprised the new government. The Borbidge-Sheldon review of the 2015 electoral loss concluded that:

> The overwhelming election win of 2012 led to hubris and a false sense of security, consolidating an energetic and reformist government leadership team, but without parliamentary experience. The huge influx of new MPs and a leader without parliamentary background contributed to a lack of corporate history in the conduct of parliament and the party room… The political tactic of importing a leader from outside the parliament without parliamentary or state leadership experience and policy knowledge carried inherent risks which were not immediately apparent and in the short term worked well. (Borbidge and Sheldon 2015: 1.5, 1.8)

Newman reversed machinery of government changes and the move to mega-departments mandated by Anna Bligh in 2009. He appointed 19 ministers, each with their own department—immediately increasing the number of DGs from 12 to 19 and bringing yet more disruption and change for Queensland departments. Early in its term, the government appointed former Liberal Federal Treasurer Peter Costello to lead a Commission of Audit into Queensland's finances—a decision Newman acknowledges now was a mistake (King 2015). It concluded the state was living beyond its means and recommended significant cuts to reduce recurrent expenditure. Eventually, the government agreed to cut 14,000 public service jobs, with savings from corporate and policy areas to be redirected towards front-line services. A Public Sector Renewal Board, chaired by former Borbidge government Under-Treasurer Dr. Doug McTaggart, was appointed to drive reform and change in departments.

McTaggart also became Chair of the PSC. He phoned me shortly after the government changed to advise (very politely) that my services and those of my fellow PSC Board Members were no longer required. That was not unexpected; our appointments had been extended for twelve months in 2011 to avoid binding the incoming government. I did what I always do at a change of government in Queensland—I explained that I am here to support the people who support the government of the day and that I and other Griffith colleagues would be available as and when the incoming government might decide help was needed. I developed a good working relationship with the DG of DPC and through him with the Premier.

It soon became clear though that Cabinet processes were a casualty of the further loss of experience and expertise. The language of routines—once an article of faith among core executive actors—fell into disuse. This may be because of frequent turnover and a governing cadre that lacked awareness of the significance of routines and processes in providing the direction and coherence necessary to achieve the government's agenda.

It was also quickly apparent that Newman was a paradoxical Premier. Despite his pugnacious and combative personality, he was not a 'strong Premier' in the Queensland tradition. From early in his tenure, I heard stories that Newman did not control, nor did he seem to know how to work the cabinet process—that he was frequently out-voted. This made subsequent assertions by his colleagues that the electoral defeat was Newman's personal fault all the more difficult to accept. It seems the Premier dominated a limited number of quite specific priorities, while more experienced hands fashioned the wider agenda. Newman admits as much in the biography authored by former LNP Member for Cairns, Gavin King (2015).

The Borbidge-Sheldon review concluded: 'It is a simple fact that no government can function without the cooperation of the public service' (Borbidge-Sheldon 2015). This was something the Newman government learned the hard way. Its unexpected defeat in January 2015 was widely attributed to its handling of the public service and, by the party's own admission, its failure to respect the institutions of the state. In addition to picking a fight with nearly every Queensland constituency, Newman had offended a number of the Fitzgerald principles—something the former Royal Commissioner was only too happy to point out in the days leading up to the poll.

The anxieties that I alluded to at the start of this chapter following the 2015 election were vindicated in the wake of the Newman government's defeat and Annastacia Palaszczuk's unexpected ascension to the Queensland Premiership. It emerged that some agencies had not, as required under the Cabinet Handbook, prepared two sets of incoming government briefs. Whether they did not understand the requirement, or the prospect of a change of government seemed remote, is an empirical question to which I have not yet managed to get a straight answer.

Where Are We Now?

During her first week in office, the Premier emailed the Queensland Public Service assuring them:

> The Queensland government has the highest regard for its professionalism and independence… That is why I have committed to restoring fairness for public servants and ensuring that the proper conditions exist for them to provide frank and fearless advice to Government. As part of this commitment, we will return to a Westminster-style model that values and supports a permanent public service… Also, I want to acknowledge that previous machinery of government changes have caused significant disruption and reassure you that we will do everything we can to keep changes to a minimum.

She accepted the damage done by incessant 'reform'.

It has become fashionable to blame the Newman government for the 'culture of fear' that is said to grip Queensland Public Service. But as I have shown, there is clear evidence that the starting point of the recent malaise was around 2005. In slow, insidious increments, the traditions and beliefs that had guided practice in Queensland in the post-Fitzgerald years came under sustained assault. They deteriorated steadily through the accumulation of dilemmas that could not be reconciled. Shocks to the system from the Beattie (2005–2007), the Bligh and Newman premierships diminished the numbers of senior leaders socialised to operating in accordance with Westminster norms that at least attempted to clearly demarcate between the political and administrative domains.

Rhodes and Tiernan (2016) have documented the dying days of the Bligh government. Their study highlighted four dilemmas that confronted political-administrators as the spectre of defeat loomed over Queensland's long-term Labor government. These were:

- Contingency, which continuously frustrated agenda-setting and other efforts to plan for the medium-term;
- The problem of fragmentation and coordination, which arguably is greater because of states' service delivery responsibilities;
- The primacy of coping and survival in the calculus of political-administrative elites, especially as electoral defeat looms; and
- The tendency of a besieged leader to rely on an ever-decreasing circle of close advisers who, because of their close relationship with and loyalty to the leader, cannot or are unwilling to offer alternative advice.

My decentred account of the period before and since reinforces the claim that Queensland governments face recurring dilemmas that frequent 'reform' efforts have been unable to resolve and indeed may have exacerbated. My account identifies at least two more dilemmas.

- The problem of distrust that has destabilised the senior ranks of the state's public service for more than 30 years, with consequent effects on policy capacity and institutional memory.
- The relative impunity with which the political executive is able to change and reshape the public service, including and perhaps especially through the appointment of agency heads.

Successive governments' practice of purging and personalising chief executive appointments has diminished the pool of talent, skills and experience. It has created a climate of fear and insecurity among the middle ranks that is debilitating and self-reinforcing. Again, this assessment is not new. A Crime and Misconduct Commission (CMC) review of child protection in 2004 noted the Department of Families had five DGs responsible to five different ministers in the preceding ten years. In 2005, consultant Peter Forster who conducted the Health Systems review in the wake of the Bundaberg Hospital controversy noted that contract employment for senior officials had been deleterious to robust advice. Whether reality or neurosis is hard to tell. Queensland public servants have often feared their political masters. This is balanced by the public service itself being an electorally powerful constituency that in 2012 helped defeat Anna Bligh and in 2015 turned savagely on the Newman government.

The lack of constraints on executive power became especially apparent during the Newman years, when individuals of substantial professional experience, but who lacked a Westminster narrative, or an appreciation of state government, were appointed to lead public service departments. Two possible explanations can account for their failure to abide by the caretaker conventions to ensure incoming government briefs were prepared. Perhaps (like the rest of Queensland) they assumed the LNP government would be returned (even if under a different leader); or they lacked awareness and understanding of the conventions. Neither bodes well for the accumulated consequences of decades of partisan incursions into areas of administration more appropriately the province of a career public service.

Ministers decry the loss of policy capacity, but they might more accurately lament the loss of craft (Tiernan 2015). Rhodes (2016) distinguishes between the craft skills of three occupational groups: political-administrators at the heads of government departments who exercise 'dual leadership' of the public sector in partnership with ministers; service delivery managers and front-line workers. At the sub-national level and certainly in Queensland, ministers have little respect or patience for such distinctions. They want and expect agency heads to serve and support them, but to also oversee and know intimately the details of large, decentralised delivery systems. The ubiquity of problems that arise out of complex delivery networks and the tendency to favour short-term 'fixes' that defer rather than 'solve' problems overwhelms political leaders. Their fear that their ministerial career will be undermined by bureaucratic incompetence is palpable. It drives the cycle of distrust. But ministers themselves are strangely unprepared for their roles. They make the wrong choices in choosing to surround themselves with young, often inexperienced issues managers rather than experts. Career politics has weakened their connections to the sources of intelligence and early warning that might assist them to stay on the 'right side' of the political-administrative divide, at a sensible distance from implementation problems that are legion in Queensland where so much—not least accountability for performance—remains internal to government.

There is much to recommend a decentred perspective, but it is not without challenges, particularly for the active member researcher. The need to account for the historical background to the development of beliefs and practices creates an empirical challenge; it is difficult to strike an appropriate balance between description and analysis. In the next section, I discuss some of the more important strengths and limitations of decentred analysis.

Strengths and Limitations

There are four strengths to my approach.

First, it provides opportunities to see continuities and changes over the long-term. Presentism leads to the misleading proposition that all of the problems I have described began with Campbell Newman. The Newman era was a major break, but I have shown that his government likely exacerbated dilemmas already in evidence under previous governments.

Second, a decentred analysis is especially valuable in Queensland because the victors (i.e. Labor reformers) wrote history. Engaging with a wider range of voices helped me to develop a more nuanced view. It made me appreciate the extent to which the LNP is shackled to the Bjelke-Petersen years. The Newman experiment has only reinforced the party's troubled relationship with the Fitzgerald legacy. Taking a longer view of the development of current beliefs helped to reveal the dilemmas posed by contending partisan traditions.

Third, I provide an actor-centred account that reveals how competition and infighting among and between ministers and their staff on one hand (court politics) and departments on the other (bureaucratic politics) shape not only policies, but also the fate of governments.

Fourth, decentred perspectives allow dominant narratives to be scrutinised and reinterpreted. By standing back and reflecting on my insider's experience of more than twenty years, I developed a stronger appreciation of the Queensland Public Service's strong service delivery tradition. I have come to the view this tradition has been diminished and disrespected by a 'policy class' whose traditions and norms were shaped in other jurisdictions and other tiers of government and who sought to impose these onto a bureaucracy that remains, by virtue of Queensland's governance traditions, primarily delivery-focused.

Finally, the active member researcher needs to be cognisant that his or her relationships with key players provides opportunities to develop deep insights into their beliefs and practices. Thus, the role of 'insider' confers privileges, but also responsibilities. In my experience, the researcher's professional obligation to strike an appropriate balance is not always appreciated, nor well understood. I am always at pains to explain that while I respect their work, I am not a colleague. I do not owe allegiance to their department or their political party. I am not their friend. I have been around for such a long time that they give me access and expect me to be sympathetic. It can be difficult when they mind, are hurt by, or want to contest my construction of the stories I have been told about events. This happened with members of the court that surrounded Anna Bligh. I received feedback that they were angry and felt I should have accepted their version as the definitive account of what really happened. I am sorry they were offended. It is never my intention. I have access because they trust me, but that trust is fragile and can be damaged if they find my version of their stories too frank and fearless. Individuals, their relationships and their stories matter much more than allowed by political scientists. I may be too close to the game, but contemporary history is always rewritten and that rewriting must take account of those who were there. I was there.

Notes

1. Annastacia Palaszczuk challenged me about this when she and I were both guests on ABC Television's Q&A programme in July 2015. She claimed she had always thought Labor would win.
2. Since November 2015, at the request of the DG of the DPC, I serve as 'critical friend' to the Queensland Government Leadership Board (which comprises the heads of 19 public service departments and the Public Service, Police and Fire and Emergency Services Commissioners).
3. For example, when facilitating strategic planning processes for central departments (which I have done on and off since 2007); moderating strategic retreats for the Leadership Board and its antecedents (which I have done on and off since 2006); undertaking consultancy projects; designing professional development programmes for officials and ministerial staff, etc.
4. http://www.queenslandspeaks.com.au/.

5. The Legislative Council, the state's upper house, was abolished in 1922 on the vote of a majority of then ALP members, known colloquially as 'the suicide squad' (Wanna and Arklay 2010).
6. A Griffith University research team that I led was contracted by the QSA to review the 1986 Cabinet papers and to prepare them for public release. A summary of their findings is available at: https://medium.com/the-machinery-of-government/the-1986-queensland-cabinet-minutes-f77b90853468#.s2w7yi946.
7. Nuttall would later be charged and convicted of numerous official corruption offences. He served more than seven years' jail.

References

Adler, P. A., & Adler, P. (1987). *Membership Roles in Field Research*. Newbury Park, CA: Sage.

Bevir, M., & Rhodes, R. A. W. (2016). The Three Rs in Rethinking Governance: Ruling, Rationalities and Resistance. In M. Bevir & R. A. W. Rhodes (Eds.), *Rethinking Governance*. Abingdon, Oxon: Routledge.

Borbidge, R. (2011, March 28). Rob Borbidge, AO. Interviewed by Roger Scott and Maree Stanley. *Queensland Speaks*. Available at http://www.queenslandspeaks.com.au/rob-borbidge.

Borbidge, R., & Sheldon, J. (2015, May 28). *Election Review: Report and Recommendations*. Available at: https://lnp.org.au/wp-content/uploads/2015/05/Borbidge-Sheldon-Election-Review-.pdf.

Coaldrake, P. (1991). Opportunities and Digestive Difficulties Associated with Queensland's Public Sector Reform Agenda. In G. Davis (1993) (Ed.), *Public Sector Reform Under the First Goss Government: A Documentary Sourcebook*. Brisbane: Royal Australian Institute of Public Administration (Queensland Division) and the Centre for Australian Public Management at Griffith University.

Corbett, J. (2014). Practicing Reflection: Empathy, Emotion and Intuition in Political Life Writing. *Life Writing, 11*(3), 349–365.

Davis, G. (1995). *A Government of Routines: Executive Coordination in an Australian State*. South Melbourne: Macmillan.

Davis, G., & Rhodes, R. A. W. (2014). *The Craft of Governing*. Crows Nest: Allen & Unwin.

Head, B. (2009, December 7). Brian Head, Interviewed by Roger Scott and Peter Spearitt. *Queensland Speaks*. Available at: http://www.queenslandspeaks.com.au/brian-head.

Hogan, T. (2016). *Coming of Age: Griffith University in the Unified National System*. Carlton, VIC: MUP Academic.

King, G. (2015). *Can Do: Campbell Newman and the Challenge of Reform*. Brisbane: Connor Court.

Menzies, J. (2005, September). *The Circus Animals' Desertion: The Challenge for Longevity (or the Limitations of Personalisation)*. Paper presented at 53rd Australasian Political Studies Association Conference, Dunedin, 28–30.

Norell, P. O. (2007). Governing Karlstad; An Insider Story. In R. A. W. Rhodes, P. 't Hart, & M. Noordegraaf (Eds.), *Observing Government Elites: Up Close and Personal* (pp. 103–128). Houndmills, Basingstoke: Palgrave-Macmillan.

Palaszczuk, A. (2015, February 18). Special Broadcast: A Message from the Premier. Email to the Queensland Public Service.

Rhodes, R. A. W., & Tiernan, A. (2016). Court Politics in a Federal Polity. *Australian Journal of Political Science, 51*(2), 338–354.

Sosso, J. (2011, December 19). John Sosso, Interviewed by Helen McMonagle and Roger Scott. *Queensland Speak*s. Available at: www.queenslandspeaks.com.au/john-sosso.

Tiernan, A. (2015). Craft and Capacity in the Public Service. *Australian Journal of Public Administration, 74*(1), 53–62.

Wanna, J., & Arklay, T. (2010). *The Ayes Have It: The History of the Queensland Parliament, 1957–1989*. Canberra: ANU EPress.

CHAPTER 9

How Do Local Government Chief Executives Engage with Policy Dilemmas?

Kevin Orr and Mike Bennett

INTRODUCTION

Local government is an arena filled with stories and narratives that offer competing accounts of the past, the present and the future—the stuff of policymaking. In this light, this chapter examines how local government chief executives shape narratives and utilise storytelling as part of pursuing influence within complex policymaking arenas. In our study, stories emerge as a facilitative resource in decentred policymaking, inviting others to contribute to how the present is understood and the future is imagined. We explore a relational perspective that directs attention to communication practices, such as stories and narratives, through which policy 'realities' are constructed. Our contribution to the book is to provide insights into the ways in which storytelling and narrative practices mediate the policymaking process.

K. Orr (✉) · M. Bennett
School of Management, University of St Andrews, St Andrews, UK
e-mail: kmo2@st-andrews.ac.uk

M. Bennett
e-mail: mike.bennett@publicintelligence.co.uk

© The Author(s) 2018
R. A. W. Rhodes (ed.), *Narrative Policy Analysis*, Understanding Governance, https://doi.org/10.1007/978-3-319-76635-5_9

There is no essentialist account of the state, of governance, or of policymaking. Instead, social scientists need to pay thoughtful and critical attention to the stories of the participants in these processes. In this chapter, we embrace the potential of a decentred approach to policymaking, one in which we listen to and learn from accounts (stories of storying) of a particular group of front-line actors—chief executives of local councils. We suggest that the polyphony of policymaking can be understood through appreciating the importance of the beliefs and traditions of those involved. We end the chapter by considering the implications for practitioners and the limits of a decentred approach.

Local government in the UK is an interesting setting for this work, given its policy and service delivery responsibilities for areas such as social care, public housing, planning and transport. It is also the only directly elected part of the public sector and is, therefore, part of the fabric of representative democracy. For policymaking, these features of local government mean that it is enmeshed in complex central–local relations, a melange of local professional and political influences, a complex organisational landscape of service providers, partners, and inspectorates, and an expectant chorus of community or consumer interests. Local government organisations abound with traditions: a cacophony of voices, interests and assumptions about how to organise, prioritise and mobilise action (Orr and Vince 2009). From a social science perspective, therefore, this is a rich and challenging setting in which to explore decentred policymaking.

We understand decentring in the context of the move from public sector bureaucracies to markets and networks, or what Bevir calls 'a new politics' (2013: 9). The complexity and fragmentation of service delivery mean a plurality of actors, and interests are at large in the policy process. Local government practitioners—professionals, managers or politicians—often have at best influence rather than direct control and operate in interdependent relationships with other bodies, private and public, third sector and community-based. This arena is therefore infused with the dynamics of decentring.

In exploring the dynamics of a decentred policy process, the focus of our fieldwork is on the practices of the chief executives of these organisations. Our empirical method stems from a deep and sustained engagement with this set of policy actors. This work began in 2008 when we started a programme of jointly interviewing local council chief executives about storytelling. For this chapter, we have supplemented this long-standing engagement with this practitioner group, with a fresh wave of interviewing specifically undertaken (November 2016–July 2017) with this book in mind. In this work, we step away from a reified notion of local government organisations and their policymaking apparatus and towards narratives and storytelling.

Decentred Policymaking

We engage with the concept of governance developed in the work of Mark Bevir and R. A. W. Rhodes as all processes of governing, including those undertaken by power, language and social practices. For Bevir (2013), 'Governance is explained by the narratives that… actors first inherit as historical traditions and then revise in response to dilemmas' (see also Chapter 1 above). We therefore explore a decentred theory of governance that is interested in understanding a diversity of governing practices through which the day-to-day work of policymaking is accomplished.

We pay particular attention to the narrative practices of chief executives and to the dilemmas they encounter and respond to. In terms of decentred theory, and the related idea of the state as cultural practice, narrative practices are 'meaningful'. They are meaningful in that they draw upon, and contribute to, the creation, recreation and disruption of traditions. We explore the narrative practices involved in how policymaking is accomplished. It is an approach that pays attention to the contested and contingent aspects of the setting. Situated actors share stories to make sense of the organisational action or of context, or to shape policy choices. This is an approach that takes seriously the languages, meanings and beliefs used to cast and recast governance and policy. It focuses on meanings in action and recognises contingency. Embracing contingency means accepting that neither institution nor practices fix actors' interpretations or responses to their circumstances and the responses that follow. The task for fieldworkers engaging with decentred theory of governance is to engage with the local reasoning and situated agency of those involved. We need to look at the webs of meaning which provide a backcloth for people's actions (Bevir and Rhodes 2003; Bevir 2013). This represents a shift of topos from institutions to meanings in action (Bevir and Rhodes 2016; and Chapter 1 above). A decentred theory of governance demands a change from focussing on reified networks to the beliefs and stories of social actors.

Similarly, in relation to policymaking, an implication of a decentred theory of governance is that what come to be treated as policy drivers, influences or imperatives do not stand as immutable unambiguous facts. Factors seen as important focal points for attention are constructed as dilemmas arising from particular traditions. Policy positions are crafted in response to how such drivers and influences are conceived and interpreted. Local reasoning and understanding become a key focus for social scientists. How do local practitioners understand and interpret the policy environment and their relationships with other actors and arrive at the priorities for organisational action? And how is such action accomplished?

STORYTELLING AND NARRATIVE PRACTICES

An interest in narrative is part of an interpretive turn in the social sciences (Berger and Luckmann 1966; Rabinow and Sullivan 1987), one which has come to span disciplinary boundaries in the social sciences. Such a turn has extended to, for example, anthropology (Geertz 1988; Levi-Strauss 1963); history (Carr 1986; White 1987); philosophy (Ricoeur 1983); and psychology (Sarbin 1986; White and Epston 1990). Organisation studies have seen its own related developments, manifested in growing interest in the mediation of organisational action—for example leadership and change, sense-making, organisational learning and the generation of knowledge—through narratives and stories. Such an interest, and methodological focus, is encapsulated by Boje's framing of stories as 'the blood vessels through which changes pulsate in the heart of organisational life' (1991: 8).

In this tradition of scholarship, the spaces and places of organisational action (such as policymaking) emerge as narratively constructed from webs of conversations. Landmark work has explored the stories managers tell to each other (Hummel 1991) and the narratives of street level bureaucrats (Maynard-Moody and Musheno 2003). In the study of public policy, scholars have offered a challenge to the deductive orthodoxy that values ideas of objective assessment of policy outcomes and instead seek to highlight the socially constructed complexity of meanings which play out in different policy contexts.

Finally, and crucial to this book, the contributions of Bevir and Rhodes (e.g. 2003, 2015, 2016) have been important in encouraging a growing interest in local practices, and in particular the importance of stories and narratives in governance. Their work advocates the importance of storytelling in governance and encourages an approach that embraces the idea that the study of public administration is concerned with understanding, and crafting stories about, beliefs, actions, practices and their contexts.

Our study seeks to build on this scholarship by exploring the narrative practices of senior public administrators—UK local government chief executives. We provide an understanding of how stories and narratives are used as part of their day-to-day practices, especially in relation to their leadership roles in a decentred policy process. In this context, our study explores two interrelated research questions:

- How does decentring find expression in chief executives' accounts of the local policymaking process?
- How do stories and narratives help chief executives mediate a decentred policy process?

Methodology

The chief executive is a vital officer position focusing on translating the political will of local politicians (the elected members or councillors) into organisational action. It evolved from previous position of town clerk, following the Bains Report (1972), which concluded that local government needed greater management capacity. The job has also been shaped by new public management ideas, which promoted the importance of strategic management and leadership. It is best understood as a managerial and leadership position: leading change programs in complex organisations; setting tone, influencing culture and developing staff; and ensuring priorities are delivered. The role therefore involves elements of leadership, strategy, communication and political management.

Councils are complex organisations, not least in relation to the range of front-line services for which they have responsibility, taking difficult decisions in the face of competing demands from different stakeholders, meeting statutory obligations in the midst of financial constraint and addressing wicked social or economic issues. At the same time, the chief executive plays an important part in supporting the democratic role of councils. Chief executives pivot between professional officers and elected politicians, providing managerial leadership (including translating political direction to staff), advice to the politicians on strategy and policy, and acting in an executive capacity. Their responsibilities include ensuring good governance by 'speaking truth to power' (SOLACE 2014: 3). Chief executives operate at the boundaries of what is achievable organisationally and what is viable politically.

We have had a long-term and ongoing engagement with local government chief executives. Chief executives are an elite level of highly paid, powerful government managers who operate high levels of prioritisation of their time. They employ staff who control access accordingly. Our research, particularly in the earlier years of the project, was helped by Bennett's role as a director of the professional association, and in different ways we continue to have considerable professional interactions with this network. These connections have enabled us to gain research access to this organisational elite and to sense check our emerging interpretations with members of that network.

Between 2008 and 2017, we interviewed jointly 98 local council chief executives. There have been many phases in this work, beginning with 'being struck' by the richness of the practice its significance as a topic for inquiry; the potential to use it as a basis of academic-practitioner research collaboration between the authors; engagement with literatures (most recently public policy scholarship) to steer our work in the field; and an early small-scale study to 'test' some ideas and assess our prospects.

In the most recent 18 interviews (2016–2017), we moved from a more open-ended interest in storytelling practices to a set of research conversations with an especial interest in discussing stories, narratives and their part in the policymaking process. Taken together, we have engaged our participants in thinking about 'How and why do you use stories?' and more recently in 'How and why do you use stories in the policy process?' In this chapter, we focus on the 18 policy process interviews. However, we have also revisited our data set as a whole and interrogated those earlier interviews for insights into this topic, paying particular attention to material relating to policymaking and relations with politicians and council leaders.

Interpretive research can never entail 'random' or perfectly controlled participant selection (Schwartz-Shea and Yanow 2012). However, ours has been a long-term engagement in which we have taken an inclusive approach to gain exposure to factors such as professional backgrounds, gender, length of service or level of experience and so on. Across all phases, we included unitary authorities; county, metropolitan and district

Table 9.1 Interviews: by number and type of authority

Type of UK council	Number of chief executives interviewed
Unitary authorities	26
County councils	9
District councils	25
London boroughs	20
Metropolitan/city councils	18

councils; and London boroughs (see Table 9.1). The fieldwork encompassed different geographical locations across the four nations of the UK. We have aimed to include a multiplicity of organisational types, without making scientific claims to representativeness. In assembling, shaking and adding to our pieces of field interviews, we are drawing together a mosaic that we feel has a close resemblance to the features of the sector and of the network. As part of that process, a regular check on our sampling has been asking the question about whose voices are we missing?

The constructive use of language is an important focal point for research into organisational practices (Grant et al. 1998; Reissner 2011). Language is constitutive and central to how we construct social and organisational realities (Gabriel 2015), and that insight provided the grounding for our data analysis. Our study explores one way in which chief executives try to influence these realities through their use of stories and narrative techniques as part of the policymaking process. Our analysis involves zooming in on chief executives' storytelling through their reflective accounts of their practices. It is an approach based on an understanding that 'local concepts and practices are where organizational structure and process come to life' (Agar 2010: 298). We explore how our research participants see the world and to learn from their 'vantage point on politics' (Fenno 1990: 2), as a basis for interpretive analysis.

From the outset, our study design enshrined a collaborative method of academics and practitioners 'coproducing' research knowledge. For the first three years of the fieldwork, Bennett worked alongside council chief executives as director of their professional body. Academic-practitioner coproduction of knowledge has been a core feature of our research. This research practice builds on the legacy of the early 'pracademics' and the tradition of public administration as an inclusive field of study (Perry 2012; Posner 2009). Like any social science research, we understand coproduction to be a political undertaking (Orr and Bennett 2012a, b), involving the negotiation of interests and values, but one in which the potential of such a collaborative endeavour is to generate knowledge that has interest and value to academics and practitioner communities.

Rigour or robustness depends on reflexivity and 'self-monitoring' (Schwartz-Shea and Yanow 2012). We used cross-checking of our interpretations at many stages—beginning immediately after interviews on trains or in coffee shops whilst the encounter was still fresh in the mind; subsequent phone conversations; email exchanges; and through taking stock of the emerging themes in preparation for subsequent interviews.

The make-up of the research team enabled us to bring to bear Bennett's perspective as someone closer to the chief executives' own setting and everyday discourse and concerns, adding sharpness and shading to our interpretive capacity. We also 'member-checked' our interpretations through follow-up email exchanges with many of our interviewees, and supplementary face-to-face conversation with a further selection of respondents. We also shared drafts of this chapter with two critical commentators from the practitioner network. In the next section, we consider our interview data and set out the themes that emerged from our research conversations with the chief executives.

Findings

Expressions of Decentring in Chief Executives' Accounts of the Policy Process

Closed Loops and Fraying Seams
Our respondents paint a similar picture of what they often describe as a familiar or fairly classical model of policymaking within councils. Commonly, it is sketched as involving processes of dialogue between officers and members, which to varying degrees will be dominated by politicians or by a strong officer cadre. It will be more or less inclusive of a range of views. The chief executive will exercise varying degrees of autonomy in relation to (or achieve influence over) the key politicians. In many ways, the accounts offered and the dynamics therein are of a piece with fifty years of academic debate about officer–member relations

in local government. The accounts also resonate with the management, professional and democratic traditions of local government as drawn by Orr and Vince (2009). One respondent summarises the 'classical' policy process in this way:

> I think there's a traditional model, and we are still figuring out how we change that model ... I've experienced it everywhere. The most powerful aspects of decision-making I think within the authority are really the officer or professional agenda if you like, plus some evidence, meeting the political process. Somewhere in that space is how policy decisions get made.

Another chief executive offers a similar view of 'that space', extending her perspective to a reflection based upon working in several different local councils across the past three decades:

> The traditional model in a council ... is quite a closed loop within the organisation ... I've worked for all political parties over the years, and mainly all political parties over the years have been quite comfortable with a world where, in different degrees, an officer-member discussion, results in the administration taking a view and then we kind of roll that out to the population. The default mode that people are most comfortable with is, you know, bring an Officer perspective, bring some evidence, bring political interests and values to bear and in that room, which is not usually a public room, [and] there's a product. Maybe, either in advance of that discussion or after that discussion, there's some public engagement goes on, depending what the issue is. I think that's the tradition that we come from and are there still.

However, many of our respondents also point to disruptions to such traditions of policymaking. They experience the traditional closed loop model coming under pressure from the effects of austerity and downward pressure on public budgets. As one chief executive reflects:

> There's various things that are kind of pressing in on that model. One is just the fact we're operating in low resource, because resources are tight it becomes harder and harder to come up with creative solutions that defuse political problems or trade-offs - space for creativity might have meant you could help kind of defuse some of the political issues in the way you implement something. I think the longer austerity's gone on it's just harder to be in a world where you're not impacting people in a negative way. That therefore brings political issues to the fore in a decision-making process.

In such accounts, we see the somewhat reluctant acknowledgement of networked governance. As another respondent puts it, '…the seams are starting to fray, and we're having to start to respond in a slightly different way'. One of the reasons given for these fraying seams, of the process becoming less self-contained, involves an appreciation of the increasingly pluralistic environment in which chief executives and elected members operate as policy actors.

This pluralism is described by one respondent as bringing an unsettling of local assumptions and practices. In particular, he describes a loss of control in the face of ever more complex demands and expectations on local councils:

> It really feels we're trying to do more complicated things now than perhaps we were. We know how to build things, we know how to invest in the expansion of a service, we know how to make things more efficient. But we're really in a world now where we're trying to care about outcomes in a serious way, we're trying to do complicated things like demand management and they are more complicated deliverables. And they require partnership working where you're not in control of everything.

Another chief executive of a large county council characterises this pluralism in terms of the confusion of different stories and narratives that are deployed in a network of policy actors in which policy coherence can be elusive:

> It's a very complex place. We've got lots of districts and boroughs, and unitaries that are part of our county, loads of Clinical Commissioning Groups, we've got a very complex health landscape … A lot of it is policymaking in partnership, which makes having the 'one story' and the 'one evidence base' quite difficult because you've got health colleagues standing up saying one story, us saying another, and if you're a resident hearing those different stories it is quite fragmented. Because of the twelve districts there's a very complex picture… And I don't think we've negotiated that between us.

This sense of searching for coherence in the midst of ambiguity and contestation was developed by another respondent who had experienced cultural challenges involved in moving from a way of working that assumes the council's voice to be first amongst equals to an acceptance of shared autonomy and interdependence. In this respect, he identifies a double hurdle.

He explains that even if such changes are achieved successfully through the adoption of new values and practices within the organisation, their partners, long used to a more directive stance from the council, may regard such shifts of behaviour or orientation with scepticism.

> We want to tell people what to do because we're public bodies that know everything, so creating an environment and the space where there's parity and equality of view but that then leads to decisive action is very difficult, so we're having to learn to be less controlling and more enabling and that feels very counterintuitive, countercultural. We are struggling for other parties to recognise that we're trying to play a very different role where all the time we've been fairly controlling, very autocratic. And that actually we're trying to be open. That's very difficult.

Grasping the Political Realities of Networked Governance and Decentred Policymaking

Out of this fragmentation and complexity emerge challenges for chief executives, charged with managing in this decentred environment, and tasked with supporting the elected members who themselves are confronted with the tribulations of a decentred political arena. Chief executives engage with members to explain the realities of political influence—the opportunities and limitations of their mandate. One chief executive explains how she tries to enable officers and members to understand the wider context in which they operate and to be better able to navigate the different stakeholders and interests at play in that environment. She describes this in terms of embracing humility (or a more circumscribed view of their own autonomy) but also in terms of apprehending that their influence is located within a wider system of distributed autonomy:

> A key part of my role is to develop the leadership capability, within the officer corps but also the political arena as well and I'm doing that very overtly… Because I do actually believe that that's a critical factor in good policy-making, not just about your competency as a leader but how open you are to challenge - the humility of leadership. I've been trying to broker, create the discussion around what it's like to be part of the system. And that's played better in the officer corps then it has in the political corps, because broadly the Members will say 'Well we're the democratic leaders and that therefore sod the system…' But that is my role - to bring that piece together as part of the system.

Discussions over resources reveal competing priorities for action and illuminate different professional traditions and expectations in a system. A further layer of complexity, adding to the decentred policy process, is the scrutiny of local decisions by national bodies. One chief executive spoke animatedly of his travails with local health professionals over whether to fund anti-smoking initiatives as part of a public health strategy focusing on prevention. When funding was diverted, it left the politicians exposed to accusations by the national education and social care inspectorate, Ofsted, of ignoring professionals' expert advice for reasons of political expediency or policy weakness:

> We put three million pounds a year into promoting smoking cessation, right? So when we look at the budget, there's a consideration because we don't need to do that. So the Members have a policy discussion about the benefit of that against the saving of three million pounds. So they'll debate that in the context of adult social care, children's social care, parks, waste, everything else in our remit... and if we don't take that three million we've got to take three million somewhere else because I've got to take three million out the pot somewhere, so it'll lead to a change somewhere. Members are saying... people know that to smoke is bad, why are we spending three million pounds telling people what they know? So let's keep the money for something else. Of course the professionals, the Public Health people, will say, that's terrible. And the Public Health people are my staff but even more than that, there are also Clinical Commissioning Group professionals rallying on behalf of the hospital. They say well if you stop that then twenty years down the line, we're going to have a massive impact on mortality. What the Ofsted Inspectors said is that 'Your Members don't listen to professional advice on policy.' Well they do listen to it. The fact that they don't agree with it is different from them not listening to it.

They also told us of the need to create spaces in which differences of context, values and traditions can be shared between different policy participants. One chief executive offered the example of education policy in her council in a deprived area of England. Dialogues between the management team and politicians and local teaching professionals explored a particular local education initiative that did not fit the template of guidance from central government and the inspectorate Ofsted, another key player in the policy environment. She challenged colleagues to think beyond the specific Ofsted requirements in shaping local policy change, yet she identifies the risk involved:

And then of course when you get your Ofsted call out, the inspection, and think God Almighty, I might get hammered on this. But actually it was the right thing to do, rather than it just being the Ofsted approved model. So we got Requires Improvement but a strong RI. The conversations allowed people to see the things differently, so it created that space to startle people's thinking, because habit's the biggest enemy of policy innovation - people say oh well we do that already or, you know, we've always done it like that… So, how do you put them in a space where they, their thinking is challenged or their perspective is startled?

Here, a centralising tradition of the primacy of inspectorates and national policy interacts with a tradition of local autonomy and choice. This coming together of traditions of centralisation and professionalism is experienced as a dilemma. It involves the extent to which policy and practice are determined by agents external to the authority and locality, or can be shaped by professionals with local knowledge in line with the council's strategic vision. The two examples above highlight dilemmas of agency and of strategy. How far to push back at a central inspectorate? To what extent to champion local sovereignty in the face of central scrutiny and critique? And can the national policy narratives of such inspectorates be used to harness organisational commitment to a local way of doing things? We see the flux and interactions of different centralising traditions and local and professional traditions.

How Do Stories and Narratives Help Chief Executives Mediate the Policy Process?

In this chapter, we add to our previous contribution to understanding the significance of participants' constitutive stories about local government (Orr and Vince 2009; Orr and Bennett 2017). Chief executives engage in an array of narrative work and storytelling to manage their interactions with others. Elsewhere we examine how these narrative practices extend to different areas of chief executives' everyday practices. These include inviting an emotional connection with public service—for example to encourage a realignment between colleagues in different parts of the organisation. Narrative practices can also involve making sense of organisational realities—for example, how a collective sense of the organisational landscape is constructed, within a network of relations, and in the face of competing narratives and interpretations. They can entail provoking reflection on practices and assumptions: telling stories which offer critique and aim to generate change. Fourth, they can extend to managing political relations with council leaders—how chief executives manage interactions to help leaders get what they need.

Overall, we found a commitment to stories and narratives amongst our chief executives, who recognise it as an important part of their practice in relation to policymaking. Our interviews offer us examples of where the chief executives are authoring stories in interventionist ways to influence the action. But the chief executives are also alive to the importance of others' stories. Here their job is to listen to and understand the beliefs, concerns or aspirations that play through these. They include examples of stories that exert a catalysing effect in the policy process and become a focal point for the mobilisation of organisational action or local political change.

Taking the first of these, the interventionist storytelling, the chief executives' practice is underpinned by a quest to offer meaning amidst the chaos of different voices, demands, disruption and changes in the local government arena. In that context, a reliance on dry facts is seen as insufficient:

> Evidence is never enough you've got to find meaning in all the noise. And storytelling is the best way of doing that, and you've got to connect people to a purpose, because it's complicated. You know, you can't describe all the technical aspects and the richness of it all, it's too long and too dull. You've got to find a way to encapsulate what your policy journey is about and engage people, because it's about culture and values… that's the level of engagement you need it to be on really, so I do think it's very important.

Another chief executive accounted for the power of her storying practice in this way:

> A good story is a distillation, a synthesis of evidence, emotion, values, and therefore it is the most powerful and when done well it's incredibly effective way to communicate, because it shows emotion and values. It's very important when you're having the discussion when people are losing something. Quite a lot of what we've had to do in the last six years needs doing in the next five. You know, normally leaders will say this is change and there's a pain of change but, but where we're going to is much better than where we've come from. It's not as simple as that. In the last five years, some of the change has been as a cost to people, definitely the staff

who lost their jobs, sometimes for the communities, and having an emotional value strand to the way you communicate that is incredibly important, there's loss to people.

In the case of stories told by other actors, the role of the chief executive is to listen, interpret, translate and manage the organisational or policy response. Such stories can have a catalysing effect. One respondent reflected upon the case of the state of local health care in the borough and a successful campaigning effort to support health provision:

> Stories which are anecdotal to individual families of members and officers are powerful. Because the majority of those live locally and therefore the experience of our local hospital is shared in those stories, it becomes incredibly real. It becomes about when Gran was in the ambulance for two hours because she couldn't go into A&E, why is that? And then that plays back into our professional lives… It is individual stories which are real to individuals and told with conviction, that mean that everybody understands the consequence of what's happening… 'We've got to do something about this'… 'This is us, it's affecting us'… So there is an emotional content to that, a poignant nature to it which has impact.

The chief executive feels implicated in a policy arena which is not directly within his organisation's remit. This is because it speaks to the climate, or the public service context, and is part of the concerns and conversations taking place amongst his staff. In this sense, everything falls into the chief executive's 'centre'. As one chief executive put it, the role is coterminous with communities, not with the boundaries of the organisation. A decentred approach to understanding policymaking directs us not just to the chief executives' own stories, but those others that cut through and find purchase in policy conversations or in the local experience of a shared humanity.

Another chief executive tells of such a story which became influential in changing the thinking of elected members in relation to an aspect of policy concerning children with special educational needs and in a context of budgetary constraints:

> On the back of where we are with our finances and savings, I was having to change our policy in relation to SEN children and their transport. So the story that goes with this is there's word out there from parents of children and other professionals that Tropley provides a gold-plated service for its SEN children. I don't know if that's true or not, I haven't done the

research. So my Members, when they start to hear that say 'Look, we can't afford this…' That starting story starts to drive the Cabinet thinking… So you nail them into factual phase or research phase and say we've got this story about gold-plated service, is that true or not? So you then delve into it and you look at the facts. It's likely on the back of that positioning we will see policy changed, or policy developed differently from our existing policy and therefore we'll get that policy change on the back of that all starting with the story. It takes Members into changing policy.

Political Management: Chief Executives, Council Leaders and Relationality

The eternal dynamic of officer–member relations provides a further expression of a complex policymaking process. Many of our interviews point towards dynamics of relationality, in which policy positions are arrived at through interactions between the two groups. For chief executives, a key relationship is with the leader or mayor. The chief executive simultaneously manages the corporate body of professionals and senior managers, whilst also providing support, advice and resources to the elected members to facilitate the formulation and implementation of their programme. Entwined in this relationship are traditions of management, of professionals and of democracy, and the continuities and disjunctions between those webs of belief.

One chief executive offers a relatively harmonious picture of these local officer–member relationships and of a close cooperation between chief executive, senior management team and the elected members:

> Although it's been hard work it's been a bit of breath of fresh air… to be able to have an agreement with the Leader that this is kind of co-produced now. We have moved away from a very strong Leader model where the Leader says 'this is the policy, can somebody just write it for me?', to genuinely lead policy officers with the lead director… who work with the portfolio holder and kind of thrash out the early ideas… It is much more a kind of co-produced effort. And upfront, you know, we do sit down with portfolio holders and say 'OK, so can you just download what's in your head for us?' … and we'll try and kind of work that up into some kind of proposition.

In some other authorities, we heard of a more uneasy relationship, one in which members assumed a dominant role and in which officers' capacity to engage and shape policy ideas felt underpowered.

One chief executive told us how she tries to work with different officer and member perspectives and creates more scope for officers to provide and members to accept professional challenge and insight:

> I think there's a lack of confidence about the challenge… So what I've said to Members and to professionals here, nobody's right or wrong - you know that cartoon about is it a six or a nine? It depends what side of the number you're stood at. So you're not wrong. A professional view is absolutely right. So I might be a planner and I've got years of experience, I understand planning legislation, I know the case law and that's my advice. But, as an Elected Member I am then taking into account the people… and I make the decision. And the professionals go well that's rubbish, you know, they've ignored professional advice. No, they haven't, they've taken it into account along with other things. So I work with the Elected Members to say yes that's entirely legitimate. However the consequences of you overturning that Officer recommendation could be this, this and this. Understand that as well and then make your choice.

Other chief executives emphasise their role in providing policy challenge and explain that this can be to officers as well as to elected members. In this way, for example, one research participant describes how she tries to curtail the enthusiasms of her officers as much as the politicians:

> We employ lots of people who come up through professional routes, who not only are interested, they're passionate and some of them are zealots, right? I am the person who really challenges critically whether this idea is going to work, and I say actually it's a national policy you're dressing up locally, trying to solve this local problem and actually aren't they doing this in Tadchester? But our population is fundamentally different, so this might not work here. What I don't want is single-minded policy zealots who believe this is definitely going to work, and then they'll stick with it even for three or four years, wasting millions. And they'll then sell it politically and Mayor will agree it and then it won't work and then we're all bought into it and then we're all saying actually this hasn't worked, how do we stop this?

As part of this political management, chief executives tend to work on tuning their political antennae. A recurring theme in our research conversations and wider interactions with this group is their own 'mortality' (Orr 2014), or the way in which their own job security is intertwined with the fortunes and fancy of the leading politician. They point to the complexity of the local political landscape and of local political history. This can be a fluid picture with politicians even within the same party jockeying for position and influence. One illustration of this in policy terms is provided by a chief executive who explains the local political dynamic within the ruling Labour group in relation to policy on local taxation levels:

> They're largely managing to use the party constitution to keep control of the machine at the moment, so it doesn't feel existential in that sense. What it feels like is the way of handling that is to give a bit of ground in the policy debate. So the way my Leader would characterise it, he's got a load of middle class tax and spenders who are kind of flooding into the party. His view of is they're more the middle class residents who think why are we making a fetish of not putting a council tax up? We should be glorying in putting the council tax up. And my Leader and my Labour Group are, probably wouldn't use this term now but they're, very Blairite… They come from those battles before New Labour really, so that's an interesting dynamic.

Findings and Conclusion

Roland Barthes (1977) reminds us that the narratives of the social world are ubiquitous and numberless. Narratives are part of human strategies for dealing with change. Their representations of change (threat, positive transformation, failure, triumph) can highlight particular and perhaps hitherto obscured aspects of particular situations, and the stakes involved. In doing so, they can bring dilemmas to the surface by a new framing of a predicament in ways which call for new ways of thinking or acting (Ricoeur 1983). So, the answer to our question of how do local government chief executives engage with policy dilemmas is through storytelling and narrative practices.

Narratives offer bridges between the past, present and future. Some seem safe and solid, others more precarious or weatherworn. Policy makers are implicated in processes of trying to bridge present-day 'realities' and the potential of the future. An interest in narratives points towards an understanding of policymaking as a creative and interpretive process in which stories can engage different people and voices in shaping these future possibilities.

Our interviews suggest the significance of networks for understanding the practices of local government chief executives in relation to policymaking. Within these networks, their accounts frame dilemmas of political values, officer–member relations, relations between members of the council and wider stakeholders and interest including central government and inspectorates. These play out against the ebb and flow of traditions of democracy, professionalism, centralisation and localism (Orr and Vince 2009). Chief executives emerge as actors responding to the flux embedded in policy networks, as they interpret and respond to the competing expectations, actions and experiences of others.

Our study offers a way of understanding the politics-administration conundrum that casts the relationship between politicians and administrators as dialogical rather than dichotomous. Chief executives emerge as co-authors, sounding boards, co-developers of strategy, challengers and co-interpreters of political vision. These chief executives are therefore redolent of what Demir and Nyhan (2008) call politically active public administrators, adding value to democratic processes through purposive use of narrative in relation to political guidance and policy leadership. This insight fits well with Stone's (1997) observations of how public managers and politicians craft stories, to construct reality in ways that represent their interests and further their goals. In this way, sense-making, or giving meaning to situations and dilemmas, is a means by which leaders 'ascribe values or highlight some aspects of a situation, while ignoring or downplaying other aspects of the same situation' (Bean and Hamilton 2006: 325).

This engagement with a decentred theory of policymaking enables an appreciation of how chief executives mediate their policy networks and help us to understand the everyday production and reproduction of political power and influence through stories and narratives. Our chief executives offer a sense of a pluralistic or fragmented policy environment in which the making and remaking of policy take place. They accomplish this in a context where the seams are fraying, and the familiarity of a relatively closed loop policy system feels less sustainable. They recognise, albeit critically, the significance of networks, but nonetheless strive to ensure that the policy remains in the ambit of the manageable. Our study suggests that an important way in which they do so is by engaging with the discursive realm in which the politics and dilemmas of policy can be examined and explored together. In this way, stories and narratives enable organisational actors to understand and formulate responses to new and unfolding policy dilemmas.

Such an undertaking is by no means straightforward. The policy arena is by definition a politicised space, brimming with contestation, scepticism and competing norms and values. It is a setting in which alternative stories and interpretations 'dance together' (Boje 2008: 1) in ways which echo Bakhtin's (1981) idea of the 'polyphonic manner of story' (60).

The implication of this idea is that other actors may feel unmoved by the frames—the deliberate and purposeful attempts to frame meaning—that chief executives put forward or prefer. The action of policymaking emerges from such zones of contestation and disagreement in which narratives and stories play a pivotal role.

The decentred approach to governance highlights the melee of diverse and contingent meanings in policy arenas such as local councils. It challenges researchers to engage with local situated narratives and the ways in which local actors construct their worldviews. Their views of their local context are understood as constructed through the stories that actors share with one another. To study these networks demands scholarly engagement with the narratives around which these networks are created. Chief executives are not a homogeneous group. They have particular relationships with local politicians. As well as more or less recognisable local government traditions, there are contingent local political and organisational histories. There are parts of the process, which seem familiar to chief executives who have traversed different organisations, and yet there are no shared toolkits or uniformity of model or process. The traditional model still allows for considerable contingency. 'Somewhere in that space', as one of our participants put it, policy is made. To even the most seasoned chief executive, there is still an air of bewilderment about exactly how policy comes to be formed. Meantime, stories enable them occasionally to hold court, or to hold the ring, to hold on to influence in a decentred world.

The job description of a chief executive entails ceding the central policy role to elected members. Yet, there is a need not to abandon being at the centre of the action. But the centre is harder to plot. How do you identify and act at the centre of networks that shift and vary issue by issue or policy area by policy area? How to be at the noisy centre of polyphony, confronting many dilemmas, each contending for their attention and time?

A decentred approach holds out a radical challenge to chief executives and other participants in the policymaking process. Narrative practices in this arena at times involve authoring, at others co-authoring with politicians or professional staff, and throughout as reflexive practitioners being attuned to the stories of others. Curiosity and interested engagement with the voices and stories of others often challenges both certainty and organisational hierarchy.

Engaging in a narrative-based approach to understanding policymaking is itself a political act. It carries with it the normative implication that practitioners should take seriously stories and narratives as part of their practical repertoire: that they should attend to the stories of other actors and groups and accord them legitimacy even in situations of contestation and disagreement. In other words, stories should not be regarded as a poor substitute for facts. Rather they are sources of knowledge and understanding, a basis for action, a means for making sense of the past and of framing choices about the future. Such a view is challenging to traditions of local government that prize statistics, hard data or a weighing and measuring of the facts at hand. It rejects assumptions rooted in a positivist worldview or a modernist social science. It takes us further away from the notion of toolkits for effective governance, or a search for isomorphic best practices. It highlights the potential of learning from and through stories. Stories—telling them and attending with care to others' stories—are seen as a basis for thinking about the prospects for policy continuity or disruption, for seeking to transform practices or to judiciously shore them up. In a decentred social world, stories are a vital part of policymaking and of the ebb and flow of choices in action.

References

Agar, M. (2010). On the Ethnographic Part of the Mix. A Multi-genre Tale of the Field. *Organizational Research Methods, 13*(2), 296–303.

Bains, M. (Chairman). (1972). *The New Local Authorities: Management and Structure*. London: HMSO.

Bakhtin, M. M. (1981). *The Dialogic Imagination: Four Essays* (M. Holquist, Ed., C. Emerson & M. Holquist, Trans.). Austin: University of Texas Press.

Barthes, R. (1977). *Image Music Text* (S. Heath, Trans.). London: Fontana Press.

Bean, C. J., & Hamilton, F. E. (2006). Leader Framing and Follower Sensemaking. Responses to Downsizing in the Brave New Workplace. *Human Relations, 59*, 325–349.

Berger, P. L., & Luckmann, T. (1966). *The Social Construction of Reality*. New York: Anchor Books.

Bevir, M. (2013). *A Theory of Governance*. Berkeley: University of California Press.

Bevir, M., & Rhodes, R. A. W. (2003). *Interpreting British Governance*. London: Routledge.

Bevir, M., & Rhodes, R. A. W. (Eds.). (2015). *Routledge Handbook of Interpretive Political Science*. New York: Routledge.

Bevir, M., & Rhodes, R. A. W. (Eds.). (2016). *Rethinking Governance: Ruling, Rationalities and Resistance*. New York: Routledge.

Boje, D. M. (1991). The Storytelling Organization: A Study of Storytelling Performance in an Office Supply Firm. *Administrative Science Quarterly, 36*, 106–126.

Boje, D. M. (2008). *Storytelling Organizations*. London: Sage.

Carr, D. (1986). *Time, Narrative and History*. Bloomington, IN: Indiana University Press.

Demir, T., & Nyhan, R. C. (2008). The Politics-Administration Dichotomy: An Empirical Search for Correspondence between Theory and Practice. *Public Administration Review, 68*, 81–96.

Fenno, R. F. (1990). *Watching Politicians: Essays on Participant Observation*. Berkeley, CA: Institute of Governmental Studies.

Gabriel, Y. (2015). Storytelling. In M. Bevir & R. A. W. Rhodes (Eds.), *Routledge Handbook of Interpretive Political Science*. New York: Routledge.

Geertz, C. (1988). *Works and Lives: The Anthropologist as Author*. Stanford: Stanford University Press.

Grant, D., Keenoy, T., & Oswick, C. (1998). *Discourse and Organization Studies*. London: Sage.

Hummel, R. P. (1991). Stories Managers Tell: Why They Are as Valid as Science. *Public Administration Review, 51*(1), 31–41.

Lévi-Strauss, C. (1963). *Structural Anthropology*. New York: Basic Books.

Maynard-Moody, S., & Musheno, M. (2003). *Cops, Teachers, Counselors: Stories from the Front Lines of Public Service*. Ann Arbor: University of Michigan Press.

Orr, K. (2014). Local Government Chief Executives' Everyday Hauntings: Towards a Theory of Organizational Ghosts. *Organization Studies, 35*, 1041–1061.

Orr, K., & Bennett, M. (2012a). Down and Out in the British Library and Other Dens of Coproduction. *Management Learning, 43*(4), 427–442.

Orr, K., & Bennett, M. (2012b). Public Administration Scholarship and the Politics of Coproducing Academic-Practitioner Research. *Public Administration Review, 72*(4), 427–442.

Orr, K., & Bennett, M. (2017). Relational Leadership, Storytelling and Narratives: Practices of Local Government Chief Executives. *Public Administration Review, 77*, 517–527.

Orr, K., & Vince, R. (2009). Traditions of Local Government. *Public Administration, 87*, 655–677.

Perry, J. L. (2012). How Can We Improve Our Science to Generate More Usable Knowledge for Public Professionals? *Public Administration Review, 72*, 479–482.

Posner, P. L. (2009). The Pracademic: An Agenda for Re-engaging Practitioners and Academics. *Public Budgeting & Finance, 29*, 12–26.

Rabinow, P., & Sullivan, W. M. (Eds.). (1987). *Interpretive Social Science: A Second Look*. Berkeley: University of California Press.

Reissner, S. C. (2011). Patterns of Stories of Organisational Change. *Journal of Organizational Change Management, 24*(5), 593–609.

Ricoeur, P. (1983). *Time and Narrative*, Vol. 1 (K. McLaughlin & D. Pellauer, Trans.). Chicago: University of Chicago Press.

Sarbin, T. R. (Ed.). (1986). *Narrative Psychology, the Storied Nature of Human Conduct*. New York: Praeger.

Schwartz-Shea, P., & Yanow, D. (2012). *Interpretive Research Design*. New York: Routledge.

Society of Local Authority Chief Executives (SOLACE). (2014). *Submission to Communities and Local Government Select Committee Inquiry into Local Government Chief Officer Remuneration*. London: Solace.

Stone, D. (1997). *Policy Paradox: The Art of Political Decision Making*. New York: Norton.

White, H. (1987). *The Content of the Narrative Form: Narrative Discourse and Historical Representation*. Baltimore, MD: Johns Hopkins.

White, M., & Epston, D. (1990). *Narrative Means to Therapeutic Ends*. New York: Norton.

CHAPTER 10

How Do the Police Respond to Evidence-Based Policing?

Jenny Fleming

INTRODUCTION—WHAT WORKS CENTRES

In March 2013, the UK Cabinet Office launched the '*What Works Network*', a nationally coordinated initiative aimed at strengthening the use of research-based evidence on 'What Works' in public policymaking. Currently, there are seven research centres[1] focusing on six key areas of public policy, intended to build on existing models of delivering evidence-based policy. The What Works centres are being developed in a political environment which, it is argued, is increasingly amenable to the idea of evidence-based decision-making, particularly in the context of 'austerity' and cost-effectiveness. Government white papers, including the Cabinet Office Open Public Services White Paper (2011) and the Civil Service Reform White Paper (2012), assert government commitment to scrutiny and transparency across departments, and initiatives are in place to increase access to government administrative data for the purposes of research and evaluation (Mulgan and Puttick 2013; UK Administrative Data Research Network 2012).

J. Fleming (✉)
Department of Sociology, Social Policy and Criminology,
University of Southampton, Southampton, UK
e-mail: j.fleming@soton.ac.uk

For some years now, the College of Policing (College) and its predecessor the *National Policing Improvement Agency* (NPIA) have promoted the importance of research evidence to inform practice in policing and crime reduction. The '*What Works Centre for Crime Reduction*' (WWCCR) was established in 2013 to develop a strong evidence base for decision-making around crime reduction. The WWCCR is led by the College and until early 2017 was supported by a Commissioned Partnership Programme.[2]

A key component of the WWCCR programme has been to assist in building an evidence base; to establish a common database of knowledge; and to develop police officer skills to enable them to appraise and use evidence to inform their decision-making (see Fleming et al. 2016a, b, c). As a precursor to this task, it was agreed that a series of focus groups across four police organisations across the UK would be an appropriate opportunity to gauge an understanding as to what officers understood about evidence and research in the context of their organisation and how they felt about the changes and how those changes might be rolled out by management.

Focus Group as Method

As a way of collecting stories and getting people to reflect on their beliefs and practices, the focus group is highly applicable, particularly so when change is on the agenda and little is known of how that change may be received. The purpose of a focus group is to obtain information from a predetermined and limited number of people (Kreuger 1988: 26) ideally yielding 'a more diversified array of responses and afford [ing] a more extended basis for designing systematic research on the situation in hand…' (Merton et al. 1990: 135). Focus groups allow us to explore interactively how 'knowledge and, more importantly, ideas both develop, and operate, within a given cultural context' (Kitziger 1994: 116). The discussion is formally facilitated and the facilitator's role is to ensure that everyone participates, no one individual dominates and to encourage as much interaction between participants as possible (see Kitzinger 1994).

For the purposes of this research, a structured approach was adopted whereby open-ended questions were asked in a way that would trigger discussion among participants. At the same time, the process was more structured than normal, to increase the quality of information and the time-economy of the procedure. Such a process is not just about identifying consensus and common reflections on 'group norms and experiences'. It is equally important to explore differences of opinion and understanding (Kitzinger 1994: 113). To maximise the potential of focus group data and to minimise unhelpful deference to senior officers (see Fleming 2011), the focus groups for this research were organised by rank and location. Overall, the various discussions were frank and robust (Fleming and Fyfe 2015).

The focus groups were held in four UK constabularies between May and July 2014. A pilot for the focus groups was conducted at a UK police training institution in March 2014. All ranks were included in the invitation to participate in the focus groups. Ranks that participated in focus groups were: Constables, Sergeants, Inspectors, Chief Inspectors, Superintendents and Chief Superintendents. This chapter draws on the data from the Constable and Sergeant focus groups. There were 97 Constables and Sergeants in the focus groups under review. 49 Constables (29 male and 20 female); 48 Sergeants (35 male and 13 female). Out of a total of 160 participants (14 focus groups) overall, the Constables and Sergeants constituted 60% of the cohort and the eight groups were drawn from all four organisations.

One of the central aims of the focus groups was to better understand police officers' beliefs about, and understanding of, evidence-based practice generally[3] and how they thought it might be implemented. As with most focus group discussion, the question prompted new insights and identified aspects of the organisational culture that in this case concerned the role of senior officers and management in what was generally perceived as the new reforming 'fad'. All discussions were taped and transcribed. Drawing on the police literature to identify provisional and preliminary themes, the data were analysed thematically in order to code the focus group transcripts (Braun and Clarke 2006, 2013). The topics were reviewed and organised into potential sub-themes and then subject to a detailed analysis using NVivo©.

It has been noted elsewhere that broadly speaking, if you put a group of practitioners in a room and ask them about their job, one notes quickly the propensity for chatting and the tendency to 'group whinge' (Fleming 2011: 23). Police officers are no exception and focus groups can, if not managed well, lead to a dearth of useful content. Also, when analysing the transcripts, the danger exists that thematic analysis will lead researchers to highlight the comments that make the required point vividly. So, while such quotes are included here, the chapter also seeks to include the quotes and discussion points that came up regularly across the two ranks and the four organisations and have definitively shaped and determined the themes of this research.

Finally, focus groups can be seen as a variant of ethnographic data collection if that data are interpreted with an 'ethnographic sensibility' (Agar and MacDonald 1995; Rhodes and Tiernan 2015). In facilitating the discussion and analysing the transcripts, the emphasis falls on the meaning of utterances and those meanings can only be understood in the context of the group's understandings or traditions, i.e. in this case, the inherited beliefs and practices of officers. In other words, the focus groups are a way of decentring the meaning of evidence-based policing for two levels in the police hierarchy. Before proceeding to the focus group analysis, some context is provided for the reader.

What Works?

The emphasis on 'evidence-based policy' and employing 'What Works' in everyday police practice has had greater momentum since the establishment of the College in 2012. The move towards professionalisation has put a major emphasis on recognising and raising educational standards in policing. Promotion and advancement in today's UK police force are highly dependent on a willingness to demonstrate a commitment to professionalisation and for some, but not all, a 'real profession' means formal status, accreditation, ethical standards, qualifications (underpinned by 'evidence-based knowledge') and governance. Senior officers are committed to self-development; higher education achievements; and 'growing' the evidence base through their own or others' research efforts. Internally, they are aware that their own progress through the ranks will depend on the extent to which they can be actively seen to embrace the new scientific paradigm. Most senior officers wanting to progress successfully through the echelons of the 'top brass' belong to Evidence-Based Societies, have a Masters in Criminology from Cambridge University, and actively encourage their staff to participate in related activities (Van Dijk et al. 2015: 154–156; Fleming et al. 2015; Fleming et al. 2016a, b, c).

Despite recent changes to police governance arrangements in the UK (Lister and Rowe 2015), and a diminishment in the traditional authoritarian approach to top-down management (Marks and Sklansky 2012: 4), Chief Constables and their executive teams still lead hierarchical organisations where top-down decisions are communicated to lower ranks with little or no consultation. The 'more relaxed, informal, caring and supportive organisation' heralded by Davies and Thomas (cited in Marks and Sklansky 2012: 2) in 2001 is still about strong, top-down management. In times of transition and organisational change, the conflicting perspectives on procedure and practice between management and the lower ranks described by Reuss-Ianni (1983) become more evident as senior officers seek to 'sell' the new 'way of thinking'. At the same time, the lower ranks strive to accommodate change when all else around them in terms of values, attitudes and ways of doing things appears unchanged. Indeed, performance management targets, scant resources and general understaffing make the new horizon look daunting for junior officers.

The interactions of these two distinct cultures in policing, a street cop culture and a management culture as identified by Elizabeth Reuss-Ianni (1983) over thirty years ago are still evident. In her intensive study of the New York Police Department, Reuss-Ianni (1983) remarked on the widespread differences and conflict between 'management cops' and 'street cops'. The author noted that street cops were rarely 'in touch' with each other except through formal directives and official communications. As managers prioritised administrative processes and street-level 'cops' exhibited 'operational pragmatism', there was invariably a lack of 'a common context for interpretation or action,' which in turn ensured a negative impact on morale and communication generally (1983: 118). Reuss-Ianni's work provides a framework from which we can identify and consider the bottom-up responses in the UK to 'evidence-based policing' and the role of management in pushing this new agenda.

We met the focus group participants at the beginning of a transitional period during which the UK's police national body, the NPIA, had been dissolved less than a year previously and replaced by the College. At the time the focus groups were conducted between March and July of 2014, the College's activities (at least for Constables and Sergeants) were largely the stuff of rumour and hearsay. Many knew little about the concept, and others were apprehensive about what it might mean for them. Others considered it 'another change fad' to contend with and the more cynical recognised it as another way for senior officers to 'mark their card' for promotion.

Against this background, there were three overarching characteristics of the dominant organisational culture[4] that shaped the police response to evidence-based policing in the focus groups—organisational change (and the fatigue that accompanied it); lack of consultation and the importance of buy-in for the lower ranks, and the promotional opportunities that change inevitably brings to management. Before discussing the participants' responses under these three headings, I describe what officers understood by evidence-based policing and their reactions to the 'doing' it.

Evidence? What Evidence?

In varying degrees, there was a lack of understanding overall of what constituted evidence-based research in the context of policing.

> I haven't heard of it, no. But I [think] that we as practitioners will be the ones putting it into place with very little feedback or support from people above us (Constable, Male)

> Can I just clarify because I'm a bit confused, what do you mean by evidence, do you mean DNA samples, documentation at a scene, or evidence as in research? (Constable, Female)

> Having recognisable outcomes in everything we do, so everything can be logged to get the statistics together (Con. F)

> It's how people best receive information from us, it's on the intranet (Con. F)

Sergeants had a little more understanding but not much:

> Still not clear to me what the College are suggesting, what this evidence-based model should look like and what potentially PCs do at that level, we're commenting on something and we don't know what it looks like or how different that's going to be (Sergeant, Male)

> People doing things on the basis of past knowledge and history? (Sergeant, Female)

> Target your resourcing to a particular problem using the correct evidence that's out there, statistics, crime stats, that sort of thing (Sgt. M)

> Yes I have heard of this, it's about making objective decisions in terms of resourcing and policing tactics based on something tangible, that's my summary (Sgt. M)

Many of the officers thought they had heard the term evidence-based policing, although few could provide a strong definition and most overlapped their understanding of 'evidence' with gathering facts in an investigation—that is, 'gathering evidence for a crime'. Such 'facts' would cover the use of police statistics and any associated analysis. For those officers who were unclear about the concept, evidence-based policing was explained to the whole group by the facilitator before the focus groups progressed. It became evident with both Sergeants and Constables across the groups that the beliefs and practices of how hierarchy and progression worked in their individual police organisations were a major factor in how they framed evidence-based policing as part of their responses. Challenges and dilemmas identified with evidence-based policing in practice included time, resources, capacity, operational policing realities and culture. These issues have been discussed elsewhere (see Fleming and Fyfe 2015; Fleming and Wingrove 2017). This chapter explores how the inherited beliefs and practices about hierarchy undermined the concept of evidence-based policing as a permanent organisational change strategy.

While Sergeants saw themselves as the rank that would be called upon by management to move the concept forward, Constables were reasonably sure that their formal 'buy-in' would not be required. The following section is a series of linked quotes involving three officers interacting and expressing a sense of perceived inevitability about a Constable's 'place' and the powerlessness associated with change and transition:

> I think we are the practitioners at our rank and my experience of … police is they involve practitioners at a very late stage if at all, so it's not something we'd have any involvement in until we're told this is what we're doing, probably wouldn't even be told why we were doing it or the basis for it (Con. F) ↓

> Or a consultation will have already decided what we're doing anyway (Con. M) ↓

> Yeah and a consultation will involve specific people who already knew about it in the first place (Con. F) ↓

> It makes it difficult, we're the ones who are going to have to make it work, you know anyone below Chief Inspector tends not to be involved in these discussions unless they are in a specific piece of planning, so people on the ground trying to make it work have no faith because of the way it's being operated (Con. M) ↓

> Foisted upon them (Con. F) ↓

> We're the ones who've got to make it work, so you'd like to think we'd be asked at the beginning, our views, because often the decisions are made from above us from people who have been removed from the lower end and haven't had to deal with those situations for some time and they don't appreciate how we're going to put it into practice (Con. F)

This particular exchange was not unusual in itself. 'Operational pragmatism' (Reuss-Ianni 1983: 118) was a strong thread of the Constables' narrative:

> I think from a policing perspective, Constables' perspective, we have really little input into policy making apart from tokenistic consultation. The other thing is when you're out on the ground and research is quoted, basically what it tells you is common sense things that any common sense police officer should know, should realise when they're out on the ground, it generally looks like a lot of money being spent on research for research purposes to back up stuff that generally should be taken as Carte Blanche (Con. M)

Some Constables considered that it would be their 'natural' role to shoulder the 'grunt work' of a new scheme without complaint.

> Constables do what Sergeants tell them to do, we're not free thinkers, at this rank we are a sausage factory, shouldn't be thinking for ourselves, shouldn't be thinking outside the box, we're a sausage factory. Once you get to the next rank it's different, you can do that, at constable level you can't do that, you just do what you're told by the person above you (Con. F)

> It's for the rank structure to make the policies and procedures and that's what we follow, that's what we do… (Con. M)

Others, however, recognised their own sense of agency and the levels of discretion afforded to them as street-level bureaucrats (Lipsky 1980: 13–18) and were confident about the value and importance of the hierarchy getting the buy-in from them:

> It's a hearts and minds thing, you need to get people to buy into it and that's what the police are bad at, the buy in factor. If people don't buy into it, it won't work because police officers are simple (Con. F)

Sergeants saw themselves as the group that had to be brought in if they were going to successfully 'sell it' to the lower ranks.

Buying in the '*Doing*' Rank

The advantage of the Sergeants doing it is that if that buys us in then it's more likely to be done on the street because, we've all had training and if the Sergeant doesn't agree with it they walk out that room and say don't bother doing that, if you get us bought in and we agree with it and we deliver the training then it's more likely it's going to happen (Sgt. M)

It's a very insipid thing, I sit in meetings and the poor old PCs, the way they are spoken about it's like they are a different being. They don't have the morale support, even of the organisation at the moment, which I think is terribly sad. We need to start believing in ourselves so we'll want to be professional and buy into things like this (Sgt. F)

What might buy us in a little bit more and certainly buy me in, if we can do this training, if we can come up with solutions as we've talked about and be trusted to implement them and not be overruled by the bosses as you were because that happens all the time, you go to do something and the bosses say no, ... we're supposed to be leaders but you never get to make the decision because it always gets changed by someone higher up. If you want to buy us in we need that guarantee that we're going to be doing something that is practical and will be supported (Sgt. M)

I think with the delivery of anything, how this is taken forward and delivered to officers, there's going to be two key principles and it's all going to fall under value. We have to value this so much so that we ensure our officers have protected time to take this on board, we want you to engage in this, we really want you to have some sort of a buy in into it (Sgt. M)

This is the rank that gets done, this is the most important rank in the police force and when you hear the Government say they want to get rid of Sergeants it really annoys me because this is the rank that sells the difficult messages to the PCs on the ground. This is the rank that's the first port of call for any serious incident, this is the rank that gets things done. The Sergeants are the doing rank and the rank that will sell it to the PCs and if you don't get the buy in from the Sergeants you won't get the PC's buy in (Sgt. M)

Engel and Peterson (2014: 409) point out that in general, 'the influence of supervisor attitudes on officer attitudes and subsequent behaviour appears to be fairly weak'. However, this lack of influence does not apparently detract from the belief that the 'doing' rank can make things happen on the ground. Yet, the change-weary response of Constables and their views on 'waiting out the fads' would be a challenge for any supervising rank.

> One thing in this organisation that I think is our greatest weakness is, we have implemented that much change you can understand why people have taken their eye off the ball (Sgt. M)

> I think there's not the understanding where the change comes from, we have a lot of change all the time and I think that's the frustrating issue, people are probably fed up with it, but maybe if there was better consultation with the ranks about what needed to be changed so they're more involved from the start, that might be better (Con. M)

> I'm just drawing on what ... just said, managers coming in and wanting to put their stamp on change, innovative ideas (Sgt. M)

> Nobody likes change, this organisation has had so much change over the years, it's unbelievable, its change for the sake of change (Sgt. M)

> When we got a new boss the first thing I asked was how long are you going to be here for (Sgt. M)

> That just creates problems because every boss that comes in he or she comes with new ideas and the idea is to tick a change box if you want to go on further, the whole thing just gets turned upside down (Sgt. M)

> I'm just drawing on what was just said, managers coming in and wanting to put their stamp on change, innovative ideas (Sgt. M)

A general overview of the focus group responses of both Constables and Sergeants suggests a strong sense of cynicism and of the 'wheel turning' again, usually for the benefit of management. In a reform context, managers are largely perceived to be 'out of touch with the realities of operational police work' (Bacon 2014: 114). A major thread in the focus groups of Constables and Sergeants was the role of senior officers and their role in perpetuating new 'fads'. It was generally agreed that senior officers would benefit from a new idea while others did the work. The recurring metaphor was that of the wheel, which was forever-turning full circle; they held a circuitous notion of change.

Promoting the Wheel

> It's for promotion, so if new things come along it gets the tick in the box for the promotion at the expense of us on the ground, we are getting hammered and crucified (Con, F)

> ... In the past it's always been a standing joke within the police that a Chief Inspector will come up with an idea, get promoted to

Superintendent and the next Chief Inspector will come in, change it and get promoted again on that and then the wheel turns. The wheel constantly turns in this job, one minute we do one thing, I mean I'm doing things now I can remember us doing in the 90's, we are still moving forward but the wheel turns and you go back to what works, or in some cases what didn't work (Sgt. M)

A Sergeant from another group made a similar observation:

Where does this fit in with service delivery? Because that's what it's all about now, we're down to the bare bones and it's all about … answering calls and dealing with people and that doesn't fit into this quant measurement I'm afraid, service delivery is the new mandate, we've now got a new boss who's turned up and every time a new boss turns up it's a new broom and you know it wears you down. It's like water torture, God here we go again … it's hilarious if you watch it, you couldn't make this stuff up (Sgt. M)

The inevitability of the wheel turning was acknowledged by a long-serving Constable:

At this rank everything changes every five years and after ten years you're doing exactly the same as you were at the beginning but it's brought in as someone's new idea, someone's got a promotion, so everyone's used to something brand new being brought in and then going back a few years later, so there's that level of scepticism … everything is presented to you as 'yes this is the fantastic answer to solve all our problems', well it wasn't ten years ago so what makes it different now? So it just goes round. There's … when a brand new idea is brought in with very little explanation, there's a lot of jadedness (Con M)

Benefits accrued to senior officers or management included the perception that new ideas were often the springboard to promotion.

All the things they have to hit to get their board, so they come up with this great plan and the people who carry that out are the Constables on the ground whether it's right or wrong we do what we're told, and because of people trying to get promoted you get these hair brain schemes making us look like idiots on the ground and an organisation as a whole (Con. M).

If you start going Inspector upwards you then start talking political agendas and promotion, gathering evidence for promotion, and they all arrive with a new idea, they want to change things, 'this is what I've done and this is the mark I made (Sgt. M)

I think we've got an organisation which has a big fat middle body which people are looking to latch themselves onto and guide and steer and take control of and possibly step off onto the next rank (Sgt. M)

There's too many new initiatives and competing initiatives and it comes from competing people trying to get promoted, let's call a spade a spade, these initiatives by in large come from Chief Inspectors looking to write a report on what they have done, for example, with their community engagement (Con M)

… because I've not been chasing promotion I've not had to worry about that because I got to a level I was happy at fairly early on in my career … I think what we're saying is targets do not work because you merely get people who are chasing promotion to be fair, looking to tick that particular box (Sgt. M)

PCs won't be interested, supervisors will shut down PCs that are interested, you'll have Chief Inspectors that are quite interested if they're going for a Superintendent's board but no one's really going to want to invest that much time and money when they've got other things they're getting hassle for (Con. M)

In my time in the police things have gone full circle again and again, what we're doing now we decided not to do ten years ago because it didn't work ten years ago, they'll always be change because it ticks a box and helps them further up the ladder (Sgt. M).

A lot of it is just for promotion, I mean the reducing offenders [programme], when that first kicked off we were the pilot scheme but the number of guys that were just sucked into it and knew nothing about it but wanted to be a part of it just to get up the ranks was unreal, trying to latch onto it (Sgt. M)

That thing about neighbourhood qualifications is a brilliant example of somebody who needs promotion, at some point they must have got promoted because then it just died a death and we never heard about it again (Sgt. M)

Constables and Sergeants had a lot to say about senior officers and their promotion prospects. Most, sometimes with no hint of cynicism, acknowledged that any change was embraced by senior officers purely for promotional prospects or getting yourself noticed in a positive way. The author speaking to a Chief Constable about how you get 'buy-in' to radical change activity in a police organisation was told:

> In terms of selling it - I'd go to the next round of promotion applicants … they're ambitious, they work, they stretch themselves, they produce, they deliver, they're working to a deadline (Chief Constable. M)

A conversation with an Inspector from another organisation reflected the importance of 'marking your card' for future prospects:

> … from a senior level, if you start an initiative it doesn't really matter about the results as long as you can say I put this in place, for example the hate crime stuff, we look the public in the eye and say this is what we're doing. Six months down the line no-one ever really asks if it works, we just say we did it and there's credit given to the senior officer, and that's maybe the problem with the Individual Performance Review thing, you can write what you want on it and unless you're blatantly telling lies your supervisor is going to say fair enough (Inspector. M)

The short-termism often associated with targets, performance management and promotional prospects is seen to be a particularly irritating trait of management's result-oriented focus.

> I have used business objects but it can be quite dangerous because people come to conclusions from it which aren't accurate. … This is one thing that frustrates me with senior officers especially, is cause and effect, they mistake the two. So recently we had a spike of burglary in our rural area so the Chief Inspector was jumping up and down, put in massive resources and in three months the spike went down. He made the assumption it went down because of what we've done, now they've got this proactive unit. Coming from a science background I know you're got to be really rigorous in your testing, how do we know that wouldn't have gone down on its own anyway? The bosses seem to leap on these spikes and then react whereby it might not actually be the right approach, so although stats can be useful, it's how you interpret them that's the big issue (Sgt. M) ↓

> I agree. Interpretation is the key, it's that professional capacity to interpret subjectively objective data, and as you go up the ladder, up the chain of command, they seem to lose touch with the reality and just look at

> numbers, but there are things that sit outside the numbers that aren't part of that series and the people on the ground, beat officer, PCSO, residents, all of those people will know that but our interpretation at senior management level of the data can skew things quite badly (Sgt. M)

> I do feel the risk averse things a trait of senior management, we are willing to try things, but the number of times you get overruled, let's not do this (Sgt. M)

The need for senior officers to do 'some real work' was also articulated—particularly by Constables.

> If senior officers came out on the ground with us, not just for one day but a month and see how we have to deal with domestics and so forth and get a better insight (Con. M)

> All the things they have to hit to get their board [promotion], so they come up with this great plan and the people who carry that out are the Constables on the ground whether it's right or wrong we do what we're told, and because of people trying to get promoted you get these hair brain schemes making us look like idiots on the ground and an organisation as a whole (Con. M)

> It seems to me that at a point in your career after promotion you stop becoming a police officer, and yes I understand that you become more of a politician because of the nature of the work you do but what I would like to see is more supervision from the top rather than politicking, concentrate on supervising and supporting the officers. Go out on the ground (Con. M)

Overall, the disconnection between Constables and Sergeants and those of higher rank was apparent. In Lipsky's terms, street-level police officers are interested in 'processing work consistent with their own preferences'. Managers are 'result-oriented'. They are 'concerned with performance, the cost of securing performance, and only those aspects of process that expose them to critical scrutiny' (1980: 19). Ironically, this disconnect, or sense of 'other', is also apparent in research with more senior officers. Later research in this particular project demonstrates that Inspectors, Chief Inspectors and Superintendents in their discussions of evidence-based practice, training and application also refer to the higher ranks in somewhat cynical terms. Chief Superintendents, Assistant and Deputy Chief Constables and Chief Constables were in varying degrees described as, too political, too concerned about poor media exposure, risk averse, not willing to allow for failure or mistakes or to restructure management performance frameworks to allow for innovation. Senior officers are apparently never involved in the delivery and therefore less likely to appreciate the challenges of 'the pointy end' (see Fleming and Wingrove 2017). However, it should be noted that amongst their peers such officers were always quick to assure the audience that evidence-based policy and practice was in essence a positive move in the right direction for professional policing (Fleming and Wingrove 2017).

Discussion

Recent research supports the analysis here. It is senior officers who are more involved with the evidence-based programmes. Those officers with a demonstrated commitment to higher education (i.e. funding their own postgraduate programmes) are also more likely to be associated with positive reactions to the ideals of evidence-based practice (Fleming and Wingrove 2017). With direct entry recruitment at the senior level and fast-track internal programmes for those wishing to move quickly up the once seniority-based ladder (College of Policing 2017), senior officers are in many ways compelled to commit to the new paradigm that is evidence-based policing. There is no doubt that without this commitment it is unlikely at this stage that these officers will progress to the top of UK policing.

Thirty-five years on, the divide between management and the rank and file can still in part be discussed in Reuss-Ianni's terms. The bureaucratisation of management imported from government and business sectors has been a feature of policing in the UK for almost three decades. Despite improvements over time, street-level officers still see problems emanating from bureaucratic controls, management aspirations, 'unnecessary' change structures and resource allocation as compounding the difficulties they experience on the street. They are cynical about what they see as the relentless cycle of change and the senior officers whose careers are based on its implementation. We know that animosity between management and non-management is not specific to policing. As Reuss-Ianni (1983: 121) points out, 'it is a situation which might be expected in any dynamic large scale organisation in transition'. We know that much of the organisational literature has identified a web of resigned understanding between those who do the work and those who supervise it (e.g. Lipsky 1980). An interpretive approach, however, allows us to look specifically at what might be at the bottom of a set of beliefs and practices that often drives such attitudes. In this context, understanding Constables' and Sergeants' grasp of evidence-based policing has revealed a web of beliefs about management (at all levels) and their practices. Interestingly, not about leadership per se, but about management, about targets, performance management and the core belief that senior officers (of whatever rank) are unlikely to appreciate the challenges and hardships that those of the lower ranks have to contend with.

The hierarchical nature of policing has been a core feature of its organisation and structure in western industrial societies for a century or more and is an ever-present part of the story-telling ethos and the 'canteen culture' (see Waddington 1999) that informs the rank and file of policing. Strong, formal police unions in most of these countries attest to the strength of the divide between the lower and senior ranks. Indeed, the state of Queensland in Australia has two police unions, one for the rank and file and one for the Commissioned Officers. Never the twain shall meet (Fleming et al. 2006). In the UK, the rank and file enjoy the membership of the Federation, the Superintendents have their own association and the Executive ranks are now part of the National Police Chiefs' Council, the representative body for British police chief officers.

The introduction of managerialism in the UK with its flatter structures, decentralisation and notions of merit, accountability and professionalism overriding principals of seniority has not changed the culture of police organisations in any significant way (Fleming and Lafferty 2003). Arguably, it has reinforced the management vs. rank and file divide. Add large-scale organisational change to the mix, and you have the somewhat predictable tales of the pencil pushers vs. the real police workers, the administrators vs., in Reuss-Ianni's terms (1983: 118), the 'operational pragmatists'.

So what does this decentred analysis of police ranks, or 'bottom-up' approach, tell us? What practical policy lessons might be drawn from this account which identifies the beliefs and practices around hierarchy; around the role of management in facilitating change and rank and file understandings of organisational change? It has been argued elsewhere that 'a genuinely bottom-up approach cannot incorporate top-down direction without seriously compromising its ethos' (cited in Beech et al. 2015: 271). Yet surely at some stage we need to take on board the views of the would-be 'implementers'. Their buy-in is as important to the successful implementation as the blueprint itself. Beech et al's. (2015) account of organisational change in Police Scotland suggests a hybrid approach that provides for strong consultation in the early phases that drive the foundational objectives and takes the organisation with them through the full change programme. It remains to be seen whether such an approach proves amenable to the rank and file. However, it is clear that identifying bottom-up narratives allows for a more nuanced understanding of the webs of belief that drive attitudes and practices and provides a picture of the underlying traditions that hold these sets of beliefs in place. Narratives help to identify the dilemmas and unintended consequences and shed light on how these beliefs are continuously recreated and sustained.

Notes

1. National Institute for Health and Care Excellence (NICE), Sutton Trust/Educational Endowment Foundation, College of Policing What Works Centre for Crime Reduction, Early Intervention Foundation, What Works for Local Economic Growth, the Centre for Ageing Better and the What Works Centre for Wellbeing.
2. University College London, Institute of Education University of London, London School of Hygiene and Tropical Medicine, University of Southampton, Birkbeck, University of Surrey, Cardiff University and University of Dundee.
3. Other aims included:
    - To better understand the extent to which research/evaluation is currently pursued in police organisations.
    - To better understand the challenges and perceived risks and barriers to greater evidence use.
    - To gauge what would be perceived as a useful training tool/programme in order to 'instruct' officers in the value/use of Evidence-based Research.
4. Bacon reminds us that the existence of a dominant culture does not mean that police culture is monolithic, universal or static (2014: 112).

References

Agar, M., & MacDonald, J. (1995). Focus Groups and Ethnography. *Human Organization, 54*, 78–86.

Bacon, M. (2014). Police Culture and the New Policing Context. In J. M. Brown (Ed.). *The Future of Policing* (pp. 103–119). London: Routledge.

Beech, N., Gullidge, E., & Stewart, D. (2015). Change Leadership the Application of Alternative Models in Structural Policing Changes. In J. Fleming (Ed.). *Rising to the Top: Lessons from Police Leadership* (pp. 257–274). Oxford: Oxford University Press.

Braun, V., & Clarke, V. (2006). Using Thematic Analysis in Psychology. *Qualitative Research in Psychology, 3,* 77–101.

Braun, V., & Clarke, V. (2013). *Successful Qualitative Research: A Practical Guide for Beginners.* London: Sage.

Cabinet Office. (2011). *Open Public Services White Paper.* London: Cabinet Office.

Cabinet Office. (2012). *Civil Service Reform Plan.* London: Cabinet Office.

College of Policing. (2017). *About Us.* http://www.college.police.uk/About/Pages/default.aspx. Accessed December 9, 2017.

Engel, R. S., & Peterson, S. (2014). Leading by Example: The Untapped Resource of Front-Line Supervisors. In J. M. Brown (Ed.). *The Future of Policing* (pp. 398–413). London: Routledge.

Fleming, J. (2011). Qualitative Encounters in Policing Research. In *Qualitative Criminology: Stories from the Field* (pp. 13–24). Leichhardt, NSW: Federation Press.

Fleming, J., & Fyfe, N. (2015, February). *We Can Read and Write You Know! Selling the Idea of Research* (Focus Group Report) (pp. 1–56). Sunningdale, Berks: College of Policing.

Fleming, J., Fyfe, N., & Marshall, A. (2015). Making Connections Between Research and Practice: Tackling the Paradox of Policing Research. In J. Fleming (Ed.). *Rising to the Top: Lessons from Police Leadership* (pp. 237–256). Oxford: Oxford University Press.

Fleming, J., Fyfe, N., & Wingrove, J. (2016a). *'Evidence-Informed Policing: An Introduction to EMMIE and the Crime Reduction Toolkit': The Design of a Pilot Training Programme* (Report submitted to the College of Policing).

Fleming, J., Fyfe, N., & Wingrove, J. (2016b). *'Evidence-Informed Policing: An Introduction to EMMIE and the Crime Reduction Toolkit': A Pilot Training Evaluation* (Report submitted to the College of Policing).

Fleming, J., Fyfe, N., & Wingrove, J. (2016c). *'Evidence-Informed Policing: An Introduction to EMMIE and the Crime Reduction Toolkit': Trainer Guide* (Report submitted to the College of Policing).

Fleming, J., & Lafferty, G. (2003). Equity Confounded: The Impact of New Managerialism and Organisational Restructuring on the Recruitment of Women in Australian Police Services. *Labour and Industry, 13*(3), 37–39.

Fleming, J., Marks, M., & Wood, J. (2006). 'Standing on the Inside Looking Out': The Significance of Police Unions in Networks of Police Governance. *Australian and New Zealand Journal of Criminology, 39*(1), 71–89.

Fleming, J., & Wingrove, J. (2017). We Would If We Could … but Not Sure If We Can': Implementing Evidence-Based Practice: The Evidence-Based Practice Agenda in the UK. *Policing, 11*(2), 202–213.

Kitzinger, J. (1994). The Methodology of Focus Groups: The Importance of Interaction Between Research Participants. *Sociology of Health & Illness, 16*(1), 103–121.

Kreuger, R. A. (1988). *Focus Groups: A Practical Guide for Applied Research.* London: Sage.

Lipsky, M. (1980). *Street-Level Bureaucracy: Dilemmas of the Individual in Public Services.* New York: Russell Sage Foundation.

Lister, S., & Rowe, M. (2015). Electing Police and Crime Commissioners in England and Wales: Prospecting for the Democratisation of Policing. *Policing and Society, 25*(4), 358–377.

Marks, M., & Sklansky, D. (Eds.). (2012). *Police Reform from the Bottom Up: Officers and their Unions as Agents of Change.* London: Routledge.

Merton, R. K., Fiske, M., & Kendall, P. L. (1990). *The Focused Interview: A Manual of Problems and Procedures* (2nd ed.). London: Collier MacMillan.

Mulgan, G., & Puttick, R. (2013). *Making Evidence Useful: The Case for New Institutions.* London: Nesta.

Reuss-Ianni, E. (1983). *Two Cultures of Policing: Street Cops and Management Cops.* New Brunswick: Transaction Publishers.

Rhodes, R. A. W., & Tiernan, Anne. (2015). Focus Groups as Ethnography: The Case of Prime Ministers' Chiefs of Staff. *Journal of Organizational Ethnography, 4,* 208–222.

UK Administrative Data Research Network. (2012, December). *Improving Access for Research and Policy Report from the Administrative Data Taskforce.* London UK: Statistics Authority.

Van Dijk, A., Hoggewoning, F., & Punch, M. (2015). *What Matters in Policing.* Bristol: Policy Press.

Waddington, P. A. (1999). Police (Canteen) Sub-Culture. An Appreciation. *British Journal of Criminology, 39*(2), 287–309.

CHAPTER 11

What Do UK Citizens Understand About Austerity?

Anna Killick

INTRODUCTION

In this chapter, I use an interpretivist approach to explore how UK citizens make sense of the economics underpinning austerity policy, a policy that has dominated politics from the time of the 2008 crash.

For a long time, survey evidence indicated that a majority of the British public supported austerity despite the pain it caused, because they believed the pain was necessary to achieve the long-term benefit of reducing the national debt. There was an outpouring of political economic literature on the subject of the 'resilience' of the Osborne austerity narrative. Many writers argued that the narrative appealed because it chimed with a pre-existing 'public common sense', which was usually presented in the singular as if it did not vary across the population (Gamble 2013; Blyth 2013). However, this writing was not based on in-depth qualitative empirical research of what people believed. Therefore, political scientists did not have much insight into *why* in the surveys people said they supported austerity, whether their reasons were

---

A. Killick (✉)
University of Southampton, Southampton, UK
e-mail: ak9g15@soton.ac.uk

economic or social, and what they understood of the arguments about the seriousness of the debt or about the possible solutions. The lack of qualitative research may have contributed to political scientists overestimating support for austerity, so that they were taken by surprise by the resentment displayed in the 2016 referendum result and the surge in support for Labour's anti-austerity policies in 2017 (Dorling et al. 2016; Hopkin 2017). However, recently, researchers have begun to recognise the need for qualitative research to complement the surveys (Dunatchik et al. 2016), so we understand public opinion better. This chapter contributes by exploring everyday sense-making of the economics of austerity and asking whether there is one dominant 'public common sense' on reducing debt.

Part I of this book decentres policy by examining the beliefs of the elite actors who make it. However, interpretivist political scientists also have a strong track record of exploring the beliefs of everyday actors; how they make sense of and contest policy, the conceptual underpinnings of their understanding and variations in those patterns of understanding (Danziger and Lin 2009; Van Wessell 2017). I apply the Bevir and Rhodes (2003, 2015) interpretivist approach to explore citizens' beliefs about austerity. I explore the beliefs of sixty people from two contrasting districts of a southern city, asking what they believe about austerity and the underlying economics of it:

- Do participants believe that the national debt is serious and needs to be reduced?
- How do participants conceptualise government spending and the need for it to be either reduced or increased and what are their related beliefs about taxation?
- Is there one common sense on austerity or does it vary and, if so, how?

I first set out the dominant argument in the literature that austerity chimed with public common sense, at least during the 2010–2015 period, to highlight the pitfalls of making assumptions about people's beliefs based on quantitative research alone. I then outline my interpretivist approach, the fieldwork conducted in 2016–2017, the main findings and, finally I conclude that 'common sense' is socially constructed and historically contingent.

Does Austerity Chime with 'Public Common Sense'?

In this section, I provide a brief review of the, mainly constructivist, political economists writing on austerity.[1] They proposed the thesis that austerity chimed with one dominant public common sense.

Like most commentators, they perceived Chancellor of the Exchequer Osborne as carrying out austerity policies between 2010 and 2016. His original aim was to achieve a reduction in the proportion of GDP spent by government on public services from 21.2 to 12.6% by 2019–2020 (Office Budget Responsibility 2014). This reduction in government spending would contribute to eliminating the deficit by 2015–2016 and hence ultimately to reductions in debt.

Most recognise that, despite the eventual abandonment of the deficit reduction target in 2016, the spending cuts have been significant. They have hit welfare recipients, low-paid workers and people who use public services like libraries and drop-in centres disproportionately, and their impact is continuing (Office Budget Responsibility 2016). At the time of writing, Theresa May's government, while sometimes seeming to abandon some austerity policies in the face of increasingly powerful Labour attacks, is still committed to a public spending and debt reduction programme.

How did constructivist writers like Mark Blyth (2013) explain the resilience of public support for austerity? They eschewed a structuralist analysis of powerful interests in the media and corporations helping politicians manipulate public opinion (Harvey 2005). They also, rightly, rejected narrow institutionalism, because its focus on path-dependency in institutions downplayed the power of ideas to effect change. Instead, they argued that the reasons for the resilience of support lay, in part, in the nature of the austerity ideas themselves and how they resonated with pre-existing 'common sense', which they characterised as shared beliefs based on everyday understanding.

The austerity ideas appeared more simple and coherent as a solution than those of Osborne's more 'counter-intuitive' rivals, the Keynesians. Andrew Gamble (2013) argued austerity ideas chimed with a historical British political economic tradition of fiscal conservatism, a desire to 'balance the books', dominant from the nineteenth century onwards. The nineteenth-century tradition harks back further to the ancient division of liberal political economy into three 'households': private, state and corporate. Even though private households no longer make money in the same way they once did, many people still believe that the household is analogous to the state and that the consequences of debt for the state are the same as for households. Osborne used the household debt analogy, as Thatcher had done before him, attempting to convince people that, because they avoided household debt due to moral reasons and to avoid the serious consequences of bailiffs and repossession, the state should have the same approach. Both personal debt and government debt were framed as irresponsible.

Therefore, some constructivists argue that austerity's appeal to 'common sense' understanding has a moral component that debt is wrong. Liam Stanley (2014) conducted one of the few qualitative political science tests of such propositions. Working from a constructivist and everyday IPE perspective and wanting to analyse the public 'mood of the times' following 2008, his findings show that the framing of 2008 as a 'debt crisis' and subsequent acceptance of austerity only worked because it chimed with the public 'mood of the times'. People were not 'duped' by austerity; they were already receptive to it. His qualitative study of middle-class homeowners indicated they had what he terms 'shared beliefs' with three elements:

- that debt was an 'unambiguous moral obligation',
- that financialisation meant that people had lived beyond their means and therefore were in some way complicit in the behaviour of those banks that lived beyond their means,
- and that the state had been profligate.

Stanley's study indicates that people may have based some of their interpretation of the 2008 crisis on their own personal experience of debt and on strong moral beliefs about debt which made them receptive to Osborne's 'funnelling' of the household debt analogy. However, his research did not cover lower-income groups in depth.

Constructivist writers also argued pro-austerity ideas were powerful because they were simple; the fact that austerity was easy to understand gave it 'strength in public discourse' (Schmidt and Thatcher 2013). For instance, Blyth argues that the narrative 'more debt doesn't cure debt' is 'seductive' in its simplicity (2013: 10). Hay says alternative narratives would have to 'be sufficiently general and simple' to help people make sense of their experiences of 2008 (Hay 2010: 467). Pro-austerity ideas are simple because they are intuitive, relating to everyday personal experience of personal debt through the use of the household debt analogy. Keynesians refute the household debt analogy, arguing that in certain conditions of low-interest rates governments can borrow more to invest and subsequently have higher growth and tax receipts with which to pay off debt. It is a more complex argument. It takes both knowledge that is more formal and effort to understand what Schmidt and Thatcher characterise as the 'improbable' (2013: 32) Keynesian argument. Gamble echoes this sentiment with his statement that Keynesian ideas about the difference between the household and national economy have 'never been easy to communicate to citizens' (2013: 72). However, the claim that people found Keynesian ideas harder to understand was not supported by empirical research.

There was ample survey evidence such as in British Social Attitudes reports that people supported austerity (Park et al. 2011). There was some qualitative empirical research about the middle class's common sense (Stanley 2014). There was little qualitative political science research into the nature of people's beliefs and understanding of austerity to back the constructivists writers' claims that there was one dominant common sense supporting it.

Exploring People's Beliefs Using an Interpretivist Approach

What advantages does an interpretivist political science approach (Bevir and Rhodes 2003, 2015) have for conducting the necessary qualitative research in this area? Interpretivists do not believe methods like process tracing, often used in constructivist research, are sufficient. They also baulk at structuralist approaches, which interpret people's reasons for action as determined by their social position. Instead, they argue we must explore what people believe by asking them.

Interpretivists approach researching people's beliefs with an open mind about what traditions they might have inherited, what webs of beliefs they hold and what dilemmas they face—in the shape of competing beliefs or material circumstances—which might make them use their creative reasoning to adapt their existing beliefs. Researchers have to work harder; they *may* find that people's beliefs are patterned according to occupation, or age or some other demographic factor, but they cannot assume it from the outset.

Interpretivists often use abductive research designs. This means the researcher has the flexibility of entering the field with broad questions such as 'what do people believe about debt or austerity?' and can keep refining methods in the light of what they find in the field (Schwartz-Shea and Yanow 2012). I used an ethnographic approach, which helps researchers take agency and the situated aspect of that agency seriously. I chose to interview people from two contrasting districts of one city so that I could describe the local environment. I interviewed people mostly in their homes and kept a detailed field diary, taking into account my reactions and reflections on the interviews and positionality as a researcher. However, aside from attending tenants' meetings, my participant observation was limited; I relied mainly on semi-structured interviews and therefore describe the research as having an ethnographic sensibility rather than being ethnography.

I chose to interview in a southern city because it was near where I was based and because it was not one of the more prosperous of southern English cities. It had experienced some of the problems of deindustrialisation faced in other regions of the UK. I have not named the city or districts within it in order to protect the participants' anonymity (Tsai et al. 2016).[2]

I interviewed 28 people who lived in the 'Hill district' part of the city. Hill district contains 1970s' blocks of four-storey flats and a huge council estate built in the interwar period. This council estate comprises generous-sized semi-detached houses with big gardens front and back, large living rooms with big windows, plenty of space and sound structures. Hill district used to have a functioning mixed shopping street, which is now largely devoted to fast food to supply the growing student population to the south. It has a high proportion of social housing and people on low wages and benefits; 26 of the 28 interviewees come from low-income backgrounds and would be categorised as from occupational groups C1 to E,[3] 14 are women and 14 men, and they come from a range of ages from 18 to 80s.

I interviewed 17 people who lived in Church district. Church district has a high proportion of owner-occupied housing and a strong association with the university and professional public sector work such as in education and health. It contains a couple of classical grey stone spired churches and lots of huge trees, chestnuts and beeches. It comprises wealthy residential roads built from Edwardian times through the 1920s. Fifteen out of 17 interviewees would be categorised as from occupational groups A or B, 6 were women and 11 men, and they came from a range of ages from 18 to 80s. I also interviewed 15 people from other areas of the city, making 60 participants in all.

I recruited using gatekeepers and snowballing, and by delivering letters in each district and then knocking on doors a few days later. I conducted lengthy interviews, on average fifty minutes long, about people's understanding of the economy. In the 20–30 minutes sections of those interviews that are relevant to this chapter on austerity, I asked the broad questions set out in the Table 11.1.

Thematic Analysis

I analysed the transcripts using thematic analysis, a flexible method developed by psychologists Braun and Clarke (2013). It involves a rigorous six stage coding, where transcripts are read through for codes first which are then grouped into themes. I present the themes that emerged

Table 11.1 Interview questions relevant to austerity

Broad questioning	Rationale
What is your economic life story? Jobs of parents, adult employment and housing, economic experiences	To achieve a rich understanding of the interviewees' context, traditions they inherited and dilemmas they faced
What do you understand about debt?	I use the term understand rather than believe because it incorporates an extra dimension inviting discussion for instance about awareness of debt or whether there are key terms they do not understand. I do not stipulate whether I mean personal or government debt because interviewees' interpretation of the question may itself reveal which is uppermost in their minds. If they interpret the question as being about personal debt, I ask follow-up questions about government debt and vice versa
Follow-up questions on beliefs about austerity and the household debt analogy	
What do you understand about government spending?	Understanding of government spending and beliefs about levels of it may help illuminate beliefs about debt
What do you understand about taxation?	Understanding of taxation and beliefs about levels of and type may help illuminate beliefs about debt

from the interviews in the following findings section. In some cases, the pattern of the themes, such as on beliefs about debt, was strikingly related to each of the districts because it reflected different income levels. In other cases, such as beliefs about tax evasion, themes were common across most participants regardless of which district or demographic feature. In some cases, such as for support for Keynesian ideas, beliefs were patterned according to political affiliation. However, there were always cases of participants who reacted differently to others and did not correspond to a 'pattern', and where space allows I acknowledge them. In presenting what interviewees say, I give some demographic detail including age, sometimes in brackets after the interviewee's name.

Findings Hill District: Fear of Personal Debt

A dominant pattern among Hill district interviewees, who are mostly on low incomes, is to speak of life as survival and a day-to-day struggle. Mainly, I analyse the interviews for saliency rather than frequency, but the frequency with which interviewees use words can sometimes reveal insights. A count using Nvivo finds 115 references to 'survival', 'managing', 'struggling' in interviews of participants in occupational groups C1 to E but only three in those of occupational groups A and B. I expected a degree of income-related patterning but not to this radical extent. Callum at 18 already says 'as long as I can manage okay...I guess that's all I want' about his life. Clare aged 18 talks of struggle and things being difficult. Elena, in her 30s, hopes they are going to 'be able to bear' the future. Gary has two children and is training for promotion in his NHS health assistant job. For the last two years, he says 'it's been a struggle it really has, you don't go out anymore. You buy your food and pay your bills and that's about it, our life at the moment'. Several of the older Hill district interviewees express pride that they have managed; Jean, in her 70s, living on the state pension, says 'We managed, we got through life (laughs). We still do manage now.' The struggle manifests itself in food in some cases. Rosa (40s) has had a lot of egg and chip dinners, Shelley (50s) beans on toast for days. Steven (80s) 'got through'.

It is a striking pattern that all those expressing fear of personal debt and perceiving it as hard to avoid are from Hill district. Many in Hill district respond to my neutrally worded question 'what do you know and understand about debt?' by assuming I mean personal debt, not government or national debt. I deal with what Hill district interviewees understand about personal debt in some detail because their fear of it makes them view it as more important than government debt.

Some interviewees express their fear of personal debt by using words like 'thankfully' (Adam age 30s) to describe currently being debt free and Lidia, in her 40s, is 'so proud now because we haven't got any more loans, we paid it all'.

Diane's life (30s) is profoundly affected by debt. She has only ever earned the minimum wage, working long hours in respite care and as a cleaner as well as caring for her children. She and her partner, a painter and decorator, decided to buy a house when the market was rising. They saved all the deposits and fees, bought the house and then he lost most of his work following the 2008 crash. She says 'we struggled along, kept trying to pay, finding all the monies and then we said "enough's enough". It was out of our control we were going to lose it so we had to sell it'. They were not profligate in their lifestyle but were forced to sell the house after only a year at a loss, incurring a debt that they are still paying off eight years later. In this quote, Diane expresses optimism that in the end they will pay it off but also a weight of revulsion that 'it' is still there. The quote also shows how the debt controls them because they feel they have to subject themselves to the debt adviser's direction:

> Diane: We got into debt so we're still paying for it now, but we'll get there. Yeah.
> Interviewer: And did you get any help with that?
> Diane: Not really no, just all out of our wages bit by bit what we could afford went into pay plan and paid off. Then, we got told to come out of that and wait until we had a bit of money behind us so we could keep on top of the bills, and then still pay bills off as and when we can. But there is still debt there.

Out of all the interviewees, Diane mentions words like managing or surviving most frequently, with several variants of the theme that she just lives from day-to-day. 'I just take every day as it comes now after what we've been we've gone through, that black hole (laughs). You know we just take every day as it comes.' She is vehement that they will never buy again, 'never go back that way'.

Most of the other interviewees in debt, such as Linda, have got into debt to pay bills:

> Debts are crippling because it's so easy, so, so easy when you're unemployed and you've got no money and somebody says to you, 'I'll give you £200 today you'll pay me back about £400 at £20 a week'. You think 'oh yes God, yes, I can run and go and get a hundred pounds worth of shopping in the food cupboard. I can go and get the shoes that the kids need'. And then lo and behold that £20 a week never ends, it never ends…I've been trapped in it for years and years and years… I can't see a way out of it because there is always somebody there to give it to you. (Linda age 50s)

Some who believe they have been too materialistic are critical of themselves. Julie (age 60s) says that when she was depressed she had an attack of 'havingness' consumer spending, and she was only able to clear the debt because she was made redundant from her job as an administrative assistant. Martin (age 50s) blames the broader social context because he thinks material pressures are strong and identifies the 1980s as the point when the 'avoid debt' tradition his working-class parents had grown up in changed:

> I think that [the 1980s expansion in credit] was the biggest change. We were all victims of corporate finance multinational companies especially around that time. It was around that time it was rammed that you can own your own house, you can own your own car and everything else and that was what came from America. It was all on credit you know. You end up in a trap. It doesn't help that people are chasing the dream existence. I think they see it on telly all the time, Relocation [TV programme], you look at all the houses so they're always chasing that next goalpost sort of thing, but you become a victim. (Martin age 50s)

Martin and some other interviewees are even more fearful for the younger generation. Rosa has already had to pay her son's debts off twice because he was, in her view irresponsibly, offered credit cards too young. Debt exercises a particular hold over the 18-year-old college students interviewed, some of whom are contemplating university. But even here, there is a marked distinction between how Clare, from a low-income background, talks about forthcoming student debt, compared with Phoebe, from a higher-income background. Both seem passionate about their art-related subjects; Clare wants to study English, Phoebe Art. Clare, who worries about the debt her mother is already in, says of future student loan debt that it is 'something hanging over your head all the time because money pretty much stresses me out all the time and having that, it's just kind of an inevitable thing that we're going to have to deal with' (Clare). For a while, her fear of future debt made her question her desire to go to university. She has already had difficult conversations with her council tenant mother about the financial impact of her leaving because of the bedroom tax. These conversations and doubts are common in her friendship groups but not Phoebe's. Whereas Clare 'knows her own income', fellow student Phoebe, who sees herself as 'quite privileged', does not even look at her part-time job pay cheque. Phoebe worries about future debt but says:

> it's always been a conversation that we had but it was just 'do what you want to do' because it [Art] is such a diverse degree you can really do anything with it and take what you want from it. So [future earnings and debt] has always been there but it's never been an issue, is what I'm trying to say. (Phoebe aged 18)

Mica, in her early 30s, is less critical of either herself or society for getting into debt. She jokes about how she cannot curb her interest in 'shiny, new things' and, despite attempts of others to give her debt advice, she just accepts that her debt will probably be a permanent feature.

In summary, most Hill district interviewees believe life is a struggle with much mention of terms like surviving, getting through and day to day. Their low incomes and insecurity make them fear debt and, even if they are not living with debt now, they can imagine circumstances where it might be impossible to avoid. They offer often grim narratives of debt as either a consuming addiction or a trap and have sympathy for those, particularly the young, who get lured into it. Because they do not perceive debt as easy to avoid, they do not morally condemn it. It is a striking pattern that all those expressing 'fear' of personal debt and perceiving it as hard to avoid are from Hill district.

HILL DISTRICT: LACK OF CONCERN ABOUT GOVERNMENT DEBT

Hill district participants fear personal debt. What do they believe about government debt? Do they believe the Osborne narrative that government debt is a serious issue? Do they support the analogy he draws between household and government debt; that in the same way a household should cut spending to get out of debt, however painful, so should a government? Do they believe it is morally wrong for the government to be in debt?

The first theme that emerges from 15 interviewees from both Hill and Church district is that some people are not even aware the government is in debt. It is surprising, given the salience of the message, that interviewees from across income levels and ages such as Alice (80s), Beverley (60s), Gary (40s) and Lucie (18) are unaware of, or immediately profess lack of knowledge about, the scale of government debt.

In Hill district, some, such as Elena in her 30s, who are aware of the debt, are nevertheless unconcerned about it:

> Interviewer: Have you ever been aware of the country being in debt, the government being in debt?
> Elena: Oh apparently, yes apparently, yes everyone says that about borrowing and borrowing too much, yeah.
> Interviewer: Does it worry you?
> Elena: Not really, not really.

In Hill district, some are aware of government debt, but blame the government for it. There are three 'levels of blame'. First, there are those who believe the government has exaggerated the debt for their own ends. Tel (60s) believes Osborne's austerity is ideologically motivated; 'I think it's a lie. I think they're just using it as a cover to decimate services and of course I'm being political here'. Some may not be as cynical about Osborne's motives but see him as attempting to shift blame for the 2008 banking crisis onto the whole population:

> So at one point it was the banks and now it's all us. So it's become more our responsibility and the language seems to have affected our psyche in the fact that it's all our responsibility together. (Martha 40s)

The second level of distrust of government is based on a more generalised distrust of politicians as a class. This distrust manifests first as belief in secrecy and massaging of figures; Colin (60s) thinks government debt is 'all hidden away'. The government is directly to blame for the debt due to incompetence: Shelley (50s) says, 'Yeah I could understand about how bad the government debt was. I don't know, aren't they to blame, really, the government, for getting us in this situation?'

An even stronger 'distrust' claim is that politicians are lining their own pockets. Jean in her 70s says 'In [Osborne's] pocket yeah! (Laughs). They run around in these big posh cars don't they…they don't have to pay for it. That's right, this is how it goes along'. Elliott also in his 70s, says, 'They're all right they've got their little contained package and a good pension at the end and handshake. But the likes of Joe public, we never see any of that'.

Linda distrusts politicians so much she has never voted and would like to start a non-voting campaign:

> I'd love to say to the world 'stop voting!' Stop voting, let's see what happens. Let's see what happens when we stop voting for them arseholes to get rich, see what happens. (Linda 50s)

Even if they are aware, or are made aware in the interview, that the government is in debt, again a surprising number have not registered the Osborne message of the household debt analogy, saying they have never heard it expressed. However, many could be perceived as rejecting the analogy at an implicit level. I judge rejecting the household debt analogy implicitly to include beliefs that personal debt is much more of a problem than government debt. Shirley says 'I would worry more about us getting into debt than about the government getting into debt'. Those who think the government is exaggerating or that the debt is due to their incompetence also fit in this group. Those who believe there are other ways to reduce debt than by cutting government spending reject the household debt analogy explicitly, and I consider their beliefs in one of the following sections.

Church District: Personal Debt Is Avoidable

In Church district, instead of believing that personal debt is to be feared and hard to avoid, most believe it is due to profligacy and easy to avoid. Most in Church district who see debt as profligacy say their lives are comfortable. Medical consultant David (70s) encapsulates the perception of life as comfortable when he says, 'Oh yeah there was never any doubt that we would be secure. And there was never any doubt that we would have enough to live on quite comfortably'. James (70s) says:

> I had a reasonably good job… and we had a very good employee share scheme, which actually worked out unbelievably well for us, it made a big difference to our financial situation. I can't believe how lucky we were actually to be in that place at that time and that was fortunate.

Many believe it is moral to avoid debt. Fawad (40s) and Harry (50s) talk of money as precious and are among several to talk about the need for prudence. Mary (70s) remembers worrying greatly about the only time they were ever in debt even though it was only for £10.00. Rachel (50s) says:

> I'm not very good on debt, the only debt I have is my mortgage, never had a loan…and I've always been brought up, you don't have hire purchase, you pay for what you have and so I think perhaps my gut reaction is the country shouldn't be on too much debt actually. To be honest, yeah, probably I would come down on that. (Rachel)

In terms of the personal experiences underpinning this perception of debt as profligacy, most interviewees have only ever had one debt and that was a mortgage. They are awed by how much money they have made from their 'debts' in property and conscious their own children may not be so lucky. My interviewees with mortgages are much more positive about their mortgage debt than Stanley's (2014) middle-class homeowners. Perhaps this reflects the greater rise in house prices in the South. Church district interviewees do not class mortgages as irresponsible and, when they talk about 'immoral' debt, tend to mean debt due to excessive spending. They do condemn such debt as profligate and therefore immoral.

There are many comments that reflect a desire to reduce expectations of what the government can achieve. This view is sometimes linked with the belief that excessive personal spending and debt reflects unrealistic expectations. Thus, Rachel comments:

> I don't agree with people being in a lot of debt and I do think these days people want things that they can't have… So I think it's time we contracted our ideals really would be my take on it. (Rachel 50s)

This sentiment is echoed by Stephanie (50s) 'our expectations are greater than they ever have been'. Rachel comes to the general conclusion about government debt that 'I think overall we have to reduce our expectations of what is possible in order to reduce our [government] debt, we can't have it both ways'.

The Church district interviewees who see debt as profligacy back Stanley's (2014) conclusion that common sense has a definite moral component. However, debt as profligacy is a concept that mainly seems to work for those on higher incomes, such as in Church district, than those on lower incomes, such as in Hill district.

Church District: 'Our Country's Debt Is Too High'

In response to the question, 'what do you know and understand about debt?' many Church district interviewees interpret the question as being about government rather than personal debt, in sharp contrast with Hill district interviewees. This response may reflect the fact that the interview as a whole is about understanding of the economy, but also that their own personal debt is less serious than for many of the Hill district interviewees. Many express concerns about the level of government debt saying immediately it is 'billions' or 'serious' or a 'problem' even though they do not know exact figures. Alan is one of the few with detailed knowledge of the level of government debt:

> 60 billion a year, which is enormous…what [Osborne] has done is manage to convince the financial markets that this country is very serious about getting the deficit down, and they've given him the benefit of the doubt, which has kept long term interest rates down, which has benefited business…but it could be big problem, could be a real problem if we can't get it down. (Alan 40s)

Support for the possibility that we could all be 'in it together' to reduce debt is reflected in Harry's comment 'the idea that we were in it altogether was important'. However he believes, like many in Church district who support austerity but feel uneasy about its implementation, that Osborne did not follow through on this promise, hitting the poor disproportionately:

I don't feel that was carried through because difference in wages is showing that it's…become rather impossible for some people at the bottom of the pile. I'm not sure that's really been understood….The way in which austerity hits the poor is very regrettable and anyway to ameliorate that would have been helpful in ways that don't seem to have happened… we're going to get a lot of very alienated people with impossible situations. (Harry)

Rachel (50s) and some other older Church district interviewees identify the problem with austerity's implementation as a lack of social cohesion more generally. The British people no longer unite to sacrifice for the common good in part because class divisions have become more acute; 'because I don't think we feel part of the club, because we are a class society we don't have this feeling of we are in this together …'. Nevertheless, however uneasy, she concludes 'I do think, I do think we should have had austerity'. Stephanie (50s), after expressing similar unease also ends with 'but I still believe the government should be balancing its books and not borrowing'.

Many Hill district interviewees reject the household debt analogy, but there are many Church district interviewees who support it, suggesting that it resonates more with the 'common sense' of those on high incomes. For those who support it, there is much talk of 'cutting your cloth' and how 'we as a household' would discuss reducing our debt. Fawad (40s) says that not 'living beyond your means' is common sense; 'everyone knows that's good practice, that's the first thing you tell a child, if you want to buy something you save up'. Helen (40s) says 'Yes I do I think it's good not to have any debt…It's important to be a more sustainable economic model and so living within your means is good. So it's a good idea to try and reduce the government debt'.

Beliefs About Government Spending and the Effects of Austerity

I ask interviewees what they understand about government spending to contextualise their beliefs about austerity. The most commonly cited area of spending cuts they condemn in both districts is the NHS, a topic that was dominant in news stories during these interviews. In Hill district, there is less support for benefit cuts than in Church district, and many feel government spending cuts have hit them hard and should be reversed. Many of the interviewees who are most concerned about personal debt and on low incomes are least concerned about waste in government spending and want spending to increase. Mica says:

> I don't think you could ever spend too much on schools and hospitals because I think that those are the main things that probably you should be spending [taxes] on, because everybody needs healthcare and everybody needs a fair education. (Mica 30s)

Rosa echoes interviewees from both districts when she says the government spends too much on bailing out the banks:

> And at the start of the recession 'oh we'll have to be in a recession because we can't afford the national health system but, hey, let's throw a few billion pounds into the stock market so the rich don't get poorer and we'll just take all the money from the poor and let them be poorer'. I do feel that has been done in the last few years big time. (Rosa 40s)

Five interviewees from both districts believe there has been too much privatisation. Rosa notices in her community centre work that Capita is inefficient and unaccountable compared with the old local government employees, and that the council has imposed political restrictions on their campaigning work. George, in his 70s, is explicit on the need to 're-nationalise' the NHS.

There is a theme of comments from Hill district in particular that show strong opposition to austerity and the principle behind austerity—that we could somehow all be 'in it together'. Instead, any version of austerity that includes cutting spending on social services is seen as endangering the social fabric of the country. All those on benefits, including tax credits, report having been hurt by the cuts, Elena (30s) feels 'dread', Gary (40s) 'a sinking feeling', some that government is squeezing people who are most vulnerable such as the disabled. Rosa (40s) and Rebecca (50s), both working in schools, argue preventative policies such as Sure Start should not be cut because it is cheaper than the consequences of inaction. Shelley (50s) volunteers at a food bank, where austerity-inspired sanctions on benefits leave already 'depressed' people even more hopeless. Shirley (70s) worries that austerity has undermined the vulnerable and says 'I think with any structure you've got to have a sound base'. A few argue that society is about to break down and talk of returns to Victorian times; some interviewees from Church district echo that concern, but in a more detached way.

In considering spending cuts, Hill district interviewees are more likely to express frustration that politicians are out of touch. Gary says, 'they have it all backwards, they're not in touch with people you know' (Gary 40s). Mica is one of the several to urge politicians to live at least for a while on lower incomes so that they can become better at directing social policy:

> Because I feel like they grow up in such a different world than that which they're trying to impact. 'Okay you lot need to do this, you lot needs to do that.' Have you ever met people like this before? Have you ever experienced what they're doing with their lives? Like, how can you say how they need to live if you have never actually lived in that sort of environment to know whether it affects you or not? (Mica 30s)

In contrast, in Church district, there is spontaneous mention of waste in response to my question 'what do you know and understand about government spending?' Prudence is often reflected in disapproval of government spending unless it is 'spent wisely'. Alan (40s) shows unease when he says, 'I'm not opposed to… government spending rising, if I was sure it was being spent wisely, but I don't think it is', and James (70s) thinks 'there are things that the government needs to do but it seems to be wasteful'.

To sum up this theme, it seems likely that those who are struggling and fear personal debt also want spending for social services on which they rely on to be maintained, and question whether it is even possible, as Osborne argued, for spending cuts to be designed in such a way that 'we are all in it together'. Many Church district interviewees also express opposition to the scale of the cuts on the NHS and in work benefits, but they are more likely to also mention waste. Their perception of the social problems caused by cuts is more detached.

Common Pattern of Beliefs on Tax

Beliefs about tax are relevant because raising them is an alternative to spending cuts as a debt reduction measure. Answers to questions on tax are less income patterned than on spending or debt. Not all interviewees would categorise themselves as paying tax, such as those on benefits or pensions, even though they do all pay indirect taxes such as VAT. However, while people who pay income tax might complain more than those who do not, there are some similarities in responses on tax between the districts.

In answer to the question 'what do you know and understand about tax?' over twenty interviewees from both districts voluntarily mention tax evasion or avoidance by companies and 'minted' (Colin 60s) individuals. Therefore, there is an implicit or explicit theme running through many interviews that some government debt could be reduced by clamping down on tax avoidance. Seventeen interviewees believe that the tax burden has shifted too far from the rich and that they should pay more. This comment by Julie on Hill district reflects that view:

> I think years and years ago, the really rich people were well and truly hammered, in the old money every 19s 6d I think went on tax and the six pennies they kept. Well, never should that have ever happened, but at the same time it's gone too far the other way now and there's too many loopholes and the very rich seem to know how to use them. Quite frankly, the country needs all of the money! The very rich people, there's only so many houses they need whether they like it or not. They would say they've been gifted to earn so much money, why don't they just put up what they should be paying and that's that! (Julie 60s)

While not all interviewees advocate increasing taxes on the rich, only four out of the 60 interviewees explicitly oppose doing so.

Explicit Rejection of Osborne's Economic Case

There is a group composed of interviewees from both districts who explicitly reject Osborne's household analogy. This group of ten reject it because they support the Keynesian alternative. The 'Keynesian ten' are all politically aware. They argue that government debt, particularly if it is to finance infrastructure investment, should not be perceived as a problem, and they are explicitly Keynesian in a combined rejection of the household debt analogy and the spending cuts prescription. They argue from a basis of economic knowledge of the Keynesian alternative. Clearly, they undermine the Blyth/Hay thesis that Keynesian doctrines are hard to understand. Paul (50s) says 'I think as individuals we are always reluctant to be in debt, but for the country you know, it's a way of building the economy'. Jane is another example:

> I know that there is an economic theory which says that if you are in low growth you should spend your way out of the difficult situation by going into debt to finance, for example, infrastructure projects in order to create employment so that people will earn money and spend that and that will somehow boost the economy. I suppose on a personal level running your own budget going into debt and having a deficit is always worrying, but I think that on a national level it is a completely different matter. (Jane 70s)

All of the 'Keynesian ten' see themselves as left of centre and show throughout their interviews that they are politically engaged.

Only a couple of interviewees support the Hay/Blyth thesis that Keynesianism is hard to understand. David is uncomfortable with austerity because it hits the poor, wants to believe in the Keynesian argument, which he is vaguely aware of, but expresses a lack of confidence in the detail of it. He mentions 'these economic mechanisms which I really don't understand; you know, the idea that if you spend more and borrow more you can borrow out of debt'. He expands:

> There is a view that you shouldn't spend more than you've got which logically would certainly apply to me as a private individual. We've never bought anything, except our house, with a debt. If we want a new television we saved the money to get it. If we want a new car everybody said take out a loan, but we didn't, we paid cash. We've never owed anything and to my mind, at a simple level, I could say it would be nice if the government was in such a situation that they never spent more than they got. (David)

He knows some economists dispute the 'austerity' approach but 'that's when I begin to not understand'. He also expresses anxiety about this division between economists in itself, a theme echoed by many others throughout the interviews.

Discussion

Some political economists have assumed that there is a dominant 'common sense' on austerity based on shared beliefs and everyday moral and economic understanding. However, these interviews show that there are differences in both moral and economic everyday understanding between the two districts, one lower income and the other higher income. Most of the Hill district interviewees do not have a common sense belief that personal debt is due to profligacy. In fact, they do not express strong moral condemnation of it. For most of them, because they do not have mortgages, personal debt takes the form of payday loans or credit card debt that spirals quickly out of control. If they are not in debt themselves, they know others who are, and they are particularly fearful about young people getting into debt. Those on low incomes considering university are more fearful of the consequences of it than higher-income students. Hill district interviewees used creative agency to adapt inherited traditions about frugality passed to them by their parents. They confront the dilemmas of increasingly available credit (even if sometimes only of the payday loan variety), consumerist pressures, less availability of cheap social housing, stagnating low incomes, declining in work benefits and greater job insecurity. Not everyone adapts in the same way. Some battle to be debt free and succeed. Others are more fatalistic about debt and are resigned to it as a permanent feature of their lives.

Hill district interviewees' understanding of personal debt affects their beliefs about government debt. Many do not express much knowledge of the seriousness of government debt or of Osborne's use of the household analogy to argue for the need to get the government debt down. It may be that conducting these interviews in 2016–2017 accounts for some of this lack of awareness of the seriousness of government debt because government debt was no longer the dominant issue, replaced by Brexit. Yet, Church district interviewees *are* still conscious of it. An alternative explanation is that the Hill district understanding of the seriousness of personal debt, combined with their greater tendency to distrust politicians, means that they do not believe government debt is as serious as the Church district interviewees believe it is. They do not trust the politicians' claims about its seriousness. This belief contributes to them having less 'common sense' that spending cuts are necessary. They fear the effects of the spending cuts both as it has already adversely affected them and could affect their community in the future.

In short, these interviews suggest that many Hill district interviewees do not have the common sense that Blyth and Hay described. These findings show the importance of conducting in-depth interviews with people from lower-income backgrounds, whose voices are often not heard by political scientists.

In contrast, Church district interviewees have a 'common sense' that is far more similar to that described by Blyth and Hay. They have similar traditions of frugality to those of many of the Hill district interviewees, but have established comfortable and secure lifestyles which mean they fear debt less. It is surprising that none really have an alternative, more throwaway tradition regarding personal debt, but this may reflect the times they were brought up in; for those over forty, their parents were profoundly influenced by the 30s depression and war and post-war austerity. Most in Church district do see debt as profligacy, and for the overwhelming majority, the only debt they have ever accumulated is a mortgage on what has turned out to be a safe and ever appreciating asset.

The debt that other people have worries them because it is debt due to spending, which they do see as profligate. Other people's expectations about both standards of living and of what governments can provide need to be reined in. Church district interviewees are far more likely to recognise and express support for Osborne's use of the household debt analogy than in Hill district. They are also more likely to believe that some spending cuts, particularly as they claim there is some waste in the system, are necessary. However, many are uneasy about the scale of the cuts and the perception that the rich have not shared the pain with the poor. This unease may have grown over time as the cuts progressed, outweighing their original unease about the debt.

These interviews suggest that in the particular case of austerity, common sense is based on economic experience. It may be that starting the interview by asking about the person's economic life history skews answers in the later parts of the interview. Nevertheless, I am struck that while some interviewees show that they follow the news closely, or have accurate and detailed factual knowledge, still they characterise their understanding in personal terms, using their own everyday experience to illustrate what they mean. Are there any patterns in those experiences depending on demographic factors aside from income, such as age or gender? I find less variation between men and women than I had anticipated. However, there are some differences according to age. The 18-year-olds whom I interviewed did not on the whole express an in-depth understanding of government spending, debt or taxation because, as they repeatedly told me, they had not yet had to deal with these issues. It may take them a while to reflect on their own family traditions of economic experiences as they encounter material realities in their adult lives. Among those in their 20s or 30s, there do not appear to be striking differences in beliefs about either debt or austerity compared with those over 60. For those over 60 who are keener on spending cuts, these beliefs seem to be linked more with their income level than age itself. Political awareness or affiliation makes a difference in discussion of Keynesian alternatives. Some on the left made more effort to seek out the ideas out and understand them, although they do not seem to be as difficult to understand as Hay and Blyth claimed.

Conclusion

What conclusions can we draw about austerity and the value of the interpretivist approach to researching citizens' beliefs for political science?

Firstly, this research, conducted 2016–2017 in a southern English city, is historically contingent; if I had conducted it at the height of austerity then maybe support for austerity would have been stronger and based on a greater shared understanding. However, while beliefs may change more quickly, it is unlikely that underlying everyday understanding could change greatly. So, we should not assume there is one dominant version of 'common sense'. It is context dependent. People know what they need to know. They learn from their everyday economic experiences. We should always explore particular voices, especially the silent voices of the more marginalised members of society. And we need an ethnographic sensibility and detailed interviews, not surveys, to draw out such beliefs.

Secondly, as political scientists, we may draw on research of social and political beliefs, but we must conduct more qualitative research that explores people's *economic* understanding. It enables us to probe and unearth surprising findings such as the ways in which inherited moral values about (say) frugality, interact with economic understandings.

Notes

1. I follow Mark Blyth's definition of austerity. He defines it as 'a form of voluntary deflation in which the economy adjusts through the reduction of wages, prices and public spending to restore competitiveness, which is (supposedly) best achieved by cutting the state's budget, debts and deficits' (Blyth 2013: 2).
2. In ethnographic studies where the districts are quite compact, Tsai et al. (2016) advise anonymising place names as well as interviewees' names.
3. According to A B C1 C2 D and E SEG classification.

References

Bevir, M., & Rhodes, R. A. W. (2003). *Interpreting British Governance*. London: Routledge.
Bevir, M., & Rhodes, R. A. W. (2015). *Routledge Handbook of Interpretive Political Science*. UK: Taylor & Francis.
Blyth, M. (2013). *Austerity: The History of a Dangerous Idea*. New York: Oxford University Press.
Braun, V., & Clarke, V. (2013). *Successful Qualitative Research*. London: Sage.
Danziger, S., & Lin, A. C. (2009). *Coping with Poverty: The Social Contexts of Neighborhood, Work, and Family in the African-American Community*. Ann Arbor: University of Michigan Press.
Dorling, D., Stuart, B., & Stubbs, J. (2016). Don't Mention This Around the Christmas Table: Brexit, Inequality and the Demographic Divide. *LSE European Politics and Policy (EUROPP) Blog*.
Dunatchik, A., Davies, M., Griggs, J., Hussain, F., Jessop, C., Kelley, N., et al. (2016). *Social and Political Attitudes of People on Low Incomes*. UK: The Joseph Rowntree Foundation.
Gamble, A. (2013). Neo-liberalism and Fiscal Conservatism. In V. Schmidt & M. Thatcher (Eds.), *Resilient Liberalism in Europe's Political Economy* (pp. 53–76). Cambridge: Cambridge University Press.
Harvey, D. (2005). *A Brief History of Neoliberalism*. Oxford: Oxford University Press.
Hay, C. (2010). Chronicles of a Death Foretold: The Winter of Discontent and Construction of the Crisis of British Keynesianism. *Parliamentary Affairs, 63*, 446–470.
Hopkin, J. (2017). *The Brexit Vote and General Election Were Both About Austerity and Inequality*. LSE (Ed.), Brexit Blog. http://blogs.lse.ac.uk/brexit/2017/06/28/the-brexit-vote-and-general-election-were-both-about-austerity-and-inequality/.
Office Budget Responsibility. (2014). *Economic and Fiscal Outlook*. December 2014. Cm 8966 HMSO. http://budgetresponsibility.org.uk/docs/dlm_uploads/December_2014_EFO-web513.pdf.
Office Budget Responsibility. (2016). *Welfare Trends Report*. Cm 9341 HMSO http://budgetresponsibility.org.uk/docs/dlm_uploads/Welfare-Trends-Report.pdf.
Park, A., Curtice, J., Clery, E., & Bryson, C. (2011). *British Social Attitudes 27th Report*. London: Sage.
Schmidt, V., & Thatcher, M. (2013). *Resilient Liberalism in Europe's Political Economy*. Cambridge: Cambridge University Press.
Schwartz-Shea, P., & Yanow, D. (2012). *Interpretive Research Design*. New York: Routledge. Available at: http://www.myilibrary.com?ID=500558.

Stanley, L. (2014). 'We're Reaping What We Sowed': Everyday Crisis Narratives and Acquiescence to the Age of Austerity. *New Political Economy, 19*(6), 895–917.

Tsai, A. C., Kohrt, B. A., Matthews, L. T., Betancourt, T. S., Lee, J. K., Papachristos, A. V., et al. (2016). Promises and Pitfalls of Data Sharing in Qualitative Research. *Social Science and Medicine, 169*, 191–198.

Van Wessel, M. (2017). Citizens as Sense-makers: Towards a Deeper Appreciation of Citizens' Understandings of Democratic Politics. *Political Studies, 65*, 127–145.

Index

A
Abductive research designs, 246
Academic-practitioner coproduction of knowledge, 203
Action Plan on Unaccompanied Minors (2010), 113
Active member researcher, 167, 168
Adversarialism, 129
Advisory referendum, 148
Advocacy
  as a club, 122, 132
  coalition, 105
  as a game, 122, 129, 132
  as a war, 122, 124
Agency heads, 186
Allowable solutions, 62
Anthropology of politics, 90
Anti-naturalism, 3
Anti-Terrorism, Crime, and Security Act 2001, 75
Attack in London, 75
Austerity, 256
  agenda, 40
  narrative, 241

Auto-ethnography, 72
Autonomous house, 59

B
Balls, Edward, 79
Beattie, Peter (Labor leader), 180, 181
  formed minority government, 178
Beddington Zero Energy Development (BedZED), 50, 60
Belief-based contingency, 162
Beliefs and practices, 162
  about hierarchy, 227
Bergqvist, Jan, 159
Best interests of the child, 103, 110
Bill committee, 88
Bioregional Development Group, 51
Bjelke-Petersen regime, 175
Blair, Tony, 74–76, 87, 92
Bligh, Anna, 182, 183
Blue collar workers, 146, 152
Blunkett, David, 75
Borbidge government, 176

Borbidge-Sheldon review, 188
Boundedly rational political actors, 161
Bricolage, 7–9, 15
Brown, Gordon, 74, 76, 79, 85, 92
Budgetary constraints, 211
Building for a Greener Future, 54
Bundaberg Hospital controversy, 180
Bureaucratic politics, 192
Bureaucratization of management, 235

C
Cabinet and policy routines, 183, 185
Cabinet Handbook, 175
Career politics, 191
Carnell, Kate, 127, 131
Carter Review, 29
Central courts, 167
Centralising tradition, 209
Chief executive officer of the Australian Food and Grocery Council, 127
Child immigrants and asylum-seekers, 112
Child participation, 103, 107, 109
Children
  'dignity/capacity rights', 99
  needs-based rights, 99
  rights narrative, 104
Civil service, 75
Clarke, Charles, 75
Climate change, 52
COBRA, 81
Code for Sustainable Homes, 54
Collaborative policy engagement, 128
Collective portrait, 171
College of Policing, 222
Common sense, 241, 256, 260, 262
Conservative Party, 157
Constructivist, 243
Contest Strategy, 77
Contingency, 72, 190, 199
Contingent, 161, 242
Contingent beliefs, 149
Convention of the Rights of the Child (CRC), 97, 98, 102, 105
Conventions, 166
Corporate capture, 133
Corruption in Queensland's public institutions, 174
Counter-narrative, 79
Counter-terrorism, 72, 74, 77, 81
Counter-Terrorism Bill, 71, 79, 84, 92
Court, 185, 187
Court politics, 185, 192
Craft, 191
Creative agency, 261
Crevice and Rhyme plots, 78
Criminal Justice Act 2003, 75
Cycle of reprisal, 177

D
Davis, David, 77
Debt, 253
Decentred analysis, 6, 16, 72, 170, 173, 236
Decentring, 136, 159, 224
  approach, 3, 10, 211, 216
  pension reform, 143
  to policy, 67
  policymaking, 197
  political arena, 207
  the reform of ATP in the 1990s, 156
  research method, 167
  theory of governance, 199
Deep green values, 57, 59, 67
Defeat in the House of Commons, 78
Defensive narrative, 104
Department of Constitutional Affairs (DCA), 34
Department of the Premier and Cabinet (DPC), 176
De-politicize, 159

DG Justice, 101
Dilemmas, 72, 73, 92, 156, 167, 170, 189, 190, 199, 214, 227, 245
Directive on Victims of Trafficking, 113
Director of Public Prosecutions, 91
Dismiss agency heads, 177
Distrust of government, 252
Dominant narratives, 192
Dunster, Bill, 50

E
Earnings-related pensions in the 1950s, 146
Ecologically modern discourse, 56
Ecological modernisation, 48, 57, 61, 62, 66, 67
Ecological modernist approach, 59, 60
Economic everyday understanding, 260
Economic modernization, 64
Electoral dynamics surrounding pension reform, 142
Employers Organization (*Svenska arbetsgivareföreningen*, SAF), 153
Energy conservation, 61
Erlander, Tage (Prime Minister), 146, 152, 153
Ethnographic, 72, 224
  fieldwork, 7
  interviewing, 9, 25
  method, 168
  sensibility, 8, 246
EU asylum law and policy, 112
EU Charter of Fundamental Rights, 101, 111
EU Family Reunification law, 111
EU human rights role, 98
Eurochild, 115
European Commission, 98
European Forum on the Rights of the Child, 107
European PassivHaus standard, 55
EU's 'Guidelines on Child Protection Systems' in 2011, 109
Everyday actors, 242
Evidence-based policymaking, 1, 7
Evidence-based practice, 234

F
Federation, 236
Federation of White Collar Unions (TCO), 157
Fiscal conservatism, 243
Fitzgerald Inquiry, 174
Fixed interests, 66
Focus group, 8, 9, 222
Food and Health Dialogue, 125
Food and pharmaceutical industries, 123
Food Standards Agency (FSA) Board, 125
Foresight (2007), 125
Foster, Don (Former Minister for Housing), 65
Fragmentation and coordination, 190
Frattini, Franco (Commissioner for Freedom, Security and Justice), 100

G
GCHQ, 81
General Comment 14 of the UN Committee on the Rights of the Child, 113
Gennser, Margit (Conservative Party), 160
Global children's rights actor, 104
Global Financial Crisis, 184
Goss, Wayne, 174
Gove, Michael (Justice Secretary), 30
Governance networks, 121

Governance traditions, 174
Government debt, 255
Government solar power initiative, 52
Grayling, Chris (Justice Secretary), 30

H
Harpsund in 1955, 147
Harvest Time, 146, 157
Hayek, Friedrich, 56
Health payroll debacle, 185
Her Majesty's Prisons and Probation Service (HMPPS), 24
Hewitt, Patricia (Secretary for Trade and Industry), 52
Hierarchical organisations, 224
Historical contingency, 149
Historicism, 4
Historicist explanations, 4
Hit-and-run fieldwork, 9
Hockerton Housing Development, 50
Home Affairs, Intelligence and Security and Joint Committee on Human Rights, 91
Home Affairs Select Committee, 80
Housebuilding industry, 56
Household debt analogy, 244, 253
House of Commons, 93
Housing 'life cycles', 57
Housing shortages, 65

I
Implementation Unit, 180
Imprisonment for Public Protection (IPP), 24
Income-tested pensions, 146
Infrastructure Bill, 63
Inscribing, 6
Insider affiliation, 168
Insiders, 130
Insider's story, 169

Institutional memory, 167
Interpretive approach, 3–5, 236
Interventionist storytelling, 210
Interviews, 73
Israelsson, Margareta, 160

J
Jenkins, Roy, 40
Joint Committee on Human Rights, 80

K
Kelly, Ruth, 53
Keynesian alternative, 259
Könberg, Bo (Liberal Minister of Social Affairs), 157
Königson, Ture, 155

L
Labor's landslide defeat in 2012, 166
Labor won the 2009 election, 184
Labour Government (1997–2010), 74
Lack of constraints on executive power, 191
Landsorganisationen (LO), 147, 149
  1946 LO conference, 150
  1950 LO Congress, 151
Language of routines, 179, 188
Leader or Mayor, 212
Legislative Programme cabinet sub-committee, 86
Liberal National Party (LNP), 165
Liberty, 82
Life cycle story-line, 58
Local government chief executives, 202
Local reasoning, 199
Local traditions, 173

INDEX

Logic of performativity, 131
Longitudinal methodological approach, 67
Longitudinal research method, 49
Lord Chancellor role, 33

M
Management culture, 225
Managerialism, 236
Mandatory individual investment accounts, 158
Martin, Nick, 51
Materiality of policy change, 49
Memoirs, 9
Metalworkers Union, 150, 151
Metaphors, 124
MI6, 81
Miliband, Edward, 79
Million Program, 158
Ministry of Justice (MoJ), 23, 26, 28, 42, 81
Möller, Gustav (The Minister of Social Affairs from 1932–1951), 146
Mood of the times, 244
Moore, Michael (Public Health Association of Australia (PHAA), CEO), 131

N
Nanny state, 127, 135
Narrative, 73, 130, 141, 144, 175, 197, 228
Narrative policy analysis, 47
National Competition Policy reforms, 176
National Police Chiefs' Council, 236
Naturalism, 1, 2
Needs-based approach, 115
Networked governance, 206

Newark and Sherwood District Council in the UK, 52
Newman, Campbell, 165, 166, 186
New politics, 198
New Public Management (NPM), 30
New punitiveness, 28
Non-genuine 'participation' mechanisms, 107
Nudge theory, 127

O
Obesity, 123
Observation, 73
Offender management paradigm, 27
Office of Cabinet, 175, 176
Office of Security and Counter-Terrorism, 81
Official Commission of Inquiry (OCI; *Statens Offentliga Utredning* (SOU)), 145
Ofsted, 208
Open up policymaking, 137
Operation Gamble, 79
Operation Seagram, 79
Organisational culture, 223
Organisation studies, 200
Organization for Retail Employers (*Handelns Arbetsgivarorganisation*), 155
Osborne, George, 64, 65
Outsiders, 130
'Over-politicisation' of the police, 77

P
Palaszczuk, Annastacia, 166
Para-ethnography, 9
Parliamentary debate, 88
Parliamentary inquiries, 125
Parliamentary scrutiny, 74
Parliamentary theatre, 90

Parole Board, 41
Participant-observer, 167, 179
Partisan conflict, 144
Partisan evidence advocates, 17
Pay-as-you-go, 147
Pensions, 142
  pension policy, 142
  pension reform, 141
Personal debt, 255
Policy advocacy, 121, 136
Policy capacity, 191
Policy Division of DPC, 180
Policy interventions, 105
Policy narrative, 5, 104, 105, 114
Policy networks, 215
Policy and operations, 36
Policy problem, 105
Political debate as a 'war', 127
Politics-administration conundrum, 215
Polyphony, 216
Prescott, John, 82
Preventative Health Taskforce (2009), 125, 127, 133
Prevention of Terrorism Act 2005, 75
Prioritization of public protection, 27
Prison capacity, 40
Prison Governors Association (PGA), 37
Probation services, 36
Problem of distrust, 190
Prohibition of child labour, 103
Project Overt, 79
Public health lobby, 126, 133, 136
Public Health Responsibility Deals, 125, 128
Public policy scholarship, 202
Public Sector Renewal Board, 187
Public Service Commission (PSC), 183
Public service's strong service delivery tradition, 192

Purging and personalising chief executive appointments, 190

Q
Queensland state election, 165

R
Rationality assumption, 141
Reflective accounts, 203
Reflexivity, 204
Reid, John, 80
Repeat interviews, 25
Research conversations, 202
Return Directive, 113
Rights-based approach, 103, 115
Rituals and exclusionary practices, 132
Role of the Commons, 85
Roles of Lord Chancellor and Justice Secretary, 28
Romanian children's case, 101

S
SAP-Agrarian coalition, break-up of, 148
Scrutiny in committee, 89
Segelov, Collin (Executive director of the Australasian Association of National Advertisers), 128
Semi-structured interviews, 49
Shared meanings and beliefs, 149
Shared traditions, 174
Shared understanding, 263
Short termism, 233
Sites of policy advocacy on obesity, 125
Site visits, 50
Smart housing, 57, 59–61
Smith, Jacqui, 85
Social Democratic-Agrarian Party coalition government, 146

Social Democratic 'Harvest Time', 143, 150
Social Democratic Minister of Social Affairs, 147
Social Democratic Party (SAP), 144, 158
Specificity, 4, 16
Spending cuts, 258
Stakeholder engagement programs, 130
State traditions, 174
Status Quo coalition, 126
Statutory earnings-related pension system (*Allmänna tilläggspension, ATP*) in 1959, 143
Stories, 73
Story lines, 48
Storytelling, 6, 16, 197, 209
Sträng, Gunnar (Minister of Social Affairs), 152
Street level police officers, 234
Strengths and limitations of decentred analysis, 192
'Strong premier' tradition, 175, 188
Strong society, 145, 150, 157
Studying up, 124

T
Tacit knowledge, 172
Taskforce and the Dialogue, 130
Tax, 258
Tax evasion, 259
Temporary Protection Directive, 113
Terrorism Act (2000), 75
Terrorism Act (2006), 77
Thematic analysis, 223, 247
Towards an EU Strategy on the Rights of the Child, 100
Tradecrafts of public administration, 172
Traditional closed loop model, 205
Tradition of engaged scholarship, 169

Tradition of the 'strong society', 143
Traditions, 25, 73, 144, 167, 199, 208, 261
and beliefs, 185
Transforming Justice, 32
Treaty of Amsterdam, 101
Treaty of Lisbon in 2009, 103

U
Union Confederation (*Landsorganisationen* (LO)), 145
Universal basic pensions, 146
Universal, obligatory supplementary pensions, 150
'Universal social protection', 143

V
Vales' Autonomous House, 51
Visual ethnography, 9

W
Waning of the 'strong society', 158
War in Iraq in 2003, 77
Waste, 258
Webs of belief, 236, 237, 245
Weighing it Up Inquiry, 134
Welfarist approach, 111
Westminster-style model, 189
What Works Centre for Crime Reduction (WWCCR), 222
Wigforss, Ernst (Finance Minister), 146

Z
Zero carbon homes (ZCH) policy, 47
2006 ZCH policy, 53
Zero Carbon Hub, 50, 64, 66

CPSIA information can be obtained
at www.ICGtesting.com
Printed in the USA
LVHW04*1241280518
578670LV00011B/744/P